regional perspectives

An Examination of America's
Literary Heritage

regional
perspectives

An Examination of America's Literary Heritage

Edited by

John Gordon Burke

American Library Association
Chicago   1973

The essays and photographs for this volume were commissioned by the ALA Editorial Committee. All, with the exception of "Archetype West," have appeared in *American Libraries*, volumes 2 (nos. 4, 7, and 9) and 3 (nos. 1, 5, and 6), with the committee's consent.

Library of Congress Cataloging in Publication Data
Burke, John Gordon, 1938–   comp.
   Regional perspectives.

   Articles originally appeared in American libraries,
v. 2 (no. 4, 7, and 9) and v. 3 (no. 1, 5, and 6)
   CONTENTS: Burke, J.G. Introduction. Carruth, H.
The New England tradition.—Garrett, G. The South—
[etc.]
   1. American literature—History and criticism.
2. Literature and society. I. American libraries.
II. Title.
PS92.B78 1973   810'.9'32   72–3595
ISBN 0–8389–3136–7

International Standard Book Number 0–8389–3136–7 (1973)

Library of Congress Catalog Card Number 72–3595

Cover photograph by Leland Payton
Book designed by Harold Rollins

contents

introduction:

John Gordon Burke

REGIONAL PERSPECTIVES is based on the premise that there is a logic of literary "place," and that its essence may be found in geography. What makes this proposition so difficult, however, is that a regional tradition can be so fleeting and ephemeral. Its exhibit at times can define its essence, and further rationalization can leave us more confused than we were when we first sought to capture a meaning to define its presence.

There is, further, a regionalism of the mind which likewise complicates this issue. Clouded by popular fiction, it can also be evoked by the most substantial writer, e.g., D. H. Lawrence and the Southwest. Such writers lead the unsuspecting to make positive and easy identifications, but at best these are artificial connections and are created solely in the imagination of the reader.

But there is a regional place in our literature, and it is assumed that through writers substantially involved with a region we can learn as much about its essence as we can from an academic and perhaps more objective critic. The assumption, of course, is that we can find the authentic by probing the resources of a writer's heritage, or asking him to do it for us. To be sure, the results will be personal, often following a tortuous logic to make a connection and to lay it "all" before us. But that is part of the risk one takes when he asks a poet or novelist to turn critic and to trace the map of a region of literature.

The tradition of this book is not new, for with the flowering of the presses in our universities, a number of authors have become publicly introspective. They have defined their craft and frequently the tradition in which they work. It is not often the case, however, that they have turned their attention to other writers and it is in this connection that this collective effort is unusual.

What follows is an assessment of writers by writers consciously trying to outline a regional tradition, and the results are startling. A redefinition of Puritanism emerges which places its influence in a more positive and socially relevant light. The myth of southern literature as a closed system is exploded, and cultural diversity in this region is brought into new perspective. The Southwest is dealt with in terms of its geography, and the threshold of a new creativity is outlined. A diversity of limitless possibilities is found in the Midwest—all there waiting the juxtaposition of space and time and ethnic consciousness. And the West, our wellspring of creativity? A strange logic of repetition is found there which suggests some even stranger historical parallels, and again brings the logic of literary "place" to the forefront.

One philosophical problem remains: What does physical place have to do with literature that our social milieu cannot explain? It is the *universal* problem, and one which runs through all the essays which follow. Taken together, this collective effort does not point to any neat solution. Yet the conceptual richness of the problem suggests that the particular can take many forms. What is normative about a *perspective* is that it can assume the dimension of a critical concept, and that perhaps is the most important lesson that can be learned from the evidence at hand which I commend to your attention.

the
new england
tradition

Hayden Carruth

Photograph by Adrien r Miles

It is not to be seen beneath the appearances
That tell of it. The steeple at Farmington
Stands glistening and Haddam shines and sways.

—Wallace Stevens

What is this thing? Where is it? Does it exist at all? Never have I sat down to write in greater puzzlement with my theme. The New England tradition: this is what I have been asked to discuss, but I can't find it. Or rather, I find too much of it. I am like a man lost in a storm in our Vermont mountains; sheets of snow twist and sprawl about me in the air, opening now and then on glimpsed peaks and gulfs, cliffs and ravines, things familiar yet falling into no remembered patterns. I am lost in my own backyard. Yet I have found my way here all my life, nearly fifty years. It is a distinctly unpleasant sensation.

For I am a New Englander born and bred. Born in western Connecticut, in the Pomperaug valley before it became the glossy habitat of exurbanites; then in the Berkshires, then in northern Vermont; moving always northward if I could, heeding Dan Chaucer's admonition to "flee fro the prees"—and surely this, at least, is a part of the New England tradition. True, like most modern Americans I have wandered, have lived elsewhere for longer and shorter periods, experimentally sometimes and sometimes in duress;

Hayden Carruth, poet and critic, lives in New England.

2

but always the sense of being a New Englander, bred in me during my early years, has been central to my self-awareness. When I have been away and then have returned, I have felt the homecomer's exhilaration and release as the land has changed at New York's frontier, the hills rising and rounding, cedar giving way to fir, and the imperceptible yet unmistakable shift of architecture. God knows there is something endearing in a New England gravel pit, something regionally recognizable, and I am a connoisseur of gravel pits from Maine to California. But what is it precisely? I have never been able to discover.

I think of those compendious and dismal volumes by Van Wyck Brooks and his fellow critics, or the compendious and perhaps less dismal volumes by scholars in the thousands, the Millers, Morrisons, Eliots, Perrys, some of whom I have read, a good many in fact; but from them all no distillation has risen. And I myself have been a "New England writer" for years, have composed scores and hundreds of poems in which aspects of the New England tradition have found concrete terms. Always I have been aware of the tradition, quite consciously aware: yet consciousness is not necessarily analytical or precise. Has no distillation risen even from my own works? Perhaps, but it is something amorphous. I recognize more clearly than ever that being a New Englander is more a matter of what I feel in my nerve and bone than of what I have said, or can ever say, in words.

This is important. The scholars and critics have labored with pertinacity to define the New England tradition, it has been a mighty intellectual endeavor, to which I am about to add my pittance; yet it is all very nearly ineffectual, a tissue of confusion and contradiction. The best it can yield is a partial, momentarily valid concept. And the reason for this is not far to seek: like all life everywhere, this living tradition is too complex, too rich, for the human mind to encompass, singly or collectively. No, the New England tradition is not in what I say about it,

3

but in my poems, and then in all the poems and other imaginative works of all the other and greater artists who have inhabited this region from the beginning, in their concretely articulated feelings, and finally in the works of the greatest artist of us all, the common New England mind that has generated, and continues to generate, our language and our lore.

Concrete articulated feelings, their interconnections, their changing patterns in the flow of time, their elastic vitality: one scarcely knows where to begin.

Begin with the land. Instinct would tell me this, even if the authorities did not. I look out my window. As it happens I live in what we call the north,[1] and the season is deep winter. Thick snow, three, four, five feet in depth, covers everything, and the channel of the brook is marked by no more than a shallow depression on the snow-surface, though I know the water, down below, is still winding blackly among the stones. The bank opposite, reaching up to a fir-pointed horizon, is snow-covered too of course, but humped here and there where great rocks lie, some as big as houses, rolled here from the distant mountaintop by glaciers long ago. Against the firs are exclamatory white birches, and bare alders and chokeberries look particularly naked on the brookside, still decorated with withered strings of wild clematis from last summer. The temperature is three degrees at two o'clock in the afternoon; it will fall sharply tonight, probably to twenty-five or thirty degrees below zero. A few snowflakes tremble in the air, and there is a touch of color in the sky where the sunlight catches a crystallized cloud. It is beautiful and terrible. "The American landscape has never been at one with the white man. Never. And white men have probably never felt so bitter anywhere, as here in America,. where the very landscape, in its very beauty, seems a bit devilish and grinning, opposed to us." So wrote a foreign observer,[2] and from his point of external vantage he saw one side of the coin of our truth, the side of bitterness, with marvelous clear directness. But he was blind to the other side. Perhaps only we Americans can know that no bitterness, no degree of alienation from our torturing, fascinating land, could make us wish in our hearts for an easier beauty. We have survived here for three hundred and fifty years. This is our home.

But my home, this little corner of New England, is not all of New England; far from it. Westerners in their disparaging way say "New England" as if we were no more than a rural county somewhere in the plains. It's true you could put all New England inside Texas and have plenty of room left over; but what we lack in extent we make up in variety. To travel from our Vermont highlands to Martha's Vineyard you would have to cross half-a-dozen distinct landscapes and as many distinct cultures. It has always been true. "Seen from a distance, the New England writers appeared like fixed stars in a constellation that grew more brilliant with every decade. In fact, they were widely scattered. Aside from the groups in the capital, they rarely met. The Cambridge authors never went to Concord; the Concord authors seldom went to Boston; Whittier, Mrs. Stowe, Thoreau, and others revolved in worlds of their own, and Ticknor's circle scarcely crossed the circles of Holmes and Lowell. Connecticut and Massachusetts were like different nations."[3] Today, in spite of jetliners and superhighways, the outlying Yankee strongholds—the western Housatonic meadows, the northern mountains, the mills and forests of Maine —lie as far as ever from sleek intellectual Cambridge, smug Boston, and glittering Newport.

There are, in fact, not one New England but many. They are united only in their Puritan ancestry long ago, that trunk from which so many disparate branches have grown. True, there is a myth of the land as well, which exerts a unitary influence, the notion of a stony, stubborn, hostile earth that somehow pervades even the salt environment of Gloucester and the Cape or the placid Connecticut downs. But the land is fertile enough in actuality, and was

5

ten times more fertile in colonial times. I am not sure that the pervasive myth of the difficult land is not more a product of the Puritan imagination than of the land itself. And here, it seems to me, we approach the heart of the matter at last.

Strange how long the popular misconceptions of Puritanism persist. They are still, I find upon consulting my eight-year-old son, taught in the public schools of Vermont, viz., that the Puritans were dour and simple-minded moralists who fled to America from the licentiousness and repression of Europe: this, twenty years after Perry Miller's summary popularization of his own and others' scholarship, showing what really occupied the minds of the first settlers:

> The migration was no retreat from Europe: it was a flank attack. We are to be a city set upon a hill, the eyes of all the world upon us; what we succeed in demonstrating, Europe will be bound to imitate, even Rome itself. These were not—despite their analogies with Moses and the tribes of Israel —refugees seeking a promised land, but English scholars, soldiers, and statesmen taking the long way about in order that someday they, or their children, or at least their friends, might rule in Lambeth.[4]

In short the Puritan leaders and probably most of the followers were far more sophisticated people than we usually imagine. They were the advance guard of the Reformation, which itself had long since changed from a reformative to a revolutionary movement. The Puritans were the radicals of their era, among the most extreme of all radical sects; far from being mere colonizers or imperialists, they were theological and political revolutionaries who expected to convert the world—even Rome!—to their way of thinking, and who were using New England as no more than a temporary base of operations. Indeed the evidence indicates that they expected to return to England within a foreseeable time after their arrival in America, and to return in triumph. Looked at in this light, the name itself, New England, which they gave to their settlements overseas, takes on deeper significance. When Cromwell, for reasons of expediency, denied them the role they thought they were destined to play in the Civil War and the administration of the Commonwealth, they were deeply disappointed and shocked. Perhaps from that moment, the moment when the Puritans found themselves removed from the corps of leadership and turned into an excluded and remote minority, we may date not only the conversion of the Puritan fathers from righteous radicalism to self-righteous conservatism, with all the subsequent oppressions and horrors we know so well, but the beginning of the whole psychology of American provincialism, which determined our cultural evolution for three hundred years to come.

But what I wish to emphasize are the positive aspects of the Puritan theocracy. It is easy enough for us to see the negative ones: how the radical purity of the early settlers turned reactionary and oppressive, and how later, under increasing pressure for material security, the elitist ethic of the Puritan fathers became an imperialist attitude toward the land and the Indians, while their doctrines of individual election and the perseverance of grace lent themselves to a laissez-faire attitude in commerce. After the Restoration in England, the hope of a radical Calvinist revolution vanished, and as the seventeenth century moved into the eighteenth the grandchildren of the original Puritan settlers lost all affinity for English ways. As the eighteenth century wore on, under successive waves of deism and Methodism, the remnants of theocracy crumbled, and the Puritans were far on their way toward becoming Americans, toward changing from Puritans to Yankees and inventing a New England culture. Allen Tate has placed the moment of irrevocable transition in 1790, when Samuel Slater thwarted a British embargo on milling machinery by memorizing the design of a cotton-spinner and bringing it to

Massachusetts.⁵ Thereafter the western spirit evolved without hindrance, culminating perhaps in Calvin Coolidge's remark that "the business of America is business." The movement from revolution to reaction in New England was complete.

This decline of Puritanism into commercial rapacity and social gentility has become a popular, easy article of historical belief, a kind of historiographic myth. But certainly other aspects of the Puritan heritage are equally important. Allen Tate has pointed out something we need to remember today, that the Puritan theocracy in New England during its first two or three decades was and still is unique, the only unitary, cohesive society ever produced by Anglo-Saxon civilization. It was held together by a single vision or a single way of apprehending the world, which permeated the entire society from top to bottom. Everything for the Puritans was not only evidence of God's will but a direct expression of His will; everything within or without their own consciousness; and the whole was organized by grace and predestination, totally beyond the recourse of individual human beings. These theocratic disciplines gave to the experience of the individual, Tate says, "an heroic proportion and a tragic mode."⁶ These are not the qualities we usually ascribe to the Puritan mind. Heroic proportion, tragic mode? We are told more often of their pettiness and emotional frigidity. Their own writings, so often inexpressive, seem to support such a view. Yet consider the burden that their doctrine of predestination placed upon them. Again and again we read that only those "endued with grace" will attain glory in the world to come or comfort in the world at hand, and God alone determines in His secret wisdom which ones will be "graced." Anne Bradstreet wrote in her journal of meditations:

> There is nothing admits of more admiration than God's various dispensation of His gifts among the sons of men, betwixt whom He hath put so vast a disproportion that they scarcely seem made of the

same lump or sprung out of the loins of one Adam, some set in the highest dignity that mortality is capable of, and some again so base that they are viler than the earth, some so wise and learned that they seem like angels among men, and some again so ignorant and sottish that they are more like beasts than men, some pious saints, some incarnate devils, some exceeding beautiful, and some extremely deformed, some so strong and healthful that their bones are full of marrow and their breasts of milk, and some again so weak and feeble that while they live they are accounted among the dead; and no other reason can be given of all this but so it pleased Him whose will is the perfect rule of righteousness.[7]

Enduring within such a dispensation, as within the fierce American wilderness, could be nothing less than a work of existential nobility for the human spirit. It seems to me that the Puritan God was in effect closer to Euripidean Fate than any intervening conception, and the lives of the Puritans, especially in America, were rooted in tragedy in the fullest sense. Nothing men could do could help them, they were up against it, yet they were obliged to carry on.

Such a doctrine as predestination was bound to degenerate into spiritual apathy in the long run, and Yvor Winters has shown how quickly Puritan ways of thought led to the allegorical, and hence disengaged, mind of the nineteenth century.[8] From there it was only a step to basic irony, then to optimism of the Emersonian type with its rejection of evil. But there were other dangers too, dangers of plain insanity. In Puritan America every stick and stone and every wind that blew was "evidence" of God's will, if men could but read them rightly. Men lived in the midst of a frightful secret. Professor H. W. Schneider wrote: "No one can live long in a Holy Commonwealth without becoming sensitive, irritable, losing his sense of values and ultimately his balance."[9] Again: "The mind of the Puritan was singularly unified and his imagination thoroughly moralized. . . . No event was merely natural; it was an act of God and was hence charged with that 'numinous' quality which gives birth to both prophetic insight and mystic illumination."[10] "God and devil were both active, scheming, hidden powers, . . . and natural events were therefore to be understood only in so far as they showed evidence of some divine or diabolical plot."[11] To live in the midst of secret plots, divine and diabolical,[12] is surely to live tragically, to pit one's human essence against the absurd; but unlike the ancient Greek in confrontation with Fate, and unlike modern man in confrontation with the depersonalizing universe, the Puritan lacked any intimation that his own suffering and endurance, however unavailing, might in some sense bestow upon him a moral superiority to the forces of destiny—what has been called dignity or authenticity. There was an existential imbalance at the heart of Puritanism, for the "heroic proportion" was all in the scale of the universal divine will while the "tragic mode" was all in the individual's own consciousness. As long as these forces were kept at full strength by the theological vitality of the Puritan movement at its height, the individual Puritan had only two spiritual choices: abject resignation and acceptance, the course enjoined upon him by his church and adopted by most church members, or the reservation to himself of something akin to a spirit of inquiry, which could be maintained only upon pain of grievous error and at the cost of constant spiritual exacerbation. If the majority chose the comfort of the former alternative, nevertheless a considerable minority chose the individualism of the latter, among whom were some who succumbed to violence and insanity, and their choice became a permanent aspect of the New England character.

One further point about the Puritans concerns me here, their attitude toward the land. It was, considering the Puritans' apparently desperate need to make a rational reconciliation of all points of doctrine, a curiously mixed and self-contradictory attitude; at least so it seems to us. On the one hand they held that the land, like all the universe, "belonged" to

God and to no one else, not even the Massachusetts Bay Company: "Our God hathe right to it, and if he be pleased to give it us, who shall controll him or his termes?"[13] But like all God's "gifts" the land was actually more in the nature of a loan, which might be called up at any time; man had no real sovereignty, but was at best a tenant; and a dutiful tenant, as John Cotton pointed out, would be sure to return the land to the Lord in better condition than he had received it.[14] This was a pervasive idea among the first settlers, and lay, I believe, behind most of their strenuous effort to apply good methods of cultivation to their new plantations and to deal fairly with the Indians.[15] On the other hand, however, the Puritans certainly held the belief that God wished them to use the land to its fullest extent, that they were under commandment to prosper, to multiply, and to make the most of their material environment. Again and again they compared themselves to the Chosen People of the Old Testament. Robert Cushman, who was a member of the original party of prospective emigrants to Massachusetts Bay, wrote in 1622 about the desirability of taking North America in spite of the prior claims of the Indians. "Their land," he wrote, "is spacious and void," and they "do but run over the grass, as do also the foxes and wild beasts," wherefore "as the ancient Patriarchs . . . removed from straiter places unto more roomthy . . . so it is lawful now to take a land, which none useth; and make use of it."[16] Another settler, John White, wrote similarly: "If it were then the minde of God, that man should possesse all parts of the earth, it must be enforced that we neglect our duty, and crosse his will, if we doe it not, when wee have occasion and opportunitie."[17] This sentiment was repeated during the early years of settlement so often that it became virtually automatic and devoid of meaning. Thus we see the Puritans entertaining two ideas about the land they had arrogated to themselves: first, that they held it in trust and were responsible to God for its safekeeping; and second, that they had been exclusively appointed by God to populate and cultivate

11

this particular sizable piece of land called New England. And we see at once what would happen to these ideas when their theopneustic content was weakened or removed: The first would change into the idea of total irresponsibility, i.e., private ownership of the land; the second would change into a sanction for indiscriminate exploitation of the land. And this is exactly what happened.

Let me summarize the elements of the original Puritan impulse that seem to me the most important for us to remember today. (1) Its radicalism. (2) Its militancy, or willingness to confront the world with demands for revolutionary change. (3) Its capacity to see the world in heroic terms. (4) Its tragic conception of human experience. (5) Its essential individualism, which is a necessary corollary of 4. (6) Its custodial attitude toward the land. And then, of course, the inevitable inversions as religious fervor waned: (1) Reactionary orthodoxy, leading to gentility. (2) Quietism, a willingness to let George do it. (3) Comedy, which is the reduction of heroism. (4) Irony, which is the reduction of tragedy, leading to fantasy, utopianism, and darker insanities. (5) Fanatical devotion to privacy. (6) Exploitation of the land and an imperialist attitude toward its inhabitants, together with an overweening pride in mere landscape. These, I believe, are the relevant themes of the New England tradition. If one word were needed to convey them all, I would choose *conscience*, either its presence in exacerbation or its absence in desuetude; or, more often, a combination of both.

None of this is exhaustive. How could anyone make such a claim in the face of the extraordinary wealth of material in our libraries dealing with Puritanism, which has been the most popular topic of American scholarship and criticism for 150 years? All I wish to do is suggest a somewhat new configuration of response to Puritanism, a configuration which will not be actually confuted by the scholars and which at the same time may prove more useful to us today than previous configurations.[18] Radicalism, heroism, conscience: are these not terms in which we find now a new cogency? It would be a vast oversimplification to say that the Puritans were the hippies of the seventeenth century. But to the extent that we can abstract Puritanism from the theocratic world-spirit of its time, the oversimplification contains a valuable truth. We are so accustomed to the pejorative meanings of the word *Puritan* that we are actually shocked when we stop to think what its basic, primary meanings are; we do an about-face. Puritanism means devotion to purity, personal and social, and opposition to injustice, greed, political or ecclesiastical corruption, lewdness and the debasement of God's gifts. Puritanism means love, as the Puritans said again and again; only love—of God and of man—could hold the holy commonwealth together. In short the Puritans, far from being the dour ancestors we have been taught to think them, the severe, the narrow, the *regrettable* ancestors, were actually as good a company as any nation could hope to have for its progenitors. True, the Puritans' doctrinal opposition to theater and the secular arts in general may have militated against our artistic evolution, though other factors in our early history, chiefly economic factors, seem to me more expressly causative. But the strengths that the Puritans infused into the beginnings of New England, and thence into the mainstream of American cultural development, are with us yet. I do not think it too much to say that whatever saving virtues we possess in our crisis of self-reproach as we make our way through the last third of the twentieth century, we owe to the Puritans.

From this base the culture of New England mounted. One hesitates to call it a "flowering"; at best a rather weedy garden. But it was vigorous, no doubt of that, becoming ultimately so complex and powerful that for a long time it was dominant in the national culture, with the result that many interconnections were established with cultures elsewhere, even abroad. Narrow at the base, increasingly

13

broad at the top, it had the shape of an inverted pyramid whose outer edges touched other pyramids on all sides; and as it became more and more top-heavy, its support was less a function of its base than of these outer contacts. Nevertheless the base was still there, still literally fundamental. Our problem is to get inside the pyramid, so to speak, and discover the essential course of building blocks that still holds it together.

Enough of metaphor. What I am saying is simply that if we are to uncover a New England tradition which is still alive and useful, we must begin by discarding immense chunks of the past, including some that have been considered not only integral to the tradition but its veritable kingpins. I am willing to wipe out, for instance, the whole eighteenth century at one stroke, and to concede at the same time my lack of scholarly prerogative for doing so; I cannot support my contention except by saying that I am aware of William Douglass, Thomas Hutchinson, Samuel Sewall, the Hartford Wits, the almanac makers, Joel Barlow, Ezra Stiles, and so on, but I am not aware that any of them contributed anything genuinely formative to the New England tradition.[19] My impression is that the force of Puritanism, as it weathered the successive waves of "foreign" religion, George Whitefield's "Great Awakening," the Deist movement, Methodism, and other Arminian developments, was weakened, was perhaps in a sense diluted, but was not altered or refashioned in a positive way; that is, the New England tradition at the end of the eighteenth century was still a Puritan tradition in its main cultural, social, and moral elements, whatever may have happened to the theology.[20] This is a generalization so broad that it may be sustained only if one concedes beforehand, as I do, all the provisions that anyone can reasonably enter against it. Yet I believe it remains a valid generalization, if only because I find the main elements of Puritanism still intact in New England long after the eighteenth century had become a dead issue.[21]

In the same way I willingly jettison the entire as-

14

pect of the nineteenth century associated with Boston and Cambridge: Brownson, Longfellow, Motley, Lowell, Holmes, Howells, Henry James, and all the rest. I mean to imply no value judgments whatever, but only that the entire thrust of this development, though originating in Puritanism, was away from New England and toward nationalism and internationalism, i.e. toward cosmopolitan high culture. It succeeded, as we know, remarkably well, forming alliances with German, French, Italian, and English literary movements; to such an extent, in fact, that a modern writer like R. P. Blackmur, born and educated in Boston, could devote his life to serious literary criticism without discussing any of the authors of his native region.[22] This Brahmin culture was a long literary evolution from provincialism to cosmopolitanism in . . . three generations? . . . four? No matter. Its ambition was to deny New England as such, and its success has removed it from our consideration.

The capital of New England, culturally, commercially, and in every other way, is the metropolitan complex comprising Boston and Cambridge. This has always been true and it is true today. Native New Englanders from one end of their region to the other are naturally oriented toward Massachusetts Bay, though newcomers and summer residents are more likely to turn toward New York. Yet the plain fact is that Boston-Cambridge, like many another capital, long ago—perhaps as long ago as the beginning of the nineteenth century—lost touch with its own constituents. Granted, occasionally the capital may make a gesture toward native culture, a Lowell may write a few poems in dialect for the *Atlantic*. But the back-country people know this is condescension, they know the dialect isn't accurate; they see that their own authors, like Rowland E. Robinson (1833–1900),[23] who could write dialect ten times better than Lowell, are largely ignored and forgotten. They themselves, when they go to Boston, are snubbed, and their loyalty to the old capital seems at best pathetic. Yet the real vitality of the New England tradition has never been a product of the sophisticated metropolitan drawing rooms in which the Brahmins played out their roles as culture heroes; it has originated in the back-country.

In 1835, when people still relied on horse transport, the back-country began somewhere east of Concord, and that was the year in which Ralph Waldo Emerson, having resigned his ministry in a high-toned Boston church, retired to Concord with the deliberate intention of making it his home for the rest of his life. It was a short but significant migration. Emerson turned his back on the Brahmin culture which was then in its first but unmistakable emergence. He would have none of it, determined to give himself to a life of contemplation. When he looked around he saw that "the landscape, the figures, Boston, London, are facts as fugitive as any institution past, or any whiff of mist or smoke, and so is society, and so is the world."[24] Against this Emerson elevated his own "soul," his mystical awareness of the meanings within appearances, but he meant no retreat into passivity. "The one thing in the world, of value, is the active soul." And if he despised the society which devoted itself to the superficial values of the world of fact, nevertheless he himself gave the greatest value to fact when rightly interpreted. "Day creeps after day," he wrote,

> each full of facts, dull, strange, despised things that we cannot enough despise,—call heavy, prosaic, and desart. And presently the aroused intellect finds gold and gems in one of these scorned facts, then finds that the day of facts is a rock of diamonds, that a fact is an Epiphany of God, that on every fact of his life he should rear a temple of wonder, joy, and praise; that in going to eat meat, to buy, or sell, to meet a friend, or thwart an adversary, to communicate a piece of news, or buy a book, he celebrates the arrival of an inconceivably remote purpose and law at last on the shores of Being, and into the ripeness and term of nature. And because nothing chances, but all is locked and wheeled and chained in Law, in these motes and

dust he can read the writing of the True Life and of a startling sublimity.

The quotation is remarkably characteristic and inclusive. On one hand it shows Emerson writing in the terms he often drew from the material world, using metaphors of gold and gems and diamonds, buying and selling, and speaking in simple optimism of the wonders of wage-earning life, which the rest of us find grubby enough most of the time. It was an optimism that Emerson could not and would not deny, springing from his deepest spiritual convictions, yet it issued in strange sentiments. "I told Jones Very that I had never suffered, that I could scarce bring myself to feel concern for the safety and life of my nearest friends that would satisfy them; that I saw clearly that if my wife, my child, my mother, should be taken from me, I should still remain whole, . . . I should not grieve." No more could he grieve for war, pestilence, shipwreck, the dark and evil underside of experience. He was blind to it, spiritually blinded by his intuition that all was "chained in Law," the law of the divine universal will, which could be nothing but total innate goodness, however separate parts of it might appear evil to man. Optimism, belief in progress: these were the factors of Emerson's thought which led Allen Tate, among other critics, to condemn it and to call Emerson the prophet of industrialism, whose perfectionist individualism and rejection of institutional morality were tailor made for "free enterprise" capitalism.[25] Santayana equally rejected Emerson's inability to comprehend the tragic view of experience: ". . . to those who are not yet free from the troublesome feelings of pity and shame, Emerson brings no comfort; he is the prophet of a fair-weather religion."[26] The criticisms are undeniably just. Yet what other writer in English has put into words as acute as Emerson's this perception of the "inconceivably remote purpose" that arrives from time to time on the "shores of Being" and reveals itself in the "ripeness and term of nature"? One must go back to Herbert, Vaughan, and

17

Donne to find it, poets with whom Emerson himself felt a distinct connection. Yet they were poets of another age and of a vastly different cultural and institutional environment.

This is no place to attempt a summation of Emerson's thought, even if I could succeed where so many others have failed. The scholars themselves are now changing their focus of attention from his "doctrine" to his private feeling, from his essays to his extraordinary journals, from his public assertions of a fixed belief to his private intellectual and mystical endeavors that unveil a soul in action.[27] This is a salutary change for us, but it doesn't alter the fact that what Emerson contributed to the New England tradition was what he contributed in public during his own lifetime. It was his unusual attitude toward nature. When he wrote of "the ripeness and term" of nature, he used language that seems strange to us. We think of him walking in the woods, perhaps near Walden Pond, looking at the trees, the wildflowers, the birds. Ripeness and term? He would better, we think, consider them as they are, living and free, not drawing to their extinctions. Yet that is exactly what he was doing; for to Emerson, who was as deep in nature as any naturalist, every tree, every tree toad, and every philosopher was a teleological event, whose end was bound by its very existence to the immanent unity of a spiritual world. Ripeness and term were precisely correct, for in fact we are ripe and terminative the moment we are born, components of universal joy. This was the joy of Emerson's anagogic vision, which we cannot doubt, but which he himself despaired of expressing:

> Am I not, one of these days, to write consecutively of the beatitude of intellect? It is too great for feeble souls, and they are over-excited. The wineglass shakes, and the wine is spilled. What then? The joy which will not let me sit in my chair, which brings me bolt upright to my feet, and sends me striding around my room, like a tiger in his cage, and I cannot have composure and concentration enough even to set down in English words

the thought which thrills me—is not that joy a certificate of the elevation? What if I never write a book or a line? for a moment, the eyes of my eyes were opened, the affirmative experience remains, and consoles through all suffering.

Yet he did write a book, he did convey to us an intimation—how much more than an intimation! —of his own spiritual energy and mystical triumph. Sometimes we have been inclined to scoff. D. H. Lawrence, whom we might have thought sympathetic to Emerson's spiritualized naturalism, complained that the Sage's "gorgeous inrushes of exaltation" only made him "sick."[28] His complaint was typical of his time. But now that phase of our sensibility is over, and Lawrence, who once seemed eternally modern, has slipped suddenly into the past, as tough and intelligent as ever but with the indefinable aura of quaintness that surrounds the thoroughly dead. Not that we have acquired "religion" or discovered new sources of mystical awareness in ourselves, alas. But our historical view is better than Lawrence's, and we see what Emerson was doing. He was restoring vitality of faith to the New England mind, he was repairing Puritanism. Granted, where he was rhapsodic the Puritans had been rational, where he celebrated cheerfulness and the spiritual perfectibility of man the Puritans had sustained themselves in the knowledge of sin and tragedy. But Emerson's spiritualized morality, his awareness of the spiritual unity of meaning and being, and his view of the natural world as the mask of spiritual reality, were close, at least functionally, to the Puritans' Covenant of Grace, their faith in the universality of God's will, and their search for "evidence" of God's meaning in the objects of the natural world. If Emerson was a "prophet of industrialism," as in some sense he was, he was not willingly so. If his belief in spiritual perfectibility suffered a sea-change when it was removed by others from the safe, cogent context of his mystical vision, if it then became a materialist faith in mere progress, we cannot blame Emerson for that, any more than we can blame Calvin for the ethics of Protestant businessmen.

What Emerson did was to reopen to the New England imagination the temptation of spiritual hope, a temptation which has obsessed and dismayed us ever since. And he did it in terms peculiarly aligned to the Yankee vision. Santayana, that alien New Englander who rejected Yankee ways and longed for the sunny regularity of the Mediterranean world, was specific in acknowledging Emerson's genius. "What such men [Spinoza, Shakespeare, Goethe] achieved by intellectual power, or just imagination or acquaintance with life, Emerson attained by his innate and happy simplicity. He had but to open his eyes, and although what happened to offer itself to his glance may have lacked richness and volume, and although his observation itself may have been desultory, yet he was a born master at looking deep and at looking straight."[29] For Emerson nature was all, man—except as a spiritual animal like any other—nothing. And in spite of his transcendent attitudes, he dealt with nature more receptively and unsentimentally than Wordsworth, for example, or any other of the European pantheists. In this he was a New Englander through and through, and quite at home as such.

As for the rest of Concord: what a fantastic village! Thoreau, of course, is the most famous of Emerson's fellow townsmen, and with good reason. His political and social radicalism, the essay on civil disobedience, his willingness to spend the night in jail to substantiate his views—a comfortable enough night compared to many that have been spent by modern (or ancient) radicals, but at least Thoreau made his point, and made it in a time and place for which going to jail was less a mark of criminality than the nadir of vulgarity. His radicalism, like his other qualities—his stubbornness, his voluntary poverty, his distrust of organized society, in short his dyed-in-the-wool Yankee character—Thoreau's radicalism, is too well-known to need further discussion, though it is worth pointing out that he stood in relationship to the Brahmin culture of Massachusetts in 1840 much as the Puritans had stood to Cavalier culture in 1620.[30] Rejection and denial were his watchwords. Yet what he did with his life was affirmative enough, and above all an affirmation precisely of his life. This seems to me in many ways the most radical thing he did. On the first page of *Walden* he wrote, as if with a Yankee twinkle in his eye: "I should not talk so much about myself if there were anybody else whom I knew as well." Nonsense. He would have written about himself in any case, even if no one would heed it, and for a long time practically no one did. Thoreau was not only celebrating himself, in the sense Whitman intended;[31] he was investigating himself, testing himself, in a sense constructing or reconstructing himself, or at least his image of himself, from the fragments of day-to-day experience. This was new in the world, something of immense importance; far more sophisticated, for example, than the Romantic notion of the auto-biographical poem, as Wordsworth's *Prelude* or Byron's *Childe Harold*. I don't mean to suggest that Thoreau was engaged in self-creative poetry in the same way that a modern poet, with a knowledge of psychoanalysis, a background in the existential authors, and a concept of poetry as action, might be.[32] But Leslie Fiedler's description of *Walden* is just: "a prose poem in the form of a journal, . . . which defines once and for all the archetypal essence of the transplanted lonely WASP in the midst of, or better, *against* the Massachusetts wilderness—in the course of which encounter, he becomes transformed into the Yankee;"[33] that is to say, into the mature and self-identifiable Thoreau. It is very significant, I feel, that Thoreau recorded his transformation in a journal, an account of random fragmentary daily experience, even though he rewrote much of it and intensified it for his published book. *Walden* was an early example, perhaps the first, of the journal of creative autobiogenesis, which became the characteristic form of American literature a hundred years later and which was, I think, a contribution of New England.[34]

Then there were the Alcotts, a houseful of bright and dithering genius, the Hawthornes in the Old Manse, all Brook Farm at one time or another, and dozens of others, originals or hangers-on: a village of gardeners and visionaries, carpenters and poets, masons and mystics.[35] Charles Ives, whose best-known composition is his second piano sonata entitled *Concord, Mass., 1840–1860*, once wrote in words his impressions of Concord:

> Concord village itself reminds one of that common virtue lying at the height and root of all the Concord divinities. As one walks down the broad-arched street—passing the white house of Emerson, ascetic guard of a former prophetic beauty—he comes presently beneath the old elms overspreading the Alcott house. It seems to stand as a kind of homely but beautiful witness of Concord's common virtue—it seems to bear a consciousness that its past is *living,* that the "mosses of the Old Manse" and the hickories of Walden are not far away. Here is the home of the "Marches"—all pervaded with the trials and happiness of the family, and telling, in a simple way, the story of "the richness of not having." Within the house, on every side, lie remembrances of what imagination can do for the better amusement of fortunate children who have to do for themselves—much-needed lessons in these days of automatic, ready-made, easy entertainments which deaden rather than stimulate the creative faculty. And there sits the little old spinet piano Sophia Thoreau gave to the Alcott children, on which Beth played the old Scotch airs, and played at the *Fifth Symphony.*
>
> There is a commonplace beauty about "Orchard House"—a kind of spiritual sturdiness underlying its quaint picturesqueness—a kind of common triad of the New England homestead, whose overtones tell us that there must have been something aesthetic fibered in the Puritan severity—the self-sacrificing part of the ideal—a value that seems to stir a deeper feeling, a stronger sense of being nearer some perfect truth than a Gothic cathedral

or an Etruscan villa. All around you, under the Concord sky, there still floats the influence of that human-faith-melody—transcendent and sentimental enough for the enthusiast or the cynic, respectively—reflecting an innate hope, a common interest in common things and common men—a tune the Concord bards are ever playing while they pound away at the immensities with a Beethovenlike sublimity, and with, we may say, a vehemence and perseverance, for that part of greatness is not so difficult to emulate.[36]

Ives wrote with a careless majesty that matched his music, and I am not sure that we ever learn from him quite what the "common virtue" of Concord really was. Nevertheless he built his two paragraphs on a good many possible touchstones. Against the "immensities" Concord propounded the idea that the "past is living," the "richness of not having," "imagination," "spiritual sturdiness," "something aesthetic fibered in the Puritan severity," "innate hope," "common interest in common things and common men" —these are the counter-themes to the Emersonian "sublimity" that dwelt in the white house of asceticism and prophetic beauty. And all the themes together are what made Concord a pivot of the New England tradition in the nineteenth century.

Meanwhile the rest of the country had embarked on its first wild surge of expansionism: commercial development, exploitation of natural resources, imperialism. Americans have become so touchy about imperialism in recent years that one hesitates to use the word; yet it is historically exact—once they were proud of it. Recently I came across an illuminating example. Everyone knows the catch-sentence, "Westward the course of empire takes its way," though everyone may not remember that it was originated by George Berkeley, the English idealist philosopher of the eighteenth century, who was much interested in North America and for four years lived in the colony of Rhode Island. Seventy years later, when George Bancroft undertook his immensely popular history of the United States, he used Berkeley's sentence as an emblematic saying stamped in gold on the bindings of all ten volumes (1834–74). The saying is explicit: westward the course of *empire* takes its way. And this was the same George Bancroft who, as acting Secretary of War in 1846, gave the command for U.S. troops to move into Texas and California, thus precipitating the Mexican War. No other war, not even the dreadful Asian conflict of our own time, has left a greater burden on the American conscience.

In New England, whatever people may have thought of the Mexican War or of Jacksonian democracy in general—neither was popular—they took to westward expansionism with a will, especially the rural people. The search for milder climates, better land, or fortune in the gold fields drew them by thousands. Farms were abandoned, sometimes almost without a thought, with results still evident in the remote mountain areas of Vermont and New Hampshire, where we commonly find old, caved-in cellar holes and rosebushes and apple orchards run wild in the forests. New England was seriously depopulated, and those who were left behind, old people, unmarried women, the ill and crippled, formed a lonely, inward-looking society, from whose winter-long broodings arose violence, insanity, and fanaticism. Joseph Smith and Brigham Young were both Vermonters, and *The Book of Mormon* was released to the world in 1830, two years before Emerson resigned his pastorate in Boston. Stranger sects followed. My father told me of a summer night, *circa* 1910, when as a young newspaper reporter in Springfield, Massachusetts, he watched the Campbellites in the countryside climb up on their barn roofs in their night-shirts to await the ending of the world. In the morning when the sun rose as usual, they had to climb down again. The ballads of the New England mountains are full of bloodshed and blood-atonement, the God of Vengeance, the dark voices of wintry evil. Rudyard Kipling, who married an American woman and lived for four years near

Brattleboro, Vermont, wrote about his neighborhood in his autobiography: "The land was denuding itself of its accustomed inhabitants, and their places had not yet been taken by the wreckage of eastern Europe or the wealthy city-folk who later bought 'pleasure farms.' What might have become characters, powers and attributes perverted themselves in that desolation as cankered trees throw out branches akimbo, and strange faiths and cruelties, born of solitude to the edge of insanity, flourished like lichen on sick bark."

Yet New Englanders—worn-out Puritans—had only themselves to blame if the west seemed more attractive than their own region. They had found a land that was rich enough when they came there. Those who settled in upper New Hampshire and Vermont in the late eighteenth century had ruined their land—they and their sons—before many years of the nineteenth century had passed, and they were among the first to take off for the west when the opportunity offered. The last otter in Otter Creek, Vermont, was shot before 1810. The white-tailed deer was extinct by mid-century. Moose and caribou, wolves and mountain lions, beaver and mink were gone. The great forests of white pine which had covered the mountains and valleys alike were gone, huge trees as splendid as the western pines and firs of today, felled and burned up for potash in a few years. Brooks turned to trickles, springs dried up, the topsoil washed and blew away. All in a few decades farms changed from fertile homesteads to stony, gravelly, weedy beds of poverty and despair. And it was not ignorance that did it; adequate methods of tillage were known, had been practiced for centuries in Europe and by the first Puritan settlers on the Massachusetts coast. It was at best carelessness and at worst deliberate exploitation, the inverse of Puritan responsibility; and the worst was far commoner than the best.

Much of this worst was transported westward, to the whole nation, in waves of emigrating New Englanders throughout the nineteenth century. A few years ago when I was driving through remote regions of Nevada I came to a tiny village named Lamoille, and then to beautiful Lamoille Canyon in the Ruby Mountains nearby. That is the name of the river which flows through my home town in Vermont; an utterly meaningless name, the result of some seventeenth-century Parisian mapmaker's inability to read the handwriting of Samuel de Champlain; yet there it was, transplanted in all its meaningless 3,000 miles to Nevada by some homesick Vermonter, who no doubt took with him also the "knowledge" that in time reduced the Nevadan prairie to a desert of sage and twisted juniper.

As the farms wore out, the mills, which had lined all New England's mountain rivers and brooks, closed down. The sheep had gone west, the wheat followed soon after, the forests of pine were decimated. A few mills remained, turning out wooden objects, bobbins and golf tees, pencils and gunstocks, toothpicks and collar buttons, until the age of plastics claimed them too. New Englanders became addicted to failure, as in a sense they had been from the beginning, with their Puritanical vision of fate. The Bitch Goddess had seldom smiled on them, but always elsewhere—the gold fields, Broadway, Timbuktu. They cultivated the virtues of failure: "spiritual sturdiness" and simple survivorship; and since most of the survivors were women, old maids living out their lives in cheerful desperation, it was natural that they should become for a time the chief bearers of the tradition, women like Sarah Orne Jewett and Mary E. Wilkins who knew Gothic New England and its mentality at first hand. The life of New Englanders had always been "a struggle, not between man and nature or between man and man, but between man and the dark powers;"[37] and in this struggle women in their housekeeping had been as deeply engaged as men in their woods and fields.

Yet one man who knew that world of spiritual terror as well as anybody was Edwin Arlington Robinson. He often remarked that he had lived "in hell," and when we learn the circumstances of his youth we see that he was being perfectly truthful. One of three brothers, he lived in Gardiner, Maine, a mill town where his father was a prosperous businessman, but later one of the brothers, Hermann, lost the family's money in western land speculations. The father died, broken and bankrupt. Robinson attended Harvard for two years, but had to go home when the money gave out. When his mother died of black diphtheria, no townsman would enter the house, neither doctor nor undertaker, and the three sons ministered to her themselves, then placed her in a coffin that had been left on the porch and buried her at night in the graveyard. Meanwhile the eldest son, Dean, whom Robinson greatly admired, had become a morphine addict, and three years later he too died, in an agony of poisoning. Stop, stop, we want to cry; no more; the human heart can't take it. Well, Robinson did take it, he survived; though there is plenty of evidence that he was damaged by it, and by the long neglect he suffered as a poet.

Robinson published his first book, *The Torrent and the Night Before,* at his own expense in 1896, when he was twenty-seven years old, and could find scarcely anyone to read it. Yet it contained not only some fine poems but some very characteristic poems. "The Torrent" is one of them:

> I found a torrent falling in a glen
> Where the sun's light shone silvered and
>   leaf-split;
> The boom, the foam, and the mad flash
>   of it
> All made a magic symphony; but when
> I thought upon the coming of hard men
> To cut those patriarchal trees away,
> And turn to gold the silver of that spray,
> I shuddered. Yet a gladness now and then
> Did wake me to myself till I was glad
> In earnest, and was welcoming the time
> For screaming saws to sound above the
>   chime
> Of idle waters, and for me to know

The jealous visionings that I had had
Were steps to the great place where trees
and torrents go.

This is a poem rooted in the natural environment,
a poem of the New England earth; then an elegy for
the destruction of the earth to satisfy commercial
ends; and finally a statement of the poet's reconciliation and an intuition of "the great place" toward
which trees and torrents, and presumably poets, are
bound. The hard earth and the equally hard men
are New England poetry *par excellence;* but so are
the poet's "jealous visionings," meaning his rebellion, and his final spiritual intuition. Louis Coxe,
the latest of Robinson's many critics, has written:
"In his [Robinson's] earlier days Emersonianism
played hell with his life and his poetry and would
in fact intrude throughout his career."[38] Coxe speaks
of the "New England Appetite for Universals"—
capitalized to mean an almost institutionalized factor of New England culture. It is what I have called
the temptation of spiritual hope. Robinson and most
of his contemporaries could not resist it, yet they
knew they should. What place had Emersonian hope
and optimism in the failing world of New England
Gothic, what could they be but delusions? This was
the great New England dilemma. In a sense the
whole effort of William James in philosophy was to
overcome it by offering a "tough-minded" alternative
to absolutistic or unitarian religion, a pluralistic and
risky view, what he called a "pragmatic or melioris-
tic type of theism." In another sense what James
was trying to do was to restore the frank and ennobling acknowledgment of human tragedy which
had been implicit in Puritan faith but had then
been eroded through two hundred and fifty years
of American pastoral sentimentalism.[39] Robinson,
writing out of a greater pessimism than James ever
knew, could make no such affirmative effort, but
instead could only veer between his despairing
realism and his visionary flashes:

28

Now in a thought, now in a shadowed
     word,
Now in a voice that thrills eternity,
Ever there comes an onward phrase to me
Of some transcendent music I have
     heard;
No piteous thing by soft hands
     dulcimered,
No trumpet crash of blood-sick victory,
But a glad strain of some vast harmony
That no brief mortal touch has ever
     stirred.

Did he mean it? So far were his life and feeling from
any gladness we can observe that we are almost inclined to think he was writing to please the fashion
or as an act of wish-fulfillment. Yet he returns to
this vision again and again in his earlier poems. I
think he really had heard "some transcendent
music," and I think every New Englander has really
heard it, unclear, unhelpful, delusive as it may (or
may not) be. My own father, a positive pragmatist
if there ever was one—he was amused by the Campbellites—once saw "a fairy sitting in a maple tree,"
and communicated with it, and received "a word
from William Blake." Robinson was no stranger to
such experience. Yet he was in the grip, too, of a
vision of failing reality, of the terror of human
nullity, and so he continued in irresolution, in al-
ternating bouts of poetry and alcoholism, until he
wore out both himself and his poetry long before
he had come to a natural terminus.

Another point to be made about Robinson could
be illustrated from virtually any poem in the 1,488
pages of his collected edition, but the poem I have
already quoted, "The Torrent," though somewhat
rudimentary, will do. In the last line "the great
place" is characteristic New England speech: ambiguity and understatement. We are not told what
the great place is; inferno or paradise?—we can't
be certain. The poem's imagery of violence suggests
the former, but the slowed, elongated movement of

the final line suggests the latter. Whichever it is, however, or whatever it is, we know that the "great place" is much more than a great place. Robinson is using simple words and common idiom to mean more than they say. This is an extremely widespread usage among poets, of course, and it would be difficult to demonstrate that Robinson's use of it derived directly from his Puritan heritage, especially since such rhetorical devices were conspicuous in the writing of the English Renaissance and had descended to the modern period by many, many routes. Yet I believe there is a direct connection between Robinson's understatement and the Puritans' concept, so important to them, that ultimate meaning is concealed and that all external reality or observable phenomena are paraphrastic of God's will. In short, appearances are deceptive and things, including words, do not mean what they seem to mean. This was such a deeply felt part of Puritan faith that it entered New England psychology permanently and became, not a literary or rhetorical attitude, but an element of the common mind and an innate mode of common speech. From this common reservoir, the great New England fund of humor that emphasizes the incongruities of knowledge and experience, New England's poets have drawn their rhetoric and diction, and not from the conscious literary tradition.

From New England this manner of thought spread throughout the west. The purest examples of New England humor I have heard have been spoken in the mountains of New Hampshire and Vermont and in the valleys of Nevada and Wyoming.[40] The importance of this is by no means limited to literary considerations, as one of the sharpest critics of Yankee ways, George Santayana, pointed out, in a singularly perceptive and advanced statement, in 1922:

> And yet I feel that there is a genuine spirit of humour abroad in America, and that it is one of the best things there. The constant sense of the in-

congruous, even if artificially stimulated and found only in trivial things, is an admission that existence is absurd; it is therefore a liberation of the spirit over against this absurd world; it is a laughing liberation, because the spirit is glad to be free; and yet it is not a scornful nor bitter liberation, because a world that lets us laugh at it and be free is after all a friendly world.[41]

It seems to me that Santayana touched very near the existential heart of the New England tradition when he wrote this. He shows us in exactly what sense our humor is serious, a very serious matter, and with unwitting prescience he diagnoses our predicament fifty years later, now when native humor has been so widely repressed.[42] One of our best human defenses against absurdity is gone and the world is now far from friendly. The more violent and desperate defenses we have been forced to adopt in its place—like Meursault's four extra shots in the *The Stranger*—may prove to be far less effectual.

Robinson, for whom this serious humor was as much second nature as it was for any other New Englander, became an important, not to say indispensable, transmitter of the tradition. There was no one else who could have brought it across the great gulf between the Cambridge poets of the mid-nineteenth century—Longfellow, Lowell, Whittier, etc.—and the poets of the twentieth century. In other respects I think we must concede that Robinson was less important than many earlier commentators have maintained. We see now that he is a poet's poet, the sort of poet from whom other writers take learning, wisdom, and pleasure, and both from his life and his work, from his few successes and his many failures. For from the whole onerous bulk of his work only a dozen or so poems still hold up. And his faults are pervasive; they can be seen in as small a poem as "The Torrent": his persistent drift away from concreteness and toward fanciful abstraction, as in "magic symphony"; his inability to rise above the dictional and rhetorical demands of what Coxe has called the "middle romantic style," as in "did wake me"; and above all his addiction to foreign forms like the sonnet; for even if a few, a very few, of his sonnets turned out to be genuinely good specimens of their kind, they had no real formal congruence with Robinson's native temperament, and this produced the same devastating weakness at the center of his writing that it had produced in the work of Longfellow a generation before.[43] Robinson probably began with as strong a talent as anyone could wish for, but it was warped, frayed, softened by his tragic New Englander's life, even though much of his adulthood was spent in "the town down the river," New York. He is a prime example of what the American nineteenth century accomplished with its persistent brutalization of spirit. Today, though we take real pleasure from such poems as "Eros Turannos," "Mr. Flood's Party," "The Pity of the Leaves," "Luke Havergal," and especially "Ben Jonson Entertains a Man from Stratford," which to my mind is the closest Robinson came to the perfection of all his resources, we end by assigning Robinson a fundamentally transitional role.[44]

We come, then, to Robert Frost, as every discussion of the New England tradition must, for in his poetry every element of the tradition is combined, there to be given the thrust of his sometimes hot and sometimes vacantly, terrifyingly cold personality. Twenty years ago Randall Jarrell wrote an essay entitled "The Other Frost," in which he complained that the popular image of Frost as a happy lyricist, a conservative editorialist, and a farmer-poet was wrong, and that most of Frost's popular poems were not among his best.[45] I agreed with this, as I think most serious readers today would also—it is a fine essay, well worth rereading—but two or three years ago, when I made up my selection of Frost's poems for an anthology I was editing, I had forgotten Jarrell's essay. It is interesting to note that in my selection of sixteen poems chosen to represent "the other Frost" there are only two which also appear in Jarrell's list of fourteen poems chosen for the same purpose.

Was Jarrell right, or was I? We may both have been wrong. The fact is that there are enough "other Frosts" for half-a-dozen readers and the collected edition of his poems is a gold mine. I suspect that if Jarrell had made up his list six months later or earlier it would have been quite different; I know mine would. A case in point is the poem I wish to quote here, "The Vanishing Red," which appears in neither of our lists, nor as far as I know in anyone else's, though it is one of his very best; at least so I have thought since I "discovered" it about a month ago.

> He is said to have been the last Red Man
> In Acton. And the Miller is said to have
>   laughed—
> If you like to call such a sound a laugh.
> But he gave no one else a laugher's license.
> For he turned suddenly grave as if to say,
> "Whose business,—if I take it on myself,
> Whose business—but why talk round
>   the barn?—
> When it's just that I hold with getting a
>   thing done with."
> You can't get back and see it as he saw it.
> It's too long a story to go into now.
> You'd have to have been there and lived it.
> Then you wouldn't have looked on it as
>   just a matter
> Of who began it between the two races.
>
> Some guttural exclamation of surprise
> The Red Man gave in poking about the
>   mill
> Over the great big thumping shuffling
>   millstone
> Disgusted the Miller physically as coming
> From one who had no right to be heard
>   from.
> "Come, John," he said, "you want to see
>   the wheel-pit?"

He took him down below a cramping rafter,
And showed him, through a manhole in
     the floor,
The water in desperate straits like
     frantic fish,
Salmon and sturgeon, lashing with their
     tails.
Then he shut down the trap door with a
     ring in it
That jangled even above the general noise,
And came upstairs alone—and gave that
     laugh,
And said something to a man with a
     meal-sack
That the man with the meal-sack didn't
     catch—then.
Oh, yes, he showed John the wheel-pit
     all right.

I take it I need add nothing to the reams already
written about Frost's closeness to nature, including
human nature; his depth of perception, sympathy,
earthiness, his New England cultural relevance. I
do wish, however, to say something about the language of this poem, though prosody is not our main
concern. Notice how all the lines are end-stopped
except the first; a brilliant way to get into a poem
and then to keep it moving, and a seemingly simple
way too—but how few poets today can approach
that simplicity. Notice also how Frost casts the
common speech, the common New England speech,
against the blank-verse measure more loosely, reck-
lessly, naturally than ever—so it seems—yet with
absolute metrical assurance. Every line is immu-
table. It is magnificent writing.

But the heart of the poem is the Miller's laugh,
and what that laugh means is the heart of Frost's
poetic temperament: the blackest, bitterest despair
in three hundred years of the New England tradition. There is nothing to match it in Hawthorne, in
James, in Robinson, or in any other writer I am
aware of. You must go back to Michael Wiggles-

worth's *Day of Doom* (1662) and then abstract the knowledge of salvation from it, to find anything like Frost's vision of the human hell. Miller or Red Man, "It's too long a story to go into now." Yes, as long as time. Man destroying himself, held in the grip of an absolute need to destroy himself, the great death-machine, pain-machine, rape-machine, the collective human heart: and what can we do but laugh? It is the greatest absurdity, as our survival somehow in spite of it, our blind, ceaseless endurance, is the greatest heroism. How many of Frost's poems give us this vision, clothed in all degrees of feeling from pathos to terror, but always the same vision. Mankind doomed. Predestined. "The Witch of Coös," "The Hill Wife," "Acquainted with the Night," "Neither Out Far Nor In Deep," "Out, Out," and many others. Yet often the vision is so quietly reported that the horror almost slips past us, and that itself adds to the horror. There is rarely a shriek in Frost. The Red Man just vanishes—not a word. The trap door says it, and then the Miller's laugh.

Understatement, the use of both objects and words to mean more than they denote: as we have seen, this is a deep-rooted New England mode of thought, and Frost is its master. It is not symbolism if you mean by symbolism the practice of the self-conscious European *symbolistes* and their imitators. It is something much deeper, more instinctive. To this day your New England farmer will prefer to shake his head and keep silent before any issue of complex feeling, and then say something about the weather. What more can be said? The trap door says it. And the Miller's laugh.

Then there is the other ox of the team, so to speak, which our look at New England's cultural evolution has led us to expect, the persistent trace of Emersonian spiritual aspiration, the temptation to hope; or better, in Frost's case, the temptation to non-despair. Many poems allude to it, though I think they are demonstrably weaker poems than the others. One is "For Once, Then, Something":

Others taunt me with having knelt at
   well-curbs
Always wrong to the light, so never seeing
Deeper down in the well than where the
   water
Gives me back in a shining surface picture
Me myself in the summer heaven godlike
Looking out of a wreath of fern and cloud
   puffs.
Once, when trying with chin against a
   well-curb,
I discerned, as I thought, beyond the
   picture,
Through the picture, a something
   white, uncertain,
Something more of the depths—and then
   I lost it.
Water came to rebuke the too clear water.
One drop fell from a fern, and lo, a ripple
Shook whatever it was lay there at bottom,
Blurred it, blotted it out. What was that
   whiteness?
Truth? A pebble of quartz? For once,
   then, something.

This is Frost using all his skill and power on a contrived poetic incident; it is marvelous to watch him
trying to convince us. "Water came to rebuke the
too clear water"—a perfect line, and the ironic
Biblical "lo" is a stroke of genius. Notice how the
living instinct of understatement is no simple or
formulaic manipulation of meaning, but a complex
of layered counter-feelings: ". . . as I thought, beyond the picture,/ Through the picture, a something
white, uncertain," and then the sharply underlined
"Once." But we end knowing that although Frost
has more than once looked down a well and more
than once *wished* he could see something else there
than water, the poem is about the wish, the "once"
that never happened. And then just as this realization completes itself we see that there actually was
something after all, something in Frost's experience,

but so vague, so remote, that it could not be accommodated in the contrived episode of the poet looking at himself in the well water. Yet did he once see something down there? My father saw a fairy in a maple tree. If only the last lines of the poem rang with a solider tone!

A more explicit poem is "The Strong Are Saying Nothing":

> The soil now gets a rumpling soft and
>   damp,
> And small regard to the future of any
>   weed.
> The final flat of the hoe's approval stamp
> Is reserved for the bed of a few selected
>   seed.
>
> There is seldom more than a man to a
>   harrowed piece.
> Men work alone, their lots plowed far
>   apart,
> One stringing a chain of seed in an open
>   crease,
> And another stumbling after a halting
>   cart.
>
> To the fresh and black of the squares of
>   early mold
> The leafless bloom of a plum is fresh and
>   white;
> Though there's more than a doubt if the
>   weather is not too cold
> For the bees to come and serve its beauty
>   aright.
>
> Wind goes from farm to farm in wave on
>   wave,
> But carries no cry of what is hoped to be.
> There may be little or much beyond the
>   grave,
> But the strong are saying nothing until
>   they see.

It is too explicit, in fact, to be characteristic: the shift from indirect statement to direct in the last two lines. Frost is writing here almost as if in exasperation with himself for having labored so long on so many other poems to say indirectly, emotively, suggestively what can be said outright. It is a feeling other poets will recognize. But of course we know, and he knew, that his first, enduring, poetic impulse was the right one, because this poem is weaker than the others, though it is worth quoting for its sexuality and its plain statement of man's solitude, modesty, nobility, and strength—that spiritual sturdiness of men who are living, not dying. Many other poems, "The Oven Bird," "A Star in a Stone-Boat," even in its desperate way "A Servant to Servants," and scores of others, say the same thing more effectively if less forthrightly. The theme has almost limitless mutations. At its bleakest it is a despair colder than anything I know in another major poet, for it is the acknowledgment of ultimate failure, the failure of love. The earth is rich, the flowers will bloom, men and women will love one another—and it changes nothing. Perhaps Frost asked too much, of love and of the world; it is an inferrable proposition. But this was his radicalism, his almost total abnegation springing from an almost total lack of faith: not just religious faith, nor even faith in humanity, but faith in any reality—he was the agonized total skeptic. Nor was he the first New Englander to find himself in such a fix, or the last. Many of his own people, the characters of his poems, were thus beset, and were driven to violence and madness because of it; but he himself chose another way out, the way of continued thinking, writing, enduring, the way of unexplainable heroism—unless the explanation lies in his creative power, secondarily over his characters, primarily over himself. I know that this is far from the whole story about Frost. There are his evasions, his masks, his patently false but strenuously enforced public image. This is a complicating factor and there are others, to which the scholars and biographers must devote themselves. What I have tried to do is get to the barest heart of the man and his poetry. He was, if I read him correctly, the furthest evolution of the New England type we have had so far, the New Englander *par excellence* and *in extremis*, who combined virtually all elements of the tradition, shaped them, gave them new impetus. We are still so close to him in time that we cannot judge him well. Envy, jealousy, and other literary animosities have hurt his reputation among younger poets and critics, and many have even held that the gulf between Frost and the "mainstream" of American literature—Pound, Eliot, Williams, etc.—is so great that readers cannot possibly give loyalty to both; but this is folly. They were all Americans and all contemporaries, sharing far more than they disputed, and even the disputes can be, if not reconciled, at least accommodated in our later understandings. If Pound and Frost considered themselves mutual antagonists, that was their misfortune; perhaps it was their necessity. I see no reason why I cannot read them both, and read them equally well.

What profit would be won from pursuing the tradition further than this, I do not know. As the tradition draws closer to us it becomes amorphous and fragmented, though to the eye of the future it may appear perfectly clear. New England has continued to be a seed-bed of poets, which I take as a sign that somewhere within the ravages of "modern education" my region has preserved at least a vestige of the liberal arts. As the centers of the nation's cultural activity have shifted elsewhere, to New York or San Francisco, many New England poets have emigrated, while still preserving the essential qualities of their tradition. Such poets as Edna St. Vincent Millay and Louise Bogan, both born in small towns in Maine, are good examples; committed wholeheartedly to the "modernity" of post-World War I, they nevertheless clung to the notions of hardihood and independence that had sustained their New England ancestors, notions which sorted well with their bitter feminism. Other poets stayed at home, struggling in the well-nigh suffocating *aura popularis* of Frost. Winfield Townley Scott of Rhode Island and Robert Francis of Massachusetts nevertheless found voices of their own within the characteristic New England idiom of their generation, as it had been defined by Robinson and Frost, and both poets produced memorable work. Other poets came into New England from outside, especially Wallace Stevens and Mark Van Doren, who both adapted large elements of the local tradition to their own prior concerns.[46] Among younger poets I think I see in Robert Creeley, who left Massachusetts as a young man and has spent the rest of his life in decidedly different cultural environments, the residue of a New England outlook, though still younger poets, like Paul Blackburn of Vermont, present a more difficult case. As I say, the closer the tradition comes to ourselves the harder it is to see it.

An even more difficult case is that of the poet who will certainly be crucial to future studies of the New England tradition, I mean Charles Olson. As mentor of the Black Mountain poets of the 1950s and 1960s, Olson was deeply involved in another tradition of American poetry altogether, that which developed generally through Whitman, Stephen Crane, Ezra Pound, and William Carlos Williams. Yet Olson remained all his life devoted to his native region, eastern Massachusetts, especially Gloucester and the other fishing villages, the heart of Puritan country; devoted not only to its history and cultural precedence but to its deepest psychology. His influence on the New England tradition was liberating and redirecting, but immensely complicating, and we cannot yet untangle all the threads.

New England's most acute critic, George Santayana, once put into a novel his view of the decline of the Puritan tradition. His hero, Oliver, the "last Puritan," spoke of the Puritan virtues in these words:

> Old-fashioned: no doubt I am old-fashioned. *Weh dir, dass du ein Enkel bist.* I was born old. It

is a dreadful inheritance, this of mine, that I need to be honest, that I need to be true, that I need to be just. That's not the fashion of today. The world is full of conscript minds, only they are in different armies, and nobody is fighting to be free, but each to make his own conscription universal. I can't catch the contagion.[47]

Santayana was writing from his standpoint in the last generation of the nineteenth century. Moreover, as a cosmopolitan he could not see beyond Boston. He thought that the Boston of the 1870s, what has been called the "genteel tradition," represented the last of Puritanism, and that its final decline as the world moved into the post-1914 era meant the end of Puritanism as a force in American life. But he was wrong. Puritanism had had many more outgrowths than gentility. It had died in Boston—long since, in fact—but it had moved farther and farther out into the New England countryside: to the mill towns, the mountains, the western borders. There the love of truth, honesty, and justice survived, there the aversion to conscript minds became stronger and stronger: there in the precincts that gave birth to Ethan Allen and Daniel Shays. The fact is that every true New Englander is the last Puritan. He goes on and on, and his children take up the role. What he has done in the ruins of his original purity—his imperialism, exploitation, and capitalist cruelty—is neither wise nor pretty, but his redemption, if he has any, is that he knows it. His conscience is finely tuned. He is his own fiercest critic, his own best conscience, and with that for his credential he can be the nation's best conscience too, if he is permitted.

The temptation to hope, the despair of failing reality, bedrock radicalism and rebellion, the vision of inner meaning in objective experience, above all the truth of independent man: these are the strains of the Puritan tradition. I do not ask that the tradition be looked at again. It has been looked at and looked at and looked at; the facts of it are there for anyone to see. I ask that we begin seeing. I ask

41

that we throw off our prejudice, so long our yoke. For one hundred and fifty years Puritanism has been the national scapegoat, but it was as good a beginning as any nation could ask, far better than most; for if its purity contained an anti-esthetic element, this was soon overcome, and in its social and political aspects it was the flower of the English Renaissance. In short it seems to me that long before the catch terms of European existentialism came to the United States in the 1940s, the Puritan evolution had brought New Englanders to the same view of themselves. Authenticity, responsibility in freedom, existence before essence, and such other catch-sayings have a European ring, but they are the modern catalysts of the New England mind, and William James was the true forerunner of Jean-Paul Sartre. Today the last Puritan is as present as ever, and as much needed. Always born old, he is eternally young. In his ultimate radicalism and existential purity he is suspicious of both the establishment and the sugary communes of the soft-headed rebels. He is our conscience, which explains why often we do not like him. But in his realism and authentic radicalism, he will ultimately become not only our conscience but our guide; as we have been guided heretofore by such men as John Dewey of Vermont, whose faith in radical social democracy came straight from the Green Mountain heritage, or as Justice Oliver Wendell Holmes, Jr., of Massachusetts, whose skeptical view of tragic human reality led to our strongest, most consistent defense of free speech and thought; for if we but knew it skepticism is the sweetness of magnanimity. "Certainty is generally illusion," Holmes wrote, "and repose is not the destiny of man," sentiments which Robinson put with greater power in "The Man Against the Sky":

> Because the weight of our humility
> Wherefrom we gain
> A little wisdom and much pain
> Falls here too sore and there too tedious,

Are we in anguish or complacency
Not looking far enough ahead
To see by what mad couriers we are led
Along the roads of the ridiculous,
To pity ourselves and laugh at faith
And while we curse life bear it?

I end by turning to a younger New England poet, Galway Kinnell, born in Rhode Island and living today in Vermont, one of the finest New England poets now writing. Like other poets of my generation, he began to write under the immense white shadow of Frost, and in a relationship to him of half-aversion, half-reverence. When Frost died, Kinnell wrote a tribute, from which I shall quote the concluding lines, because they show Frost as the New Englander *par excellence* who has been reborn a thousand times, a hundred thousand, in villages all over New England, young people committed, like Kinnell, to contemporary radicalism, committed deeply but despairingly. And that, I believe, is the necessary creative attitude of all sons and daughters of earth today.

When we think of a man who was cursed
Neither with the mystical all-lovingness
    of Walt Whitman
Nor with Melville's anguish to know and to
    suffer,
And yet cursed . . . a man, what shall
    I say,
Vain, not fully convinced he was dying,
    whose calling
Was to set up in the wilderness of his
    country,
At whatever cost, a man, who would be his
    own man,
We think of you. And from the same
    doorway
At which you lived, between the house and
    the woods,

We see your old footprints going away
  across
The great Republic, Frost, up memorized
  slopes,
Down hills floating by heart on the
  bulldozed land.[48]

Notes

[1] Just shy of the 45th parallel, half way between the Equator and the Pole. The real North extends silently above me.

[2] D. H. Lawrence in *Studies in Classic American Literature* (New York, 1964), p. 56.

[3] Van Wyck Brooks, *The Flowering of New England* (New York, 1936), p. 482.

[4] Perry Miller, *The New England Mind: From Colony to Province* (Boston, 1952), p. 5.

[5] See Tate's essay on Emily Dickinson, *Collected Essays* (Denver, 1959), p. 198.

[6] *Ibid.*, p. 199.

[7] *The Works of Anne Bradstreet*, Jeannine Hensley, ed. (Cambridge, 1967), p. 281.

[8] Yvor Winters, *In Defense of Reason* (Denver, 1947), p. 157ff.

[9] H. W. Schneider, *The Puritan Mind* (New York, 1930), p. 51.

[10] *Ibid.*, p. 48.

[11] *Ibid.*, p. 43.

[12] Anyone who doubts the subversive role played by Satan in the ordinary affairs of Puritans need only read the opening pages of Bradford's *History,* where the Serpent's schemes "to ruinate & destroy ye kingdom of Christ by . . . secrete & subtile means" are given in some detail. *Bradford's History "Of Plimoth Plantation"* (Boston, 1898), p. 5ff.

[13] John Winthrop, quoted in Richard S. Dunn, *Puritans and Yankees: The Winthrop Dynasty of New England, 1630–1717* (Princeton, 1962), p. 29.

[14] See Cotton's *The Way of Life* (London, 1641), *passim.*

[15] For an account of three white men tried and executed in 1638 for the murder of one Indian, see *Winthrop's Journal,* James Kendall Hosmer, ed. (New York, 1946), vol. I, pp. 273–74. The case was typical of its time, but its time—in the history of American race relations—was brief.

[16] Quoted in Howard Mumford Jones, *O Strange New World* (New York, 1964), pp. 189–90. Cushman, however, left the company before it embarked.

[17] *Ibid.,* p. 190.

[18] According to Van Wyck Brooks, the "root-ideas" of the New England tradition are: "Faith in the individual, the passion for justice, the sense of the potential in human nature and its world, the love of life, the belief in its ultimate goodness." See *New England: Indian Summer* (New York, 1940), p. 541. But this, especially the latter two articles, is Emersonianism, not Puritanism. The "root-ideas" of New England culture are far older, far more realistic, radical, and humane, than the optimistic spiritualism of the Sage of Concord.

[19] Though Sewall may be an exception. Without doubt he would have been if his *Diary,* first published in 1878–82, had appeared a century earlier.

[20] See Ethan Allen's *Reason the Only Oracle of Man* (Philadelphia, 1784), a remarkable document which betrays its author's Puritan character on virtually every page, although its avowed object was to broadcast Allen's determined, not to say impudent, Free Thinking.

[21] Of course in New England, as elsewhere, the eighteenth century was the political century, and I do not mean to deny either that time's political increments to the tradition or their importance as cultural paradigms later on. But I do believe that after we have made allowance for everything we have been taught about foreign models for American revolutionary thought, most of the century's basic political impulses were native and can be inferred from antecedent Puritanical ideas. In other words, Federalist theory was a reinforcement, rather than a modification or impedence, to the secular residue of Puritanism.

[22] Except, of course, Henry James, Jr., who lived for a time in Cambridge and whose American literary connections were almost exclusively with New England. But James was born in New York and lived most of his life in Europe.

[23] Robinson, a blind author who lived in Ferrisburg, Vermont, specialized in tales and sketches about life in a semifictional hamlet of the Green Mountains which he called Danvis. His work was published (in Boston) in a number of volumes, and was moderately popular during the years 1885–1910. Today he is known only to Vermonters and to only a few of them. His work merits a better fate.

[24] All quotations from Emerson are from the *Journals.*

[25] Tate, *Collected Essays,* pp. 200–201.

[26] From an early essay entitled "The Optimism of Ralph Waldo Emerson," reprinted in *George Santayana's America,* James Ballowe, ed. (Urbana, Ill., 1967), p. 84.

[27] See, for example, Stephen E. Whicher's introduction to *Selections from Ralph Waldo Emerson* (Boston, 1957), especially pp. xiii–xv.

[28] In a review of *Americans,* by Stuart P. Sherman. Re-

printed in *D. H. Lawrence: Selected Criticism,* Anthony Beal, ed. (New York, 1966), p. 418.

[29] "The Optimism of George Santayana," in *George Santayana's America,* pp. 86–87.

[30] Yet his radicalism still seems dangerous to many. Van Wyck Brooks always refers to Thoreau as "Henry," the only case of such familiarity in his otherwise Brahminical tones; as if this condescension could somehiw disguise or disarm the very maturity of Thoreau's revolutionary thought.

[31] First edition of *Walden,* 1854; first edition of *Leaves of Grass,* 1855.

[32] I have discussed these themes at some length in the essay "A Meaning of Robert Lowell," *The Hudson Review,* vol. 20, no. 3 (Autumn, 1967); reprinted in *The American Literary Anthology/2,* George Plimpton and Peter Ardery, eds. (New York, 1969), and in *Robert Lowell: A Portrait of the Artist in His Time,* Michael London and Robert Boyers, eds. (New York, 1970).

[33] Leslie Fiedler, *The Return of the Vanishing American* (New York, 1968), p. 17.

[34] I don't mean to discount earlier journal-keepers, men as diverse as John Woolman and Samuel Pepys. What I wish to stress is the autobiogenetic element—and I apologize for my inability so far to think of a less clumsy term. This, and not Thoreau's journal-keeping, is the novelty of *Walden.*

[35] See Thoreau's account of plastering his house in chapter 13 of *Walden.*

[36] Charles Ives, *Essays before a Sonata* (New York, 1962), pp. 47–48.

[37] Louis O. Coxe, *Edwin Arlington Robinson: The Life of Poetry* (New York, 1969), p. 59.

[38] *Ibid.,* p. 62.

[39] See especially chapter 8, "Pragmatism and Religion," of *Pragmatism* (New York, 1907).

[40] I have the impression, which I cannot verify, that the strain of Yankee humor in the west remains purest in areas originally settled by Mormons.

[41] From a book review in *The New Republic.* Reprinted in *George Santayana's America,* p. 176.

[42] One need only glance at their recorded utterances to see that Cal Coolidge was a barrel of fun compared to Lyndon Johnson or Richard Nixon.

[43] Robinson did move toward a formal shaping of native sources in such blank-verse poems as "Captain Craig" and "Isaac and Archibald," but then he turned from it again, more's the pity, in his Arthurian poems, even the best of which, "Merlin" and "Launcelot," seem to me far less than what I judge he might have done.

[44] Many of the things I have said about Robinson might have been said about a very different poet, Emily Dickinson.

But because she did not publish her work during her lifetime, so that it did not enter the tradition until long after it was written, I have left her out of this discussion. Another reason for dong so is that her extreme individuality puts her into a special relationship to both Puritanism and modernity, well worth investigating for its own sake—as many have done—but not relevant to my present themes.

[45] Reprinted in Randall Jarrell's *Poetry and the Age* (New York, 1953), pp. 28–36.

[46] Readers who are used to thinking of Stevens as an exotic product of modern estheticism might be surprised to find how close his early work was to the poetry of the previous generation of New Englanders, especially William Vaughn Moody. At the same time the whole effort of Stevens' later poetry was to assimilate his estheticism to Puritan realism and radicalism. Contrast his poem "The River of Rivers in Connecticut" with Emerson's "Two Rivers."

[47] George Santayana, *The Last Puritan* (New York, 1936), p. 581.

[48] From "For Robert Frost," in Galway Kinnell's *Flower Herding on Mount Monadnock* (Boston, 1964).

the south

George Garrett

Photograph by Leland Payton

The literature of the South can be deeply misleading. The plain truth is that it *has been* confusing and deceptive not alone, by any means, to those outside the South who have come to some knowledge of the region through its fiction and its poetry, but also to those native born and bred, the scholars and critics who are dedicated to the understanding of southern letters. There are many truths, deep rooted in southern life and history, which are openly expressed in southern letters. There are other things, equally true and no less important, which are not at once evident, being either taken for granted, assumed by the makers of our literature, or, in some cases, concealed out of a wishful regard for another sort of truth, the truth of myth, of the wishes and hopes, all the pure facts of the human imagination.

This should not surprise us. It is not without ample precedent. Over a glaring waste of ruined time, we know, or believe that we do, much of the truth of ancient Greece through the words of the Greeks, translated, transformed, modified, but still alive to us in the works of poets, dramatists, historians and philosophers which have somehow survived the ravages of time. But the gift of the Greeks has likewise survived its own time, appearing now at a far remove from a small country, never a nation in our sense of the word, of fractious and broiling

Novelist George Garrett teaches at the University of South Carolina.

city states, united and alike only in a common language and, perhaps, a common world of the imagination. The great words of the Greeks sing to us still; and the burden of that singing contains great truths. Without their words the remains of the Greeks would be as idle and ironic as that ruined statue Shelley restored from meaningless oblivion in "Ozymandias."

Just so. . . . And which then is true—the harsh, disunited land of petty city states, of petty politics, of much cruelty and poverty and long sorrows? Or is the truth to be found in the wisdom of those who dreamed a mythic past and looked for a shining future, an ideal which has outlasted all else? We recall, without remembering his judges or their knotty reasons, that Socrates died in discredit and dishonor for his teachings, only to become immortal, a model for all the aspirations of great teachers since.

The vague analogy of the American South is not specific or exact. It breaks down in most details, but it is still a useful one to keep in mind, a shadowy guide to understanding some of the truths of southern literature and some of those others, less easy to find, out of which that literature has grown and flowered. The analogy is also justified because, even as early as Thomas Jefferson, so many southerners were haunted by what they knew and imagined of ancient Greek ideals. It was an analogy returned to after the Civil War when many literary and intellectual southerners liked to imagine themselves as somehow *like* the Greeks who had fallen victim to the brute and half-barbaric power of rising Rome.

To begin, one must acknowledge that there is a deceptive unity in the world of southern letters. It seems easy and natural to speak of the regional literature of the South, perhaps easier than to do so of any other region. There is so much *in common* among southern writers, shared characteristics which transcend not only geographical space and differences within the region, but also time. There seems a clear unity of pattern and tradition in the history of southern writing.

It is worthwhile, at the beginning, to consider this seeming unity, to qualify it first with certain strict and disruptive facts. Because there was once, briefly in time and terribly, a separate political entity, an attempt at a sort of nationhood in the Confederacy, it would appear that at least clearcut political and social lines, if only borders on a map, could be drawn. But we know that the South spills over these vague lines of demarcation, and it always has. We have "the border states" out of which have come so many excellent "southern" writers, especially in our own times. Think of the Kentucky of Robert Penn Warren, and, more recently, of the stories (*The Shadow Knows*) and the recent novel (*Cassandra Singing*) of David Madden. West Virginia is the scene and setting for an entire mythic history of the South, in Mary Lee Settle's *Beaulah Land Trilogy*. Maryland remains debatable territory, but any number of serious studies of contemporary southern letters—of what the scholars call "the southern renaissance"—blithely include such disparate voices as John Barth, J. V. Cunningham, Adrienne Rich, and Karl Shapiro as basically *southern* writers. Similarly the overlapping of South with Southwest blurs all borders and distinctions. Scholars tend to take an awkwardly moderate position, drawing a line between, for example, east Texas and west Texas, eastern and western Arkansas. Even such a restriction allows for a baffling variety. East Texas gives us here and now such gifted writers of fiction as William Goyen, Walter Clemmons, Katherine Anne Porter, and William Humphrey. Yet not one of these lives there now. And such a list, based upon birth and background, would also have to include a variety of other talents, authors like David Westheimer or John Howard Griffin, even Allen Drury. Finally, by an arbitrary line between the black-soiled farmlands of east Texas and the wide sparse ranch country of the west, we simply eliminate certain writers who are as much a part of the southern literary tradition as anyone else. I am thinking of John Graves (*Goodbye to a River*) and of Larry McMurty (most recently, *Moving On*), for example.

The point is clear if the causes are not. To this day, as of this moment in our history, the overall borders of the South are not clearly or easily defined. And the truth is that they never were. The lines and borders of the old Confederacy were never clear from Secession through Reconstruction. They spilled over in some places, shrank back in others. Politically the Confederacy was never really unified, by definition. That in itself, the nature of union, was, after all, one of the great issues, one of the multiple, inconsistent, and contradictory things the Civil War was all about. It has been forgotten, overlooked, at times suppressed in the name of resulting unity, that the political South, the Confederacy, was, from its beginning to its end, far from unified even in theory. There were, as historians such as the novelist and historian Shelby Foote have been able to show and to prove, very large numbers of southerners by birth and heritage, who were, at the very least, "independents"; who chose to assert their own dissident liberty against not only Washington, D.C., and the Union, but against Richmond, the Confederacy, and their own state governments. Poet and novelist Thomas McAfee (*Rover Youngblood: An American Fable*) comes from Haleyville, Alabama, which, with the country around it, greeted Secession by seceding from Alabama. Haleyville was, in due and brutal course, overcome, and its white males literally enslaved in punishment. McAfee's southern heritage is a far cry from that of the Agrarians. His blood kin pulled ploughs until they dropped, to spare Alabama mules for a war far away. Or one would do well to remember that the northern counties of Mississippi, the "upcountry," furnished large numbers of volunteers to the Union cause, more per capita, it has been estimated, than any similar area in the northern states. In large part their war was against other Mississippians, the people of the Delta. And the latter, though slaveowners on a grand scale and brave soldiers in the war, were not adverse to a certain amount of advantageous trade and "consorting with the enemy" in the midst of that war.

Some of this complexity is well suggested in the fiction of William Faulkner, in *The Unvanquished*, in *Absalom, Absalom!*, in the Snopes Trilogy, in many short stories, most notably and explicitly in "Mountain Victory."

The confusion of loyalties, precisely the absence of unity of purpose, theory, or practice is there, too, in that most popular of versions of the southern myth—*Gone With the Wind.*

It should not surprise us that there was no overall political or social unity in the South. It was never there from the first settling. During the American Revolution most of the great battles between the British and the Americans took place elsewhere, though it came to its ending in Yorktown. But the South was the scene of many skirmishes and much savagery between loyalists and rebel colonists. It is widely accepted that elsewhere in the colonies *most* people were more or less neutral. This seems not to have been true in the South, where sides were taken and, even in the absence of major battles, the war was singularly brutal. Again, as in the Civil War, there is a complexity of reasons, of causes and effects. Taking South Carolina as an example, one discovers that the "lowcountry" people, the center of Charleston and the long lowland coastline of (even then) great plantations, were strong for independence despite their cosmopolitan population and their many close and practical ties with England. The loyalist strength came from the upcountry Scotch and Irish, who had fled Britain for good cause, but hated and feared their own neighbors more than they felt a need to resist distant British rule. These upcountry settlers suffered greatly during and after the Revolution. The political lines of demarcation, of separation, established first by geography and free choice, became an invisible wall cemented in blood on both sides; and that wall has not wholly vanished to this day, in South Carolina or westward where the same people moved, early and late, carrying their history and their loyalties and antipathies with them.

These qualifying observations represent a few small examples from the truth of southern history, cited because, with a few exceptions, one would have to look very deep, well below the surface of southern literature, to discover these things expressed at all.

There are other things, patterns and notions derived from the literature of the South which are dubious at best, and at worst simply untrue. In the past decade the study of southern literature has become respectable enough to generate textbooks on the subject. The best of these texts offer the student a simplified version of the general critical and scholarly consensus, a broad area of agreement from which to begin. A recurring assertion in all the textbooks I know of is that the South has always been a relatively "homogeneous" society and, white or black, largely Protestant. It may be true that today the South seems "homogeneous," having been, in large part, settled for a long time and, until fairly recently, having had a limited amount of both immigration and emigration while the rest of the nation, especially in the years following the Civil War and the rapid technological and industrial expansion, enjoyed a huge and various incoming of new peoples. But what has been overlooked from our perspective in time is the truth about the original composition of the southern population: it was considerably more various, ethnically, socially, and religiously, than the populations of the northern states at the time of the Civil War. It should be remembered that from the settled bits and pieces of Florida all along the Gulf Coast to the edge of Mexico there was (and remains) a considerable French and Spanish population, largely Roman Catholic, in Louisiana mingling with (though somewhat different from) the Acadian exiles, called Cajuns. This French and Spanish influence, a political fact until well after the American Revolution, extended north-ward along the Mississippi and remains. This area and population was in contact with its old homes in Europe and maintained quite close relations with the Caribbean islands and with much of what is now Central America. Along the coastal lowlands of the eastern South, one saw an early settled and civilized society centering around port towns—Sa-vannah, Charleston, Georgetown, Morehead, James-town, etc. And each of these centers was interna-tionally oriented, cosmopolitan by any standard. Savannah had (and has) a large Irish Catholic pop-ulation. Charleston was, it is true, chiefly Protestant, but included a rich diversity of sects and very significant minorities, religious refugees from the long wars of Europe, including French Huguenots, Dutch, Germans, Welsh, and Spanish Jews of the Sephardim, men of wealth, distinction, and some-times nobility, driven from Spain and North Africa. To preserve themselves and their values from the influences of "civilization," the Scotch and Irish moved upcountry here, as they did in North Caro-lina and Virginia. It is forgotten that there were, among the early settlers of the South, Scandinavi-ans, Danes, Swedes, and Norwegians as far south as southern South Carolina. When Quakers came to Pennsylvania, they came also in significant numbers to northern Virginia, to parts of North and South Carolina. The young poet from Leesburg, Virginia, Henry S. Taylor (*The Horseshow at Midnight* and *Breakings*) writes out of a Quaker heritage as long-standing as any in this country. The Amish and the Mennonites, somewhat later, came into the Shen-andoah Valley and settled and remained there. In the mountains which divide the eastern South from the west—the Appalachians, the Blue Ridge and the Smokeys—there are still odd ethnic pockets—peoples of Portuguese heritage, for example, and the descendants of Hessian deserters. And all along the Mississippi (including the state of Mississippi so often considered "homogeneous") there are, dating from the early and middle Nineteenth Century,

Chinese, Italians, Viennese and Central European Jews.

Though there were Indian wars in the South, some of them sufficiently savage on both sides, the Indians of the South were finally more absorbed and assimilated, through generations of intermarriage, than they were annihilated. There are still shards of Indian culture in small reservations and areas throughout the South, but in large part the nations and tribes have disappeared into the polyglot culture. Many southerners, black and white, and far more than realize it, have "Indian blood" in their heritage. Louisiana poet, and former poetry consultant of the Library of Congress, William Jay Smith, is one-quarter Cherokee and justly proud of it.

The best known now of the southern Indians are the Seminoles of Florida, and perhaps they may serve as an example of the heterogeneous society which has, in fact, characterized southern culture. The Seminoles were an artificial tribe, a gathering together of outcasts, independents, and runaways. The word Seminole means "runaway" in the language of the Creek Nation. They fled to the jungle peninsula of Florida and banded together. These bands included Indians from all the southeastern tribes and nations, and, as well, they included fugitive and outcast whites and runaway slaves. They became an interracial society, a culture, and finally a sort of tribe, though (as ever in the South) they were always a loose confederation of bands, never an Indian nation, and as eager to make war upon each other as upon the soldiers of a variety of national authorities—Spanish, British, French, American—who opposed them.

It should be clear, from these few examples, that the South never was, never could be a "homogeneous" society or culture. Insofar as this notion has been derived from the study of southern letters, it represents either a misreading or an oversimplification by the writers, or a little of both.

The textbooks tell us that the fact of slavery is

the overwhelming burden of the southern past and consequently of southern literature. There is no denying that general truth. William Styron's *Confessions of Nat Turner* bears recent witness to it. And yet it must be remembered that the overwhelming majority of southerners never owned any slaves or trafficked in slavery. It is a matter of fact and record that most southerners (even including a considerable number of slaveholders) were opposed to slavery of any kind and on many grounds; it is a fact that the preponderant majority of Abolitionists, prior to the Civil War, were southerners, where the problem, after all, existed; it is also a fact and a hard paradox that most of these, in turn, ended up fighting for the Confederacy.

Textbooks tell us that the major premise of the mythic southern past is the agrarian ideal, a celebration of agrarian and naturally aristocratic virtues, at least the possibility of a plantation culture and civilization, deriving in part from the example of Thomas Jefferson, made important in the modern literary and social scene by that great gathering of talent in and around Vanderbilt University in the 1930s. Included were such masters as John Crowe Ransom, Allen Tate and Carolyn Gordon, Andrew Lytle, Robert Penn Warren, Donald Davidson, Randall Jarrell, a tradition of teaching and learning, of historical and social attitude which is to be found now among southern writers who studied directly under these men, for example, in the work of Peter Taylor, Madison Jones, Jesse Hill Ford, and James Dickey. A myth so powerful, so influential and persuasive that it almost *ought* to be true. But there are deep and serious flaws in that widely accepted picture. Aside from the glory (and a certain gadgeteer's quackery) of Monticello overlooking Charlottesville, what can stand as the model for the agrarian dream? The great plantations of coastal South Carolina had failed, in any practical sense, a full generation before the Civil War. Their counterparts, the mansion farms of Piedmont Virginia failed, too, before the War. They were not only no longer profitable, they were no longer feasible; except, of course, as what they are now (only more so with the aid of modern technological conveniences): museum pieces, elegant, spacious, well-order, beautiful symbols of a way of life that never really came to pass. And one reason, among many, for the failure of the dream at its inception, was that these original agrarians ruthlessly and rapaciously denuded the land, on what can only in retrospect be called a "mass production" basis, for the chief purpose of quick profits; for greed, then. The land gave some of them back quick gains and then a long season, generations, of losses, not entirely ended yet. In the South lying west of the mountains, the South out of which most of the writers called "Fugitives" came and of which they wrote and have written ever since, this agrarian dream barely had a chance to begin before it was ended by the Civil War. That is to say, the South which is west of the mountains was spared the inevitable recurrence of a self-destructive pattern by the power of outside forces. Much was, of course, destroyed. But the great beauties of antebellum days which have survived in Louisiana, in the whole of the Delta country, especially the splendid remains of Natchez, for example, represent something that never really was, that was still brand new when it ended, too new to be anything but innocent. In a sense these memorials are as absurdly out of place as their distant counterparts, the columned mansion houses built by freed slaves, which stand proudly still in Liberia. But in another sense, and chiefly through the distorting nostalgia of much contemporary southern literature, these imitations of the folly of the eastern South, stand for the dream of them all. However, set squarely against the facts, they have, in time, managed, by the magic of art, a metamorphosis and given realization, a certain truth to a very old dream that was doomed the instant it was imagined. Elsewhere in the South it never existed, even as a dream. Once again one can turn to the work of William Faulkner for a sense of the complexity of the southern truth. Thomas Sutpen of *Absalom, Absalom!*, in all his passion, rage and self-contradiction (and in almost every way an offense to the agrarian myth) is a much more accurate figure for the kind of man, gifted, obsessed and ruthless, who went west to recreate, out of pride and misapprehension, the outward and visible trappings of a world he had been turned away from, whose inward and spiritual flaws he therefore never understood, even as his tragedy repeated the old pattern.

Textbooks and studies emphasize the fact that the southern writer has close ties to his native land. This is undeniable, and yet, in qualification, it must be pointed out that from the beginning most southern literature has been the creation of well-educated townspeople. Though close to the land, in fact and spirit, close to the rhythms of the seasons in what has been a chiefly rural society, close also in family kinship to those who farmed for a living, still southern literature has come from people who lived in towns and, more recently, cities and suburbs. The short stories of Peter Taylor show this truly. James Dickey's *Deliverance* is predicated on the savage contrast and conflicts between suburb and the still untamed country.

Almost all of our writers, from the beginning, have been at least one full generation removed from the day-to-day existence of rural life which is so often associated with southern literature. Farming and writing haven't joined together in a practical way, except in those instances where a writer "returned to the land," a traditional southern theme, sometimes honored in fact. For example, take the writers chosen for inclusion in the anthology *Nineteenth Century Southern Fiction* by the editor, John Caldwell Guilds. Their dates, together with the place of birth and growing up, tell the story: John Pendleton Kennedy (1795–1870) of Baltimore, Maryland; James Lane Allen (1849–1925) of Lexington, Kentucky; William Alexander Carruthers (1802–46) of Lexington, Virginia; Edgar Allen Poe (1809–49), though born in Boston, raised and lived most of his life in Richmond, Virginia; Augustus Baldwin Longstreet (1790–1870), Augusta, Georgia; Thomas Bangs Thorpe (1815–78), born in Massachusetts, educated at Wesleyan, but ended up living in Louisiana; William Gilmore Simms (1806–70), of Charleston, South Carolina; George Washington Cable (1844–1925), of New Orleans and, late in his life, a resident of New England; Charles Waddell Chesnutt (1858–1932), son of freed slaves from North Carolina, born and lived mostly in Cleveland, Ohio, though he studied and later taught school in Fayetteville, North Carolina; and Katherine O'Flaherty Chopin (1851–1904), of St. Louis, Missouri and New Orleans.

Another point, obvious from this one anthology's listings, is that the mobility of modern times, so often cited as a distinct difference from earlier days and seen by scholars as a sign of the end of southern regional literature, was there, too. Southern writers travelled as much as they could even when it was not easy. The longest interruption in the mobility of the southern writer seems to have been the Reconstruction period when financial reasons kept most of them in one place.

Today the southern writer is, like the rest of his countrymen, able to move and travel widely. But, now as then, most live in towns and cities. Today a great many are associated with colleges and universities, small or large communities overlapping into larger related communities.

It is sometimes a matter of real concern to southern writers that their "rural heritage" is falling away, replaced by burgeoning suburbia and urban life, both of which are, outwardly at least, indistinguishable from other similar enclaves from coast to coast.

A couple of years ago, I was asked to join in a panel discussion of contemporary southern literature held at Wesleyan University in Connecticut. On the same panel were Jesse Hill Ford (Tennessee), Reynolds Price (North Carolina), and William Styron (Virginia). All three of these good writers intelligently and differently lamented the passing of much of "the southern scene." With that passing they felt a sense of passing away of southern literature, since it was (it seemed to them) so closely tied to that scene, that experience, and its unique qualities. Ford, though a townsman himself, is closest to rural life by background and experience. He was less elegiac about the passing of some of the inherent rigors and hardships of "the old way." Price cited the increasing number of television aerials, perched atop farmhouses in back country North Carolina, as evidence that American life was rapidly becoming standardized beyond repair. Styron, more or less agreeing with Price, cited the increasing incidence of modern billboards and neon signs and the decline of the "Clabber Girl" and the snuff, chewing tobacco, and patent medicine advertisements, painted or tacked to the sides of barns.

It is not my intention to make much (even fun) of off-hand, casual remarks made in the context of a brief panel discussion. Rather, I think these slight things are indicative of certain larger truths about the world of southern letters in its relation to the "real" world of the southern experience. From this situation and context there are a few brief points which can be made.

The context was intellectual, a panel discussion at a highly regarded northern university. The three southern writers were perfectly at home there. All three are well-educated men. Price and Styron studied at Duke and studied writing under the same influential teacher, William Blackburn. Ford studied at Vanderbilt and at Florida, under Andrew Lytle. All three have lived out of the South at one time and another. All three have lived in Europe. They are widely travelled and essentially urbane and sophisticated men. None chews tobacco or dips snuff, nor would any of them put up a "Clabber Girl" sign except in jest. Yet their sense of loss and change was genuine and in no way condescending. In all of these things are certain paradoxes which are, and always have been, essential to a full appreciation of southern letters.

The Democratic Spirit

Thomas Jefferson is probably the best known example of a southern paradox which has remained virtually unchanged. A natural aristocrat himself, fortunate, what we would call "a member of the elite," he was nevertheless a champion of and spokesman for the democratic spirit, the value of the individual human being (excepting, of course, the slave), his spirit and dignity. In one way and another, all southern writers accept this assumption, both aristocratic stance and democratic spirit, almost without question. This manifests itself in southern letters less as a matter of "social conscience" than as an awareness that a very large part of their subject matter is in the ordinary, the day-to-day. It is part of their duty, it seems, to deal with these things. There is a sense of shared experience. All the South shared in and suffered from defeat in war and from long periods of poverty. Those who happen, by luck and circumstance, to be articulate speak for those who are not. From this point of view there should be no surprise at the ease of identification with his subjects, Depression sharecroppers, established by James Agee, in *Let Us Now Praise Famous Men*, or in the less well-known, but equally compelling book by Erskine Caldwell and Margaret Bourke-White *You Have Seen Their Faces*. It can be safely said that, regardless of genre, whether "Gothic" or "social realism," the main thrust of southern literature has been a deep interest in the extraordinary qualities present in the most humble and ordinary characters. The dangers are always those of false compassion (sentimentality) and of nostalgia.

Poetry and Prose

It is important to realize that, certainly since the times of Sidney Lanier and Edgar Allen Poe, there is a literary, an *aesthetic* assumption which is profound and unquestioned by almost all of those, including the critics and scholars, engaged in southern literature. The assumption is that poetry and prose are radically different, and that in literary value poetry is the "higher" art. Prose is reserved for the world of here and now, the captive yet chameleon present. Poetry, as poets as different as Lanier and Poe would have agreed, is closer to music, closer to a "universal language." The results of this assumption are various. Southern poetry, from the days of Lanier, Timrod, Poe, and Simms, up until our time with distinguished working poets as various as James Dickey, Vassar Miller, William Jay Smith, and Robert Penn Warren, for example, has tended to be formal and, regardless of how ordinary the subject or occasion may be, it has moved, almost invariably (excepting "light verse") into an elevated, indeed "poetic" tone and stance. Though there has been considerable use of the common things and situations of southern life in southern poetry, the language of our poetry has very seldom been experimental in the sense of making free and easy use of the many possibilities of the vernacular and the full range of public rhetoric—of the clergy, high and low, of courtroom, of politics. Experiment has been plentiful, but is most often found in the development or redevelopment of poetic forms.

This theoretical assumption and the consequent practice of poets have left for prose fiction the wide range of the language as it is, from the poetic and literary to the barnyard and monosyllabic. Style, then, and energy and all the various possibilities of the living and changing language of the South, these have been of the first order of importance to southern prose writers. All this has given them a great diversity and freedom and, yet, paradoxically, a kind of unity; for it is the language which, except for slight differences in shading, they already have in common. Moreover, since the forms of fiction are less fixed, less sacrosanct than those of poetry, southern fiction, again almost from the beginning, but notably in our time, has been characterized by restless, free-wheeling experiments in the formal ways of telling stories.

Some of this is changing slightly with the latest generation of southern poets. Our youngest published poets, though not discarding the preoccupation with verse forms, have widened the possibilities of their poetry; not only by more inclusive subject matter and occasional narrative structure, both of which are evident in the work of James Dickey, for example, or the late Randall Jarrell. Younger poets like Henry Taylor, James Seay (*Let Not Your Hart*) and James Whitehead (*Domains*) have included both the language and a kind of narrative structure once exclusively reserved for prose fiction, into their poetry. Yet, even so, the old limits of what is appropriately "poetic" and what is fit (and free) for prose, remain in place in southern literature, even as they have broken down elsewhere in our national literature.

Change and Decay

From their Jacobean beginnings, southern writers have been deeply obsessed with the ancient theme of "Mutabilitie." Change and decay have always been primary subjects in southern literature. Because it is characteristic of the southern writer (especially in prose fiction) that he feels compelled to capture in words and describe things as they are before they crumble and vanish forever. In order to do so he must create out of memory (his own and the memories of others), out of oral and taught history, a sense of what has been before. To capture the present he must define it, and the only means is through an understanding of the past. Our best writers recreate that past, making it new, changing it even as they seek to preserve it. Our lesser talents, sometimes with only a subtle difference in context and content, frame the past in pure nostalgia, freeze it, making of it something that it never was.

The Writer in Society

It is interesting to observe that this sense of purpose forces the writer to look outward. Or when he chooses to look inward, following Poe's example, he is led to create *universal* fables rather than case studies of psychology. Thus we have far less writing in southern letters, early or recent, directly concerned with "the creative process," that is, with one of the most common themes of worldwide contemporary literature, the portrait of the artist and his difficulties, what R. P. Blackmur called "the heroization of the sensibility." It is interesting that only two major southern writers, so far, have explored the subject of the literary artist in his growth and "alienation" from his society. It was, of course, the central theme of Thomas Wolfe's work. It was important to Richard Wright's remarkable autobiography, *Black Boy*. But, by and large, this has been only a peripheral subject for southern writers. Partly this is because the tradition of story-telling, of wrestling the angels of change, has led them, inevitably, in other directions. And partly it is because, in the townsman's world of southern letters, it has always been more or less respectable to write. Which does not mean that southerners are great readers of their own literature. As an audience they have had a negligible influence upon the publishing industry. They may respect their writers, may wish them well, but they do not rush to read them.

In bad times, which since about 1835 has been most of the time, writing has always been as decent a way to be poor as any other. In good times, it may not have the distinction of the old professions—law, the clergy, medicine, the military—but it is at least considered harmless.

Women and the Literary Arts

It is characteristic that ever since the middle years of the nineteenth century the profession of letters in the South has engaged the talent and dedication of many women. Consequently some of the finest and most highly regarded writers of the South are women of formidable gifts and skill. This fact was so firmly established that the late Adlai Stevenson could include it as a part of his campaign speech, "The New South," delivered at the Mosque in Richmond, Virginia, on September 20, 1952. With characteristic humor Stevenson put it this way, "Some years ago a famous American critic said that the South was the wasteland of the mind. Yet at that very moment, I am told, so many of your housewives had novels simmering with the soup—among them *Gone With the Wind*—that many husbands had to wait for supper."

That women have done well in southern writing implies a number of consequences above and beyond the inevitable social acceptability of "being a writer." It means also that writing can be regarded as a graceful accomplishment and a serious avocation (sometimes an art), but hardly a profession, not a way of earning a living. With a few notable and fortunate exceptions very few of our women writers have depended upon their writing for a living. The primary effect of this is transferable. Few of our male writers have ever managed to make a living, at least for long, directly from their literary efforts. By dint of enormous effort and expense of energy in production, Erskine Caldwell did so for many years. Tennessee Williams seems to have done well, in the long run, as a dramatist. Other writers have been successful with one book or another, but most of them have made their way by and through other, if related means. William Faulkner made most of his money, such as it was, by screenwriting. So, a generation later, does Calder Willingham. A great many others have had long careers as teachers. Some have worked in editing and publishing. The point is a simple one. Few southern writers can afford the illusory luxury that they will ever be able to live on the earnings of their art and craft. One result is that southern literature is largely divorced from practical and commercial publishing considerations.

The southern writer cannot take the commercial possibilities of his art very seriously, but, at the same time, therefore, he is freed to take the art as seriously as he pleases and is able to.

Geography

Perhaps most important is another force for variety, diversity, disunity if you insist, in southern writing. And that force is, purely and simply, geography, the lay and look and feel of the land itself which makes it possible for any southern writer to build fiction and poetry out of what Faulkner called his own "postage stamp" of territory. If the overall borders and limits of the South are vague and grow over political lines like honeysuckle over sagging fences, the same thing is true of the lesser political boundaries. All southern states are divided. All which face the sea, Atlantic Ocean or Gulf of Mexico, have a lowcountry and an upcountry. Appropriately, in the one state which might be the exception to the rule, Florida, the upcountry consists of the slight, rolling, red hills which gradually blend into the terrain of Alabama and Georgia, called West Florida, long at odds with the entire lowlands of the late-inhabited peninsula.

The lowlands are fertile, laced by rivers, still, despite towns, cities and long settlement, rich in wild game and in the sense of the sea nearby; blessed with an easier life (like Africa's Gold Coast) than the interior. Below the fierce seas of Cape Hatteras, this coastal country, from north of Charleston to the far edges of Texas on the Gulf, has much that is generally common. It is semitropical country, home of the towering knobby-kneed cypress, of the long-lived live oak and water oak, moss country, place for dunes and sea wheat, for marsh grass and cattails, for the water lily. Heavenly country for the moccasin (and in tall timber, dark cool earth and tall slash pine, for all sorts of rattlesnake cousins); home for the fugitive alligator, the vanishing wildcat, for slow, huge and crafty bass and catfish who can sometimes be outwaited by a patient boy with a cane pole when they cannot be outwitted by fancy reels and tackle and gear. Here is where the flowerings of certain southern plants—azalea, hibiscus, oleander, etc.—are richest. (The traditional magnolia does well, too, but not so well as it does in the upcountry.) It is from the settled coasts that southern literature emerged; the profession of letters is oldest there. Therefore it is not surprising that the writers of our own time, from places along that coast, tend to be among the most sophisticated, and sometimes exotic and eccentric of modern writers. Truman Capote and the lesser known, but gifted novelist (now living in Rome) Eugene Walter began their writing careers as schoolboys in competition with each other for a newspaper prize—a Shetland pony—in Mobile, a town as old and sophisticated as New Orleans. Also from the Mobile area is the gifted poet and editor Stephen Mooney. From South Carolina's lowcountry came such various modern figures as DuBose Heyward, Julia Peterkin, Josephine Pinckney, Louis Rubin, and Archibald Rutledge. From Louisiana, a few names almost at random from among many, tell the story: Lillian Hellman, Hamilton Basso, Peter Fiebleman, Shirley Ann Grau, Walker Percy, Parker Tyler. . . .

There is an absence of schools and groups here in the lowlands, a thoroughgoing individuality, wide and deep differences in intent, ways, and means of all these writers. By the beginning of our century it was an old tradition, fragmented but not uncomfortable, easily but not aggressively cultural.

For example, Walker Percy is by definition and his own design a southern writer, yet each of his novels, *The Movie Goer, The Last Gentleman,* and *Love in the Ruins,* is at once highly original and socially and intellectually sophisticated in premises and execution, and in a distinctly different manner than, for example, the obvious literary sophistication found in the novels of Robert Penn Warren.

Farther north, it could be argued that Richmond, on the James, and more or less the dividing point between Tidewater and upcountry (Piedmont) Virginia, has shown the characteristics of the older coastal culture. Two of the most prominent, productive, and strikingly different of the moderns' older generation, James Branch Cabell and Ellen Glasgow, created distinguished and well-recognized works there. Each was in many ways (Cabell the more so) a highly individual talent. Both were, also a commonplace among the modern "coastal" writers, actively and successfully engaged in all aspects of "the literary life." Today one would immediately think of William Styron, of Norfolk, and of Tom Wolfe, from Richmond, as writers who in sophistication and individuality exemplify the persistence of the "coastal" tradition.

Similarly, one might well cite the sophisticated and highly individual writers of the Mississippi Delta country, taking, as examples, Eudora Welty, in all her wonderfully wrought and precise individuality; or Shelby Foote who, after a fine and productive career as a young novelist, surprised many by turning to an epic project, already proudly realized in the two published volumes (the third and final one nearing completion) of *The Civil War: A Narrative*.

Georgia is an odd blend of the older tradition, stemming from Savannah and the long-settled coast, and the newer cities like Augusta and Atlanta, typically upcountry. From Georgia have come such diverse and extraordinary artists as Carson McCullers and Flannery O'Connor, Mac Hyman and Marion Montgomery, Conrad Aiken, Erskine Caldwell, Calder Willingham, and Frank Yerby. The range is wide; Margaret Mitchell and James Dickey both have spoken of and for Atlanta.

In general the upcountry writers are at least a generation closer to the old rural South, closer therefore to a land which is harsher than the lowlands, with more distinct extremes, and equally, though quite differently, beautiful. It should be noted that southern writers from all the South's patchwork regions have another thing in common—they have found their own land beautiful to behold, to know;

harsh and mysterious, but always beautiful in all seasons. The upcountry is hills, rolling lands, cleared land or tall forest; except for the villages, towns, centers, it was and remains fairly thinly populated. Much red clay, much pine woods, and here the red oak and the white oak, sycamore, the nut-bearing trees—pecan, hickory, walnut. It is here, when the soil is right, that the magnolia grows hugely tall, and those white, fat blossoms, so prevalent in southern fiction, offer their sweetest scent. Here the mocking-bird is an American nightingale, the jay a flashing blue and white surge of arrogant feathery energy. Possums and racoons are near neighbors, drive farm dogs and penned up hunting hounds wild by night. Up here, if a man is rich enough and has rich companions, he can wear a scarlet coat and ride horseback behind a pack of hounds, chasing the sly, quick fox. Rich or poor, he can tree a coon. It is hot as hell's hinges in midsummer (though less humid than the lowlands); wind-whipped and with mud like glue in autumn; lonesome, the ground hard, many trees bare, so many birds gone south like the tourists; but only rarely the pleasures of real snow or ice to skate on or fish through, in winter; spring is so bright and brief and dazzling it staggers senses and imagination. Comes on noisy with wood-peckers and songbirds beyond counting and naming. Comes with brightness and many colors—forsythia, dogwood, redbud, cherry, chinaberry. A rainbow, a sudden flashing of Joseph's many-colored coat, wild and free as a carnival, then gone quietly to green. And then, again, the long hot summer days.

The seasons are, while milder than places else-where, sharp and definite in the upcountry South.

In places—on opposite sides of the divide running from northern Virginia to north Georgia, spilling over into West Virginia and Kentucky, and sepa-rately in the Ozarks of Arkansas—the upcountry goes into true hill country and finally merges into old mountains with their own climates and seasons, harsher in winter and cool and crisp in summer, a hard lonesome place for only the most independent spirits, for outcasts, for the proud and poor. A sky for wheeling hawks and the high smudged circle of a lone buzzard; for evergreens and rocks and the swift crescendo of whitewater streams; for the slanting, tilting patchwork quilt farms, cleared and picked out of mountains by a weight of days, of patience and labor; of log cabins and weathered heavy-timbered barns; where fences sag and rust but are deeply serious lines; home for the gnarled apple tree and one late crop of tall sweet corn.

From Asheville Thomas Wolfe could look into those mountains and sense them and their weight and loneliness. But, except as visitors and vacationers, few writers have yet come out from the heart of the mountain country. An exception is the brilliant and original (and darkly severe) novelist and poet Fred Chappell. Though he now makes his home where he teaches, in upcountry Greensboro, he writes of those southern mountains. Even his explosive reticence seems perfectly natural. And there is the young poet from Roanoke, R. H. W. Dillard, his roots deep in the mountains of southwest Virginia, who has managed to celebrate the life of the mountains and the feeling of the mountain people in a handful of poems found in both of his published books of poems, *The Day I Stopped Dreaming about Barbara Steele* and *News of the Nile.*

But in this century and in our own time, most southern writing has come out of the upcountry areas, betwixt and between. The listing of the names of good, serious, and indeed more or less "well-known" writers coming out of the upcountry South is an implausible gesture. For example, John M. Bradbury's general study *Renaissance in the South: A Critical History of the Literature, 1920–1960* offers an excellent, but by no means complete, state-by-state listing of southern authors of that period and "of more than local prestige." Roughly one thousand names are listed there. To bring such a list up to date would at the least double it. This surge of interest and creative energy in this century, which has been named "the southern renaissance," has been characterized by a widespread productivity, joined with a controlled urgency close to passion, as if all these gifted people (though always each separately and alone) were beginning again at the beginning of things, a new naming day in Eden.

Although many of the critics and scholars of southern letters were, a decade ago, predicting the end of this renaissance, some already proclaiming its demise, they were, to say the least, premature. Many factors contributed to the original impetus, not the least the examples of a few writers of massive powers and overabundant gifts; but perhaps one of the strongest forces of this renaissance has been *educational*. It is in this century that the great state universities and the private universities (Duke, Vanderbilt, Tulane), came into their own. Pragmatic, and the source of various Populist movements over the years, the upcountry southerner has long looked to public education as essential to the improvement of his lot and of society. It is not accidental that most of the large universities of the South are situated in the upcountry. And it was here that writing was taught. Out of Vanderbilt came the teachers from the Fugitive movement, to teach all over the south. But at that same time there were others who, if less widely known, have been at least equally influential: George Williams (Rice), Jesse Rheder (Chapel Hill), William Blackburn (Duke), A. K. Davis (Virginia), Edwin Granberry (Rollins College), Ovid Pierce (East Carolina), Hudson Strode (Alabama), etc. The list of these, the "originals," is long. And given a generation and a half, in which many of their students went out to write and to teach, it has grown to such an extent that today there is scarcely a southern institution of "higher learning" which does not have at least one practicing writer on its faculty. These in turn draw others, young and gifted, to work with them; and the process, the expansion, continues.

There are some dangers in the *schooling* of southern writing. The greatest of these is a certain artificial and self-conscious uniformity, tending to-
wards mediocrity. And, in fact, there has been some
"standardization" of very recent southern literature.
But this danger is more than compensated for by
other things. The standards of "good writing," of
the "establishment," serve simultaneously as an aid
to the beginner and as something to work against,
to change, for the truly gifted and original young
writers. The constant impetus of new energy is
there in the young blacks and whites who, a generation ago, had small prospects for advanced education, let alone for the practice of the arts. New
voices are already being heard, and they express
aspects of the southern experience which have seldom been directly articulated. It is interesting to observe that the new voices of the children of poor
whites and poor blacks are, at least to the outsider,
so close as to be indistinguishable. The anthologies,
Southern Writing in the Sixties published by L.S.U.
Press, contained work by a number of young black
poets and story writers. Since in no place was the
race of the writers identified, it was assumed by
some northern reviewers that black writers had
been excluded. The real meaning was that, except
for some fine subtleties of social context, the young
writers had more in common than one might have
imagined.

It is quite possible that out of the many young
voices in southern writing today there shall not appear, again, any single and overmastering genius.
The day of the solitary masters may be gone. But,
in a sense, they have successfully created that situation themselves. One of the characteristics of
southern writing has been, precisely, the sense of
community, beginning with the family and extending outward in intricate, invisible network. In the
past this was always more an ideal than a fact, but
that, too, is changing. It is the magic of art that, in
time, what is perceived first by the imagination can

be transformed first into form, then into fact. Even as the South itself changes, a community is emerging at last, one which may be a salutary example in the larger union which seems fractioned and divided.

The contemporary southern writer is, quite as much as his antecedents, required to look to the past, his past, in order to find the boundaries of the present. The contemporary southern writer is haunted by all the old traditions, including that which we call "modern"; and, whether he believes it or not, those ghosts are real.

Although we have great cities now, with all the urban problems and pleasures, although even in small towns we have the sliding glass doors which lead to the patios and charcoal cooking of universal suburbia, although we have a plethora of TV antennae (and, for the most part, sets to be connected to them), though you will have to drive a little farther and wander afield to find a "Clabber Girl" or a bold sign announcing the merits of Mail Pouch Chewing Tobacco, though the old staples of up-country southern cooking (for black and white alike) have been named "soul food" and become an ingredient in the northern state of mind and status which a southerner named "radical chic" (while southerners in jeans and bib overalls are buying frozen "Chinese" and "Mexican" dinners at the Piggly Wiggly or the Winn Dixie), although students grow hair and beards as long and full as that of their great grandfathers (who stare at them, equally solemn, from fading daguerreotypes), still and all there seems to be no shortage at all of talented writers, ready, willing, often able, to assume tradition and to change it, as it has always been changing, even as they preserve much of it. And because that literary tradition, old and new, has never been characterized by unity or uniformity, there is and will be (in the words of an old spiritual) "room for many a more."

crossing
the midwest

John Knoepfle

Photograph by Leland Payton

The Midwest, fourteen hundred miles between the Alleghenies and the Rockies, nine hundred miles from the Canadian border above Minot, North Dakota, to the Oklahoma line below Liberal, Kansas. The wind blew down the dust of the mountains east across the Mississippi to form the Great Plains and then the grass caught them and kept them. There are four big lakes in the north and big springs and clear rivers and old mountains in Missouri. The Mississippi Valley from Cairo to St. Cloud halves the region east and west. There are high buttes in the Dakotas and hardwood forests in Ohio. And then there are the cities: Cleveland, Cincinnati, Chicago, Detroit, Minneapolis, St. Paul, Duluth, St. Louis. . . .

I will say what I can about the writers in this region, where they are or have been, those who have drawn from their environs, those who have made homes in this valley or that town. The result will be an impression of work that has been done or is being done in the larger area, not exhaustive or all inclusive, certainly, but something filled with many voices.

To begin, there is Martins Ferry, Ohio. This is about ninety miles south on the river from East Liverpool. The town is James Wright's birthplace

John Knoepfle, poet and critic, lives in Springfield, Illinois, and teaches at Sangamon State University.

and the locale for many of his poems. Below Martins Ferry the river flows dark green between darker green hills and passes some fine old, well-kept towns, Marietta and Gallipolis; but above on that horseshoe the river makes from Pittsburgh the land is scarred with industry, mills, mines, and crowded towns beyond imagining. Wright has this double aspect of the river translated into his poetry. He wonders at the loveliness of the land and is appalled by the wasted lives of men and women in the crush of that industrialized upper valley:

> I began in Ohio.
> I still dream of home.
> Near Mansfield, enormous dobbins enter
>   dark barns in autumn,
> Where they can be lazy, where they can
>   munch little apples,
> Or sleep long.
> But by night now, in the bread lines my
>   father
> Prowls, I cannot find him: So far off,
> 1500 miles or so away, and yet
> I can hardly sleep.
> In a blue rag the old man limps to my bed,
> Leading a blind horse
> Of gentleness.
> In 1932, grimy with machinery, he sang
>   me
> A lullaby of a goosegirl.
> Outside the house, the slag heaps waited.[1]

Wright's poetry is personal and lyrical, but he hammers it with place-names to the vast, submerged history of America:

> Somewhere in a vein of Bridgeport, Ohio;
> Deep in a coal hill behind Hanna's name;
> Below the tipples, and dark as a drowsy
>   woodchuck;
> A man, alone,

Stumbles upon the outside locks of a
    grave, whispering
Oh let me in.[2]

A critic has noted that Wright has created some
of the saddest poems in the language.[3] It is true: He
is a haunted poet and the America he speaks of is
a haunted land, a place where a hallowed nature is
in some inverse proportion to a depraved people.
But he has in himself a potential for transfiguration,
and his poems have a way of ending when something is about to happen: "When I stand upright in
the wind, My bones turn to dark emeralds."[4]

Farther south and west along the river there is a
congress of towns joined by a half-dozen bridges.
Cincinnati is one of these. It is hometown for the
poets Nikki Giovanni, William Matthews, Tyner
White, and the novelist Thomas Berger. Lafcadio
Hearn began a career as journalist there in 1869.
He was attracted to the steamboat landing and its
neighborhood. The sketches he wrote of the life he
saw remain the one important glimpse of a post-
Civil War black community in a northern city, a
community which had its share of orphaned children:

> Maggie Sperlock, who lives there, can also tell you
> about a little woman who comes back sometimes
> to watch over her children—the waifs that Maggie
> named and adopted, Sis and Tom and Howard. Sis
> is never whipped, for Maggie says that whenever
> the child is punished the dead mother will come in
> the night to haunt the chastiser. Sis is a pretty
> brown child, with big, dreamful eyes, and a strange
> habit of wandering in solitary places, whispering
> to herself or to somebody invisible to all others—
> perhaps the frail, fond, dark mother, who came
> back silently in the night to protect her little one.
> Maggie has become afraid of the child's elfish ways,
> and vows that old Jot, the Obi-man, must have be-
> witched her.[5]

Not all the towns along the Ohio are real. Wil-

liam H. Gass invented a place called Gilean as the
setting for his novel *Omensetter's Luck*. His novel
projects the tormented mind of the Reverend Jethro
Furber who becomes minister to the congregation at
Gilean in the same year that Brackett Omensetter
migrates down the valley with his family to settle
near the town. Furber grows to hate him; Omensetter's presence stings his mind. Even when he is
preparing his sermon, his mind is hurt with thoughts
of this natural man:

> We should all be watchmen, and we should pray
> that God will open our eyes to evil and burn our
> hearts to admonish the ungodly. Think, he often
> said, how the demons howl. Their voices are rough
> and crude; they live in fire; they scream; they sever
> their words as their heads are severed; but is not
> the justice of it sweet? In the same way the worst
> of this world signifies the best of the other. While
> saying this his voice would rise, his hands flutter,
> his eyelids squeeze rapturously together.
> Rancorous ivy. On the other side of the wall, at
> the edge of the river, the sand burned. The river
> lay afire. Kingfishers fell like spots across the eyes
> and laughter was yellow. Every Sunday Omensetter
> strolled by the river with his wife, his daughters,
> and his dog. They came by wagon, spoke to people
> who were off to church, and while Furber preached,
> they sprawled in the gravel and trailed their feet
> in the water. Lucy Omensetter lay her swollen body
> on a flat rock. Furber felt the sun lapping at her
> ears. It was like a rising blush, and his hands
> trembled when he held them out to make the bars
> of the cross. May the Lord bless you and keep you.
> . . . He closed his eyes, drifting off. They would
> see how moved he was, how intense and sincere he
> was. Cause His light to shine upon you. . . . He
> would find the footprints of the dog and the im-
> print of their bodies. All the days of your life. . . .
> The brazen parade of her infected person. Watch-
> man. Rainbows like rings of oil around her. Watch-
> man. Shouldn't we be.[6]

Omensetter is an Adam in a questionable paradise; Furber's mind burns with an imagined hell. The book's tension is based upon the opposition between Jonathan Edwards and Rousseau, or perhaps the fact that the Puritans came to the new world as educated, Renaissance men with a desire to set down an orderly plantation in the wilderness and droves of their countrymen came harried off the London docks when they were already three generations cut away from the yeoman culture of their fathers. Furber struggles to gain a coherent sense of history; Omensetter's past, such as it was, drifting back to circles of stone set out to gain magical cures, is something he accepts as adequate to his needs. Furber, no matter how hard he tries, can never uncover enough of the past to stabilize his mind.

A little north of Cincinnati is the mill town of Hamilton where William Dean Howells was born, and north of Hamilton is Dayton, Ohio, where two brothers dreamed of a lighter-than-air craft they would fly one day at Kitty Hawk and Paul Laurence Dunbar worked as an elevator operator and wrote about people who had to walk in the world wearing masks.

The young poet William J. Harris spent his boyhood in Yellow Springs, Ohio. This little college town is north of Xenia near the place where Tecumseh's village was, the Shawnee huts obliterated today beneath a cornfield. Harris, who is now in a doctoral program at Stanford University, has these lines entitled, "For Bill Hawkins, a Black Militant":

> Night, I know you are powerful and
>   artistic in your misspellings.
> How distinctively I sense your brooding,
> feel your warm breath against my face,
> hear your laughter—not cruel only
>   amused and arrogant: young—
> insisting on my guilt.
> Night, let me be part of you but in my own
>   dark way.[7]

In neighboring Indiana it is possible to trace the

wanderings of the incredible Dreiser family, first in Sullivan where the father's mill burned, then north a little to Terre Haute, then back to Sullivan, and then to Evansville on the Ohio River, the loving light city, as the steamboat roustabouts called it in those days, then off to Chicago, briefly, and finally to Warsaw near Fort Wayne in the northeastern corner of the state where Theodore attended a public high school.

Theodore Dreiser was one of the poor boys who broke through the genteel tradition in American letters and opened the way for the coming of the contemporary novel. Dreiser, with Floyd Dell, Sherwood Anderson, Carl Sandburg, and Vachel Lindsay came from an end of the century middlewestern culture that was ready for revolution and renewal. The growth of Chicago and the urbanization of the small town and the years of social unrest among farmers and workingmen and the head-on confrontation of small-town people with big city life were generating experiences that could not be contained any longer by genteel strictures.

Dale Kramer in his biographical studies of the writers of the Chicago Renaissance shows how immersed the young Dreiser was in the game of flashy success in America and how episodes from *Sister Carrie* and *Jennie Gerhart* reflect events in his own life and that of his family.[8] Larzer Ziff sees Dreiser as a ponderous new man on the American literary scene, a radical beyond his own sense of what is radical, working out detail by detail what he knows or feels to be the world of commercial America, and with nothing by way of a preconception to hamper him.[9]

The vulgarity and razzle-dazzle of American material success was not to be mocked by poor, small-town boys at the turn of the century. Dreiser saw that some were buoyed up in that limitless sea and that others drowned. He described what he saw in a massive, stolid prose, and drew no reassuring conclusions. He wounded the sensibilities of those who believed that the American experience could be modified by a proper moral education and an inherited social code.

The folk in the valley could put such detachment in more homey terms:

> Way up yonder beyond the moon,
> A blue-jay nests in a silver spoon.

> Way down yonder in a wooden trough,
> An old woman died of the whoopin' cough.

> Buckeye Jim, you can't go,
> Go weave and spin, you can't go,
> Buckeye Jim.

> Way down yonder in a hollow log,
> A red bird danced with a green bullfrog.[10]

In Indianapolis a nursery school teacher can predict the winner of the Five Hundred. She knows the work of the interplanetary Hoosier schoolmaster, Kurt Vonnegut, Jr., also. Vonnegut is very loyal to his hometown, though he often writes of it with his tongue in his cheek:

> On the trip back to Earth, Salo suspected that he had made a tragic mistake in suggesting to Constant that he return to Earth. He had begun to suspect this when Constant insisted on being taken to Indianapolis, Indiana, U.S.A.
>
> This insistence of Constant's was a dismaying development, since Indianapolis was far from an ideal place for a homeless old man.
>
> Salo wanted to let him off by a shuffleboard court in St. Petersburg, Florida, U.S.A., but Constant, after the fashion of old men, could not be shaken from his first decision. He wanted to go to Indianapolis, and that was that.
>
> Salo assumed that Constant had relatives or possibly old business connections in Indianapolis, but this turned out not to be the case.
>
> "I don't know anybody in Indianapolis, and I don't know anything about Indianapolis except for one thing," said Constant, "a thing I read in a book."

84

"What did you read in a book?" said Salo uneasily.

"Indianapolis, Indiana," said Constant, "is the first place in the United States of America where a white man was hanged for the murder of an Indian. The kind of people who'll hang a white man for murdering an Indian—" said Constant, "that's the kind of people for me."

Salo's head did a somersault in its gimbals. His feet made grieved sucking sounds on the iron floor. His passenger, obviously, knew almost nothing about the planet toward which he was being carried with a speed approaching that of light.[11]

Vonnegut as a prisoner of war in Germany worked in a factory near Dresden which manufactured a malt syrup for pregnant women. He was hidden in a bunker during the terrifying Allied bombing raid of 1945, and afterwards he helped to bury the dead, some of the one hundred and thirty-five thousand that did not survive the raid. The experience left him confused and angry and has filled him with distrust of patriotic absolutes. Campbell, in *Mother Night,* appears to be speaking for him:

"I'm not your destiny, or the Devil, either," I said. "Look at you! Came to kill evil with your bare hands, and now away you go with no more glory than a man sideswiped by a Greyhound bus! And that's all the glory you deserve!" I said. "That's all that any man at war with pure evil deserves.

"There are plenty of good reasons for fighting," I said, "but no good reason ever to hate without reservation, to imagine that God Almighty Himself hates with you, too."[12]

He is sensitive now to the fate of persons whose lives are becoming increasingly marginal, both those who have given up and those who continue to struggle:

It was the Senator's conceit that Eliot trafficked with criminals. He was mistaken. Most of Eliot's clients weren't brave enough or clever enough for lives of crime. But Eliot, particularly when he argued with his father or bankers or his lawyers, was almost equally mistaken about who his clients were. He would argue that the people he was trying to help were the same sorts of people who, in generations past, had cleared the forests, drained the swamps, built the bridges, people whose sons formed the backbone of the infantry in time of war —and so on. The people who leaned on Eliot regularly were a lot weaker than that—and dumber, too. When it came time for their sons to go into the Armed Forces, for instance, the sons were generally rejected as being mentally, morally, and physically undesirable.

There was a tough element among the Rosewater County poor who, as a matter of pride, stayed away from Eliot and his uncritical love, who had the guts to get out of Rosewater County and look for work in Indianapolis or Chicago or Detroit. Very few of them found steady work in those places, of course, but at least they tried.[13]

Vonnegut is assertive, pedantic, gentle, and when fall comes around and school begins, his books, with those of Hermann Hesse, disappear from the library shelves in Indianapolis and everywhere.

For Warren Fine, born in Arkansas and educated at the University of Kansas, the Midwest becomes a surrogate for the brooding inner awareness of a man. *In the Animal Kingdom* is a complex book, a fugal arrangement for many speakers, tangled, difficult to get through, as difficult as crossing the lowlands of southern Indiana and Illinois when the rivers are in flood.

The time of the narrative is the Revolution: Gerhard Blau has come from Europe and finds himself a member of Colonel Clark's expedition against Detroit. The movement of the characters is impeded, groping, and stumbling in a rank wilderness of nature and mind:

The river was another animal. Now even the island didn't seem to really exist within it. Both river banks, though the height of flood was past, appeared to recede; even the bank they approached diminished like the sun above it. The passengers felt tugs and pulls upon them, back and forth as if they were tide-bound objects, debris of the river, and they advanced as though only because the sun, in its sinking, had assumed a power of tide upon the river stronger than the hold of the gray, shattered sky and land behind, than the pull of the gully with its terrible mouth, the funeral clearing, the stumps about the cabin, other sun-receded things. . . .[14]

The temporal sequence is disjointed, as it is in the mind, but Blau can see, also, as if looking back on himself through time, his own death, and it may be that a man does not grow through time at all, or that his time does not stop when his life runs out on him, but he lives in different times on planes of awareness that sometimes merge and sometimes become one. Whatever, the land that Warren Fine speaks of becomes something more than a metaphor for the self; it becomes the seedbed of consciousness:

There was something Gerhard had known only in dreams and in dimly acknowledged aspirations: a sense of alteration, an othering of himself he could never lose again completely, even in the most intimate relations with Indians or any others, men or women; and it was this sense which chiefly drew him out, into America, into the continent he came to feel he had to transform in himself, this sense he thought of later as a horse sense, which kept him from lingering on that seacoast long, there dreaming the interior he must enter to try to discover the man, adult, he felt America wanted him to be.[15]

It was for Audubon the beginning of his life. He was thirty-five. He had already traveled half of the continent. He had been at work in Dr. Daniel Drake's natural history museum in Cincinnati. But now he knew what his vocation was to be, and so in 1820 when his flatboat drifted out of the Ohio River into the Mississippi, he wrote in his diary, "here the Traveller enters a New World . . . the Passenger feels a different atmosphere, a very different prospect."[16]

It was Audubon's new world, but the valley was not new: Cahokia, in what is now Illinois, had been settled a hundred and twenty-one years earlier, twenty-six after Marquette and Joliet explored the river.

Timothy Flint reported a hundred boats at the landing in one day when he visited New Madrid in 1816.[17] The town had recently been shattered by an earthquake, the disaster that created Reelfoot Lake. Flint describes the scene:

> There was a great number of severe shocks, but two series of concussions were particularly terrible; far more so than the rest. And they remark that the shocks were clearly distinguishable into two classes; those in which the motion was horizontal, and those in which it was perpendicular. The latter were attended with the explosions, and the terrible mixture of noises, that preceded and accompanied the earthquakes, in a louder degree, but were by no means so desolating and destructive as the other. When they were felt, the houses crumbled, the trees waved together, the ground sunk, and all the destructive phenomena were more conspicuous. In the interval of the earthquakes there was one evening, and that a brilliant and cloudless one, in which the western sky was a continued glare of vivid flashes of lightning, and of repeated peals of subterranean thunder, seeming to proceed, as the flashes did, from below the horizon.[18]

The country today, delta land in the Missouri Bootheel, is all sown in soybean and cotton. Up around Sikeston, forty miles west of Cairo, ditched, drained, rich, productive, the land is valued at seventeen thousand dollars an acre, what it would cost to take it out of cultivation.

West of there, extending to the Kansas-Oklahoma border, is Ozark country, mountainous, riddled with caves and enormous springs which set clear, fast rivers on their courses. The area was settled in a spill-over from Appalachia; the people who came in then had no need to go anywhere else, although settlers moved restlessly west to the north and the south of them. Vance Randolph spent his life in this rugged country, collecting the lore, tales and songs from the cabins and the towns. He shaped a style of his own for retelling the stories. It can catch the character and the humor of the speaker, as in this one:

> One time there was a young fellow named Asbury, and his daddy was a bishop in the Methodist church. They sent the boy to college back East somewheres, and then he wanted to be a congressman, so all the church people swarmed out to shell the woods for Jim Asbury. A politics committee went to every cabin on the creek, and finally they come to Seth Thompson's place. He was a smart old man, but so deef he couldn't hear himself thunder. Everybody had to take turns hollering in his ear-trumpet. Seth knowed it was about the election, but he couldn't make out who they wanted him to vote for.
>
> The folks kept a-hollering "Jim Asbury! Jim Asbury!" till finally Seth got the name all right, but he didn't seem to know who Jim Asbury was. "He's the son of a bishop! Son of a bishop!" they yelled into the ear-trumpet. "Oh, well, all them politicians is," says Seth. "How does he stand on evolution?"
>
> Old Deacon Jones allowed that Jim was against evolution, and Seth promised to vote for him, so the committee called it a day. But them pious Methodists looked kind of red in the face, and some of the young folks giggled a little on the way back to town.[19]

Stanley Elkin brings two wandering peddlers, father and son, to southern Illinois in *A Bad Man*. The crazed father knows every trick of the con game. He teaches his son that everything is salable, except himself. Young Feldman lives on uneasy terms with his father. There are distances in the old man that sound an echo in Babylon, a Jerusalem spread with salt. The boy has looked on Jordans of his own:

> He lived in a constant fear of miracles that could go against him. The wide waters of the Ohio and the Mississippi that he had seen meld from a bluff just below Cairo, Illinois, would have turned red in an instant had he entered them, split once and drowned him had he taken flight. There was the turtle death beyond, he vaguely felt, and so, like one who has come safely through danger to a given clearing, he feared to go on or to retrace his steps. He was content to stay still.[20]

But when the father dies, the boy is able to dispose of the body. It is worth fifteen dollars to a local hospital. Feldman leaves for the city then, possessed now with an obsession with selling, and there is a dark shadow hovering at his heart.

Robert Coover is from Herrin, Illinois, downstate where the country is called Egypt because it has to be leveed against flooding by the Ohio. He has written a mordant fable which describes what happens during a recent national election when the Cat in the Hat of Dr. Seuss fame blows the mind of the nation and almost carries off the presidency. The Cat is lynched, a necessity to avoid a military coup and to preserve the democratic synthesis. The lynching is arranged to take place in Pearl River, Mississippi, though anywhere else would do:

> A week later, the Cat appeared at a rally outside a small town in Mississippi, along the banks of the Pearl River. We had alerted the personnel of a nearby airbase, the White Citizens Council and the Black Nationalists, the local Minutemen, Klan, Nazis, Black Muslims, and Zionists, the National Guard and the VFW, the different student groups, the local churches, sheriffs, shopkeepers, cops, Mafia interests, farmers, Cubans, Chocktaws, country singers, and evangelists, in short, all the Good Folk of the valley. Our precautions were hardly necessary—the same thing would have happened

in Walla Walla or Concord by then—but it was only a week before the threatened coup, and since the Cat had a habit of skipping out on scheduled appearances, we were pretty nervous about it. By flattery, cajolery, and just plain hanging on to him, we kept him in sight until we could get him on the scene. Even Clark helped, though I'll never know exactly why.

That they'd kill him, we knew. That they'd do it by skinning him alive we hadn't foreseen, but those folks along the Pearl are pretty straightforward people.[21]

Coover and Elkin are both preoccupied with the nation's mammoth institutions, with baseball, politics, merchandising, radio. They create heroes who are lovingly involved in the technicalities, paraphernalia, and inner logic of their chosen fields and who embrace situations which are outrageous, eerie, and plausible. In an earlier time these heroes, with the exception of Dreiser's heroes, would have been realized as Babbitts or executives in flannel suits or unsuccessful salesmen or capitalists getting their just deserts, but in Coover and Elkin they become Jonahs swallowed by whales that obey neither the laws of nature nor the will of Jehovah.

The river country from Cairo to Alton is a broad, flat valley some ten miles wide. It used to be somber in cypress groves. Primitive hunters on the Illinois side found protection where the Mississippi had undercut the steep limestone bluffs. Their bones and artifacts have rested in the Modoc Shelter for ten thousand years. Farmers plant rows of corn in the valley now and find those niches in the bluffs handy places for storing their plows and their harrows.

St. Louis, established as a center for the fur trade, manufactures capsules for the moon. There have been writers in this city, William Marion Reedy, Sara Teasdale, Kate Chopin, and roundabout, Josephine Johnson. And T. S. Eliot who drew on the local scene for "Prufrock" and "Burnt Norton."[22] At the present time Washington University has attracted an unusual number of people in fiction and poetry, including Mona Van Duyn, Donald Finkel, Curtis Lyle, Jarvis Thurston, Stanley Elkin, William H. Gass, John Morris, and Howard Nemerov. Other writers in the area are John Hardy, Howard Schwartz, "Luke," Charles Guenther, Al Lebowitz, Constance Urdang, and Peter L. Simpson. Simpson's reviews in the *St. Louis Post Dispatch* and the *Mill Creek Valley Intelligencer* are bringing the national and the local literary scene into focus. This development is perhaps typical throughout the country; it is certainly going on in the Midwest. Groups of writers associated with the universities are beginning to have an impact, not only at large, but in an unpredictably important way on their own cities.

The St. Louis writers in the composite could never be called regional; the work, when it does touch the local, does so in terms of particularizations useful for the construction of larger themes. Mona Van Duyn can rouse rococo delectations from a visit to a neighborhood ice cream parlor:

> Poised upside down on its duncecap,
> a shrunken purple head,
> True Blueberry,
> enters its tightening frame of orange lip,
> and the cream of a child's cheek is daubed
>   with
> Zanzibar Cocoa, while
>   *Here at the Martha Washington*
>   *Ice Cream Store*
>   *we outdo the* Symbolistes.
> a fine green trickle—
> Pistachio? Mint Julep?
>   *Words have colors*
>   *and colors are tasty.*
> sweetens his chin.
> In front of me Licorice teeters like a lump
>   of coal
> on its pinkish base of Pumpkin.
>   *A Rauschenberg tongue*
>   *fondles this rich donnée*
>   *then begins to erase it.*[23]

This sugary visit, seemingly a regional delight, when returned to its context in *To See, To Take*, becomes a token of identity for a personality of fascinating range. *To See, To Take* chances human experience of all kinds, as its title implies. It is a dangerous and exhilarating book.

Constance Urdang's *Natural History* is a novel of ideas. The ideas are the real characters in the work because it is the narrator's mind that shapes and provides meaning for events and people. Among the people are three women whose lives help form the story: what they do and do not do, the kinds of decisions they make or do not make, become the material the narrator puzzles as she evolves concepts of them and of herself and of women in general. At the same time the reader is aware that these women are creating their own configurations and choosing their own meanings. The multiplicity of existences and identities grows rich and mysterious. The journal form in which the book is cast is suited to the variety of experience the narrator draws from and to the sense of process which she communicates:

THE DAY BEFORE YESTERDAY I drove down Enright. A new world. Nothing remains as I remember it. Urban Renewal has been at work during the months we stayed away—not that this should be a surprise, after all it was more than two years ago that they set up an office on Delmar and announced their plans, and we all voted "Yes" when they set up the voting machine. What makes the shock and disturbance—and I can see how this feeling would be the same after an air-raid or fire —is the bland, imperious look of the vacant lots created by the demolition of buildings ("In the enormous twilight/ Of the demolition of buildings . . . but this isn't twilight, it's clear morning sunshine decorating every leaf and grass-blade, the hard yellowish clay, the white and purple clover, shepherd's purse, ragweed, chicory, fleabane and— now that autumn is here—goldenrod). . . .[24]

East St. Louis, Illinois, has developed its own community of voices, partially an outgrowth of work done in the East St. Louis Residence Center established by Southern Illinois University in the middle-fifties. Eugene Redmond was a student there at that time:

> The way is ALWAYS up
> for people without wings;
> And the sun trudges slowly
> from State Street where day
> Prevails when the hole is dark,
> And it is then that
> Eyes peer out ahead of kerosene
> Lamps and 30-Watt bulbs.[25]

Redmond has helped to edit the poetry and prose of the late Henry Dumas who taught there when the center became the Experiment in Higher Education for the university. Dumas was master of a hard-won and honest language; any random quote reflects the high consistency of his work:

> He could hear his mother humming in the kitchen. She was up early. The sound of her voice was like the waving of a fan over a fire which had smouldered all night, and then in the morning, when a piece of good, dry wood was lain on, it would catch and rise up. Layton knew she wanted him to go to school today. He walked out of the room, through where his grandfather sat, tying his shoes and spitting tobacco juice in a can beside his cot. He spoke softly to his grandfather, but the old man's eyes hung on him suspiciously. Layton opened the front door and the sun leaped in on the old man's cot.[26]

A few miles north of East St. Louis is the place where Lewis and Clark wintered in camp before they set off on their expedition to the Pacific. They could see the Missouri River entering the Mississippi from that point. In July 1673, Father Marquette saw the Missouri entering in full flood:

I have seen nothing more frightful, a mass of large trees, entire, with branches, real floating islands came rushing down the mouth of the river Pekitanoui [Missouri], so impetuously, that we could not, without great danger, expose ourselves to pass across. The agitation was so great that the water was all muddy and could not get clear.[27]

There are steel mills and oil refineries not far from the Lewis and Clark camp, and the great temple mounds of Cahokia completed in the thirteenth century.

A hundred miles north on the Mississippi is Hannibal, Missouri, the St. Petersburg of Tom Sawyer and Huckleberry Finn. Twain went so deeply into the American psyche that he seems to be everywhere. His memory supports Disneyland confections of freckle-faced boys on the river as well as a lineage of critics from Van Wyck Brooks to T. S. Eliot to Leslie Fiedler, none of them agreeing on anything except that they all need Huck Finn on their rafts somehow. Then there is the work of the man himself, as in Huck's description of Pap Finn:

He was most fifty, and he looked it. His hair was long and tangled and greasy, and hung down, and you could see his eyes shining through like he was behind vines. It was all black, no gray; so was his long, mixed-up whiskers. There warn't no color in his face, where his face showed; it was white; not like another man's white, but a white to make a body sick, a white to make a body's flesh crawl— a tree-toad white, a fish belly white. As for his clothes—just rags, that was all. He had one ankle resting on 'tother knee; the boot on that foot was busted, and two of his toes stuck through, and he worked them now and then. His hat was laying on the floor, an old black slouch hat with the top caved in, like a lid.[28]

In central Illinois there is a dream of Lincoln, and the homes of Edgar Lee Masters and Vachel Lindsay and Carl Sandburg have been made into shrines. Strip mines desolate the cornfields, spreading unobtrusively at a distance from the roads.

Edgar Lee Masters was not interested in local color; he was interested in argument. He was the son of a lawyer who was four times mayor of Lewistown, Illinois. *Spoon River Anthology* is filled with complaints, charges and counter-charges, indictments, summations of the prosecution and the defense, pleas for clemency. The book has the resonance of gossip, the form a closed society uses to preserve its history and the germ of its legends. As a society, a small town is less closed than most. Its size is determined by numbers rather than occupation or social class. A small town is containable. It affords a writer a variety of characters with which to enrich his theme. For Masters it was a good place for dramatizing the conflict between a new and an old morality.

Vachel Lindsay loved all things. He remains a Springfield Blake, doing what he can with his genius and with his own time:

> Bad public taste is mob-law, good public
> taste is democracy.
> A crude administration is damned already.
> Let the best moods of the people rule.
> A bad designer is, to that extent, a bad
> citizen.
> A hasty prosperity may be raw and absurd,
> a well-considered poverty may be
> exquisite.
> Without an eager public, all teaching is
> vain.[29]

Carl Sandburg cannot be touched yet. A reader wants to accept all of him, but he cannot do it. He tries to put him out of his mind as a provincial poet, but he cannot do this either. He tries to separate the imagist from the chanter of people's songs, but this does not work. He tries to distinguish between the socialist and the sentimentalist, but he is not able to draw that line. Sandburg is too much a part of a

Middle America that is done with but which is still alive in most of us. He is like a wound that has not healed.

Above Hannibal is Keokuk, Iowa, where Sandburg once saw twenty-one Greeks washing their feet. Above Keokuk is Nauvoo, Illinois, where Joseph Smith and his brother are buried. The Mormons of the 1850s were what the street people are today. They were laughed at and feared.

Major Zachary Taylor lost a battle near Davenport, Iowa, to a combined force of English, Fox, Sac, Sioux, and Winnebago during the War of 1812. Davenport was a refuge for Germans who fled Europe after the Revolution of 1848. Black Hawk's village was located in sight of the town, near what is now Moline on the Illinois side:

> We had about eight hundred acres in cultivation, including what we had on the islands of Rock river. The land around our village, uncultivated, was covered with blue-grass, which made excellent pasture for our horses. Several fine springs broke out of the bluff, near by, from which we were supplied with good water. The rapids of Rock river furnished us with an abundance of excellent fish, and the land, being good, never failed to produce good crops of corn, beans, pumpkins, and squashes. We always had plenty—our children never cried with hunger, nor our people were never in want.[30]

Floyd Dell, George Cram Cook, and Susan Glaspell were all living in Davenport shortly after the turn of the century. They knew one another as young rebels in the literary set. In time they made contributions to the national and the international scene. Floyd Dell helped to spark the Chicago Renaissance. Later in New York he became editor of the *Masses* and *The Liberator*. Cook founded the Provincetown Players, then journeyed to Greece where he labored until his death to create a Greek national theatre. Susan Glaspell, influenced by Cook whom she married and by Dell, became a playwright and a novelist. The basic attitudes of these three writers

97

were confirmed before they left Davenport. Dell had picked up his agnosticism from reading Peoria's Ingersoll and his socialism from listening to street speeches in Quincy, Illinois. He found when he came to Davenport that the Turner Hall was a place where he could exchange ideas and learn. Dell talked George Cram Cook out of certain aristocratic notions that Cook had picked up reading Nietzsche, but the devotion Cook had for classical literature from his youth he kept to the end of his life. He encouraged the revival of Greek plays as well as the production of plays written on American themes when he guided the Provincetown Players. He felt at home in Greece, supposing that the virtues of the Greek peasants were the same as those of the American pioneers on the Middle Border. Susan Glaspell had decided on a career as a short story writer even before she met Dell and Cook, and she had supported herself as a reporter for the *Des Moines Daily News*.[31] Her relationship to her Iowa surroundings runs the gamut from sentimental local color to revolt against small-town morality to return in search of whatever values can be drawn from a rich and ambiguous past. Of the three, she is the only one who could be called a regionalist, and yet all of them were aware of their roots in this Mississippi rivertown and of the strange, variable sustenance it gave to them.

West of Davenport, an easy hour's drive, is Iowa City. The Writers' Workshop, the dream of Paul Engle, has been established now a quarter of a century; so many authors have studied there, or taught, or have come to read and to lecture, that in one way or another the workshop has influenced the development of the literary arts over the entire nation.

W. D. Snodgrass was a student in the workshop during the 1950s. His poem "Heart's Needle" has a setting taken from his knowledge of the State University of Iowa and of Iowa City. The poem is confessional, a contemporary mode which Snodgrass helped to perfect. The confessional mode is a refinement developed from the sudden interest in classical tragedy after the second world war. Snodgrass is able to relate his experience of marital discord, divorce, and settlement of the custody of a child, his private tragedy, to the Cold War and the stalemate in Korea. Motifs from his personal experience and from political history are set in juxtaposition to the struggle in animal and the disorder in sentient nature. The poem is a confession of personal inadequacy, a taking stock, of pain and frustration that cannot be fully exorcised. The hero is a modern, democratic man; his suffering does not deliver the state from the wrath of the gods. In the fierce ninth poem of the sequence, the speaker looks at exhibits in the university museum:

> I see the hydrocephalic goat;
> here is the curled and swollen head,
>   there, the burst skull;
>
>   skin of a limbless calf;
> a horse's foetus, mummified;
>   mounted and joined forever,
> the Siamese twin dogs that ride
> belly to belly, half and half,
>   that none shall sever.
>
>   I walk among the growths,
> by gangrenous tissue, goitre, cysts,
>   by fistulas and cancers,
> where the malignancy man loathes
> is held suspended and persists.
>   And I don't know the answers.
>
> The window's turning white.
> The world moves like a diseased heart
>   packed with snow and ice.
> Three months now we have been apart
> less than a mile. I cannot fight
>   or let you go.[32]

Those members of the Fox nation who still remain live not far from Iowa City in Tama, Iowa. They have always called themselves Meskwakies, resenting that

"Fox" fixed on them by the French in the old days when the French and the Illinois tried to starve them off the face of the earth and the Sac hid them in their own villages to prevent that. Those who live now in Tama are Ray Young Bear's people. Young Bear gained attention as a poet when he became a student in the Upward Bound Project at Luther College in Decorah, Iowa. He has kept on as a writer since then, and promises to make a long silence articulate once more:

> one chip of human bone.
>
> it is almost fitting
> to die on the railroad tracks
>
> i can easily understand
> how they felt on their
> staggered walks back.
>
> there is something about
> trains, drinking, and being
> an indian with nothing to lose.[33]

Davenport, Moline, and Rock Island are almost on a line that extends eastward to Chicago. Between, in northern Illinois, are a number of towns that provide homes for commuters from that windy place. DeKalb stands midway. Northern Illinois University is in DeKalb, and Lucien Stryk, the Zen scholar who first gathered the midwestern poets into an interesting anthology, teaches there.[34] Geneva is close by, the home of R. R. Cuscaden who used to edit *Midwest* and David Etter who lives in a house that is heavy with the presence of Lincoln.

Etter likes the small-town Midwest and he has perfected a language that corresponds to his attraction. The sheer sensuous richness of the countryside almost intoxicates him. He is a contextualist, not a moralist. He discovers, for good or ill, the secrets of people who have never made it big anywhere, and he wants everybody to know about what he has learned:

River roads of insects
rub summer in the ears
of slow farmers.
In the sweet crotch
of a sassafras tree
Janet sucks hard candy
and jabs brown toes
at her little brother.

A wind out of Kansas
carries rumors
of wild wheat fires
and the blue eyes
of young soldiers

Near the screen door
moonflowers bloom:
shy faces of farm girls.[35]

There is a hard, cold edge to Etter's poetry, a negative quality that is as amoral and as immediate as
the gorgeous images he makes of things that give
him joy. It takes him out of the humanistic tradition
of Anderson, Sandburg, Masters, and Wright, and
also away from pure imagery into uncharted relationships between the poet and his surroundings.

The Mississippi River seems endless; the country
in the northering reaches is particularly beautiful.
It is miles of high bluffs and palisades and nesting
sites for eagles. In places the river widens, creating
substantial lakes. These lakes spelled hard labor for
lograftsmen bringing timber out of Minnesota and
Wisconsin in the 1880s. Charles Edward Russell
knew these men and how they crossed the lakes:

> Sails were useful when the wind blew downstream,
> but it had a habit of blowing the other way when
> a raft came along. Oars were tried; also poling.
> Neither would work well. Rafts might be poled
> when the water was shallow, but in some parts of
> the lake it was absurdly deep. The process finally
> hit upon was to take an anchor in a skiff with a
> line about half a mile long, go out ahead and hunt

a place where bottom could be touched, drop the anchor, and then all hands pull on the line until the raft was up to the anchor. Then the yawl would be launched again and the old weary process repeated. This was kept up day and night with two crews and was no better than mankilling, but it got the raft through.[36]

There is more hard commerce on the river now than there used to be in the glory days of the steamboats. Tow pilots for the commercial lines thread barges through locks in rough wind and skittish currents with fourteen inches to spare at the lock walls. Dubuque, Iowa's Richard Bissell has worked the inland rivers as a crew member on diesel tows and barges, and he can portray the ordinary day-by-day life of the river and the language that goes with it:

"Where was you when the barge went down?" I said. I was sure worried about that barge.

"I was downstairs in the bottom of the boat cleanin' up and settin' around."

"What was your Mate doing all the time?"

"I never seen him. I can't rightly say where he was at."

"Why did that barge dive, Kid? Why did that goddam old number 36 decide to sink on us?"

"Well, I'll tell you," says the Kid, taking out a stick of Beeman's Pepsin Gum, "I've got a theory about that."

"I'll bet it's a killer," I said. "So go ahead, pride of Alton, Illinois, and tell us the theory."

"Well," says the Kid, going to work on the gum with artistic jaw motions like the dime-store clerks back in 1933, "the way I see it is like this here: the barges sure they float despite of the fact they are made of steel and filled with coal, which proves the law of gravity, but on the other hand when we landed there on the shore it seems like we might of hit some rocks or somethin.'"

"Why, we drifted in there easy," I said. "We no more than merely nudged that riprap."

"Well to make a long story short my theory is like this: I figure the river was to blame. I think some water got in that barge somehow and she sunk."

"How much did you make," I says, "when you was helping on that coal truck down at Alton?"

"Ninety-five cents an hour," he said.

"Well I hope you didn't give them no theories on the origins of coal," I said.[37]

This writing can be called picturesque or local color narrative, but it answers a need that goes deeper. There is a desire to know or perhaps a pleasure in learning of the inner life of worlds a person depends upon, but is totally removed from, something that seems to have been part of the American tradition from the very beginning because of the schizophrenic reality of town and frontier. Bissell satisfies a reader, telling him of the technicalities and the special language that define at least one of the worlds within his society.

Dubuque is also the home of Raymond Roseliep. He has taught at Loras College and over the years has helped to bring along a number of young writers. He puzzles the strange isolation of the priest, studies the scene around him, the lives of his relatives and the students in his hometown, the larger realm of art which he consciously shares. His faith permeates his thought. It is operative in these lines for his lost brother:

> I followed, and
> imagined fallow land, the desert place
> you said you would not die in, or the dry
> white wine a priest will trickle on his fast.
> But you were given to the rain that night
> and could not hear a footstep crackle sharp
> as Mass wheat in your falling street.[38]

Dennis Schmitz grew up in this town. He has achieved an enviable integration of the various strands in his background, and perhaps speaks for a generation of younger poets more at peace with themselves and less defensive than their teachers

103

were. There is a classical touch in his work, and
that he should have chosen to write a group of
eclogues seems most natural, as in this example:

>   my bedroom poised
>   between shadow & light & the light
>   was flawed by angles of glass
>   till night disappeared in a moment
>   of wonder. the farm fed
>   on the full hillsides & sheets
>   of grain seemed to fall
>   almost to the river's shore.
>   but from my window the farm
>   was less real: the river & at noon
>   the fish I could almost hear fading
>   in its cool depths distracted
>   the boy of twelve, my brother
>   beside me
>   slept. he was oldest & duty
>   has deliberate solitude: even my sisters
>   kept their dolls
>   quietly.
>   *   *   *
>   my grandfather's God
>   guided him to the river & the Holy
>   Ghost, he said, hung
>   like a white hand over this hill.[39]

Dennis Schmitz writes in the serenity of a culture that has survived. Hamlin Garland saw that
culture in its beginnings in Wisconsin, Iowa, and
South Dakota, a cruel, demanding life on farms that
wiped out pioneers, the cruelty intensified by unfair
land rentals and speculation that drained off even
the small profit from a rare good year. He came
away from that experience with no illusions: The
garden of America was a place of cankered apples.
He lived in La Crosse, Wisconsin, for a time. The
town today is best seen at sundown from Grandad
Bluff where it spreads below in the evening light
like an illuminated fan. Garland's Private Smith,
the wounded veteran on his way home from the

Civil War, saw that bluff of a morning glowing like a beacon out of a scarf of mist. That day he walked home to his mortgaged farm:

> The sun was burning hot on that slope, and his step grew slower, in spite of his iron resolution. He sat down several times to rest. Slowly he crawled up the rough, reddish-brown road, which wound along the hillside, under great trees, through dense groves of jack oaks, with treetops far below him on his left hand, and the hills far above him on his right. He crawled along like some minute wingless variety of fly.
>
> He ate some hardtack, sauced with wild berries, when he reached the summit of the ridge, and sat there for some time, looking down into his home coulé.
>
> Sombre, pathetic figure! His wide, round, gray eyes gazing down into the beautiful valley, seeing and not seeing, the splendid cloud-shadows sweeping over the western hills and across the green and yellow wheat far below. His head dropped forward on his palm, his shoulders took on a tired stoop, his cheek-bones showed painfully. An observer might have said, "He is looking down upon his own grave."[40]

Garland lived a long and successful life. He returned to Wisconsin in his age to build himself a house, but he was hard pressed to find anyone who remembered how to make a pioneer stone fireplace for it.[41]

There is a fine center for the study of contemporary poetry in La Crosse at the present time. John Judson, poet and editor, is there at the State University.

Above La Crosse, the river comes northeast from St. Paul, passing Winona (Sioux word, always given to the eldest daughter) and Red Wing where Perrot constructed a fort in 1695.

St. Paul, Minnesota, is the subject of two of the most evocative paragraphs on the theme of return in American literature. F. Scott Fitzgerald wrote

them for the voice of Nick Carraway in the final
pages of *The Great Gatsby:*

> When we pulled out into the winter night and
> the real snow, our snow, began to stretch out be-
> side us and twinkle against the windows, and the
> dim lights of small Wisconsin stations moved by,
> a sharp wild brace came suddenly into the air. We
> drew in deep breaths of it as we walked back from
> dinner through the cold vestibules, unutterably
> aware of our identity with this country for one
> strange hour, before we melted indistinguishably
> into it again.
>
> That's my Middle West—not the wheat or the
> prairies or the lost Swede towns, but the thrilling
> returning trains of my youth, and the street lamps
> and sleigh bells in the frosty dark and the shadows
> of holly wreaths thrown by lighted windows on the
> snow. I am part of that, a little solemn with the
> feel of those long winters, a little complacent from
> growing up in the Carraway house in a city where
> dwellings are still called through decades by a
> family's name. I see now that this has been a story
> of the West, after all—Tom and Gatsby, Daisy and
> Jordan and I, were all Westerners, and perhaps we
> possessed some deficiency in common which made
> us subtly unadaptable to Eastern life.[42]

Carraway's Midwest is nostalgic and collegiate,
solemnized rather than formed by "our identity with
this country." What forms Carraway's Midwest is
money, not necessarily its real presence, but its
availability and romance. If his Midwest is a memory, his East is a vision, a drunken woman in evening clothes being carried to the wrong house because no one knows her name. This East is not a
place, it is a result. In a sense these Westerners
have never left home. The East they find themselves
so inadequate to is of their own making, populated
by their own kind. Carraway's decision to go back
home is not so much a prodigal's return as the acceptance of responsibility for a beautiful premise
that was all wrong from the beginning.

106

At the University of Minnesota, John Berryman was engaged until his death in an effort to accumulate all the dream songs that can be written about Henry, the put-down man who suffers death and survives in resurrection. The songs are made in strict forms with intricate and integrating rhyme and a most unlikely marriage of minstrel show jargon to the controlled elegance of a lofty academic voice. The songs are full of comment: Jobean Henry has his comforters. The end product is poetry at once casual and tough that traps in a strange made-up voice the dis-ease and restlessness that is everywhere:

—Henry is tired of the winter,
& haircuts, & a squeamish comfy
   ruin-prone proud national
      mind,
   & Spring (in the city
so called).
Henry likes Fall.
Hé would be prepared to líve in a
world of Fáll
for ever, impenitent Henry.
But the snows and summers grieve
& dream;

thése fierce & airy occupations,
and love,
raved away so many of Henry's years
it is a wonder that, with in each hand
one of his own mad books and all,
ancient fires for eyes, his head full
& his heart full, he's making ready
to move on.[43]

Among those writers who have been in the area recently or are working there now are the poets Charles Baxter, Keith Gunderson, C. W. Truesdale, and the objectivist Carl Rakosi. The fiction writer Peter Schneenan grew up there and the novelist Alvin Greenberg has been teaching at Macalester College for the last ten years.

Greenberg brings his hero, Arthur Hoppe, back to Minnesota at the conclusion of *Going Nowhere.* Hoppe copes with the absurdity of his spaceship world of failure by giving away certificates of valueless stock.

> Most of those groups which carried him westward thus, to his unknown destination, were, of course, families, frequently on their way to or from summer vacations, their cars loaded not only with children but with games, toys, souvenirs, pets, and picnic lunches, so that Arthur frequently found himself squeezed into incredible corners, invited to play chess or cribbage or count-the-cows, enlisted to settle sibling rivalries or dispose of soiled diapers, and fed a relatively unchanging diet of bologna and cheese sandwiches, potato chips, pickles and cookies. To each member of each family that he rode with, adults and children and infants alike, and often an elderly aunt or grandmother as well, Arthur gave a share of stock in the Poughkeepsie Institute, carefully inscribing the individual's name on the certificate and in his registry, and explaining, as he did so, the nature of his gift: that it was worthless stock, that the Institute was not and never would be going anywhere, that this share of stock, therefore, laid upon the recipient no burden of obligation or worry, nothing but whatever joy he might get just from having it, for what it was, which was not much.[44]

His gesture adjusts the society a little. Everybody is happy, for a change possessing something that it feels good to have but which can be cheerfully given away.

Above Minneapolis and to the west of St. Cloud is Sauk Centre, the Gopher Prairie of *Main Street.* All the superficial details that Sherwood Anderson and Edgar Lee Masters omitted from their small towns, Sinclair Lewis has used to make his credible. Often Lewis defines people by the furniture they choose, and sometimes this is more striking than anything else he can say about them:

> Mrs. Luke Dawson, wife of the richest man in town, gaped at them piteously when they appeared. Her expensive frock of beaver-colored satin with rows, plasters and pendants of solemn brown beads was intended for a woman twice her size. She stood wringing her hands in front of nineteen folding chairs, in her front parlor with its faded photograph of Minnehaha Falls in 1890, its "colored enlargement" of Mr. Dawson, its bulbous lamp painted with sepia cows and mountains and standing on a mortuary marble column.[45]

The collection of bric-a-brac that Lewis incorporates into his novel has undergone a change over the years. The objects that he describes as signs of the cultural poverty of Gopher Prairie have taken on a curious integrity of their own. The town Lewis describes may have been bigoted, but it was not culturally impoverished. It had what it thought it needed.

Carol Kennicott's frantic search for leverage in her endeavors to change the town takes her into all corners of it and into the surrounding countryside. Here, surely, in the welter of analysis that Lewis exposes it to—Marxist, Freudian, pioneer, frontier— Gopher Prairie will emerge as visible and accurate as a photograph. It does, but by the time the book reaches the halfway mark, Gopher Prairie as a separate entity has ceased to exist. Carol Kennicott's own difficulty in defining herself and the difficulty Lewis had in deciding whether she was to be a heroine or another object of satire are as much a part of the image of Gopher Prairie as the goings on at the Thanatopsis Club and the Jolly Seventeen. *Main Street*, like *Babbitt*, ends in ambiguity. Carol Kennicott accepts an uneasy coexistence with Gopher Prairie, based on the discovery that she doesn't want to go away and that she has as much right as anyone else to be there.

Collegeville, Minnesota, is between Sauk Centre and St. Cloud. J. F. Powers taught on the staff of St. John's University there for many years. The names of the towns in that corner of the state suggest the religion of the populace: St. Anthony, St. Joseph, St. Wendel, St. Rosa, St. Francis, St. Martin, St. Anna, St. Stephen. In *Morte D'Urban* Powers examines the Roman Catholic Church, an exotic culture that flourished for decades unheeded by anybody.

As in *Main Street,* the objects with which people surround themselves and the activities in which they engage become supremely important, but Powers rejects the type of satire that Lewis would have written. There is a terror and a pathos in the romance of Father Urban, and there is an emptiness underneath the constant manipulation and projection that becomes an active source of evil:

> In a room much larger than any bedroom at the Hill, Mrs. Thwaites sat in an overstuffed wheelchair, watching television on two sets. The only light in the room came from the sets, a dead light, so that Mrs. Thwaites's face showed up like a photographic negative: a little old woman with the face of a baby bird, all eyes and beak, but with a full head of bobbed white hair. One hand was wrapped in black rosary beads the size of cranberries, and the other gripped the remote control. A humidifier steamed at her feet. To one side of her chair there was a table with dominoes stacked on it. Across the room, an elevator, door open, was waiting. In one corner, a big bed, fancier than Wilf's and higher off the floor, was also waiting. The shades were drawn in all the windows, and the temperature was equatorial.[46]

There is much of Babbitt in Father Urban. He is an active man, a booster for his religious order, and he takes pleasure in this. He can play the game, adjust to whatever the immediate polite situation demands of him. But there is much more of Jay Gatsby in Father Urban. He is a man of generous impulses who gives himself to a life of hyperactivity that is finally graceless. The heroic choices that he makes are of no particular consequence, though they help shape him in his last days as a man the organization could have predicted. This popular book reaches beyond its parochial boundaries. For Father Urban the polarities are heaven and hell, for the executive they are a life that is meaningful or pointless. In the actual living it is difficult to tell which is which.

St. Cloud, Minnesota, is the last large town on the Mississippi. North of that town the river comes out of a shepherd's crook from the west and south where it has its source in Lake Itaska. The country is one of many lakes and harvests of wild rice. Chippewa live in this river area and to the north of it. Frances Densmore who collected the music of the Chippewa recorded this very popular love song: "Do not weep I am not going to die."[47] It has the force of an anthem today.

Cleveland is on the lake, a night's journey by steamer from Detroit, a port city, leagued with Windsor, Buffalo, a culture faintly international, not spoken for yet, not quite. Hart Crane was native to the city. Edward Dahlberg was sent there as a boy to the Jewish orphanage. He knew Crane in Paris, remembers a tenuous connection in Cleveland:

> What little I had done for him had mitigated some obscure pain in me, for that part of us we do not use for others clogs our fate. I had been an inmate in an orphanage in Cleveland when Hart Crane was a soda fountain clerk in his father's fancy ice cream parlor in that city. Crane's establishment was on Euclid Avenue, Plutus's boulevard in Cleveland where John D. Rockefeller and Charles M. Schwab had their great mansions. On the rare occasions when I walked down Euclid Avenue, which smelt of Lake Erie and the windswept money of Troy, I wondered whether I would ever be rich enough to buy one of Crane's ice cream sodas.[48]

Dahlberg has perfected a style that can only be called his own, but any Tudor schoolboy in sixteenth century England could recognize how he marshals the commonplaces, the apt sentences of the ages to illuminate his meanings, offering proof that he is not just a man wandering in his time, but a witness who shares the Classical, Judaic, Christian and Humanistic heritage of the West. Even his attempt to show the orphan children in a world apart is done in reference to these worlds:

They were a separate race of stunted children who were clad in famine. Swollen heads lay on top of ashy uniformed orphans. Some had oval or oblong skulls; others gigantic occiputs that resembled the Cynocephali described by Hesiod and Pliny. The palsied and the lame were cured in the pool of Bethesda, but who had enough human spittle to heal the orphan's sore eyes and granulated lids? How little love, or hot sperm, had gone into the making of their gray-maimed bodies? The ancient Jews, who ate dove's dung in the time of dearth in Samaria, were as hungered as these waifs. Nobody can even see another without abundant affection. Whatever grace and virtue we give to others comes from our own fell needs. We pray for the face we need and call this intellectual perception. Without the feeling we are willing to give to others, the Kosmos is vacant and utterly peopleless.

Though all day long nothing was in the ailing minds of the orphan-asylum Ismaels but the cry for food, what these mutes asked for was never given. O Pharisee, when will you learn that we never came to your table for the gudgeons and the barley loaves?

Whenever Doc walked through the back yard, a covey of small oafs took hold of his scriptural sleeves and fingered the sacred buttons of them as though they were lipping the rood. The lucky ones who took hold of the hands of this Elohim of the orphanage shook with paradisiacal rapture. He could hardly loosen the grip of a three-year-old-wight with a running nose and a sore head who would hang onto his trousers. "The heart is forever inexperienced," asserts Thoreau; "Feed my lambs," says Christ.[49]

Langston Hughes began his long career as a writer in Cleveland. He had come to Cleveland from Joplin, Missouri, by way of Lawrence, Kansas. He attended Central High School, and began to write there. He had a generous talent. So many key phrases have escaped from his work and settled in the public consciousness that to reread his poems is to discover suddenly the origin of much that furnishes the memory. It is a surprise and a recognition, a return to a place that has always, mysteriously, been known. It is hard to define his special intimacy, but Hughes has already done this:

> In an envelop marked:
> PERSONAL
> God addressed me a letter.
> In an envelop marked:
> PERSONAL
> I have given my answer.[50]

One of the small towns west of Cleveland is Clyde, Ohio. Sherwood Anderson lived there for ten years during his boyhood and adolescence. It was a town of twenty-five hundred people at that time, and there were open fields around it and a nearby cattail bog left over from a receding glacier. The fields were broken with stands of beech and maple. Anderson used this setting for *Winesburg, Ohio*.

The book had a stunning impact when it appeared in 1919. Here was a collection of stories that were free from the restrictions of romantic plots. The characters were motivated by desires for beauty, truth, and goodness, but they lived in a turmoil of erotic energy and rural loneliness. Most of them had suffered some trauma, usually before the age of twenty-five, which doomed them to remain in Winesburg until the end of their lives, and only a few chosen ones escaped to Chicago to do newspaper work.

Now it is years away from 1919, and these one-chance Horatio Algers of the soul are sometimes too much to bear. The book has power still as a group of fables and myths, each with its moral lesson or its overriding emotional discharge. Episodes, and voices within them, evoke responses beyond the contexts of the stories:

> The beauty of the country about Winesburg was too much for Ray on that fall evening. That was all there was to it. He could not stand it. Of a sudden he forgot all about being a quiet old farm hand and throwing off the torn overcoat began to run across the field. As he ran he shouted a protest against his life, against all life, against everything that makes life ugly. "There was no promise made," he cried into the empty spaces that lay about him.[51]

Below Cleveland and Youngstown is Niles, Ohio. Kenneth Patchen was born there in 1911. Patchen can stand for dozens of writers who were born in the Midwest but have put their roots down elsewhere, and who do not draw especially on their knowledge of the region as a source for their works. Names that come to mind in this respect include Kenneth Koch, Cincinnati; Richard Howard, Cleveland; Michael McClure, Marysville, Kansas; Edward Dorn, Villa Grove, Illinois; Gray Burr, Omaha, Nebraska. But Patchen was an old-timer, and though this former steelworker had been away a long time, there is a special affection for him in the heartland. Frederick Eckman of Bowling Green, Ohio, and formerly director of the poetry workshop at the State University there, has been a defender and close critic of Patchen's art.

Detroit might have been a moderate town on the strait between Lake Erie and Lake St. Clair, a good place to visit with its past still gathered around it— established seventy-five years before the American Revolution—but the automobile industry and the assemblyline broke the city wide open at the turn of the century and created the Motown everybody knows.

Detroit has a good share of writers. Several are members of the faculty at Wayne State University:

John Reed, Judy McCombs, Faye Kicknosway, Stephen Tudor, and Ester Broner. Dudley Randall publishes the Broadside Press books, important volumes by black authors. Black writers working in Detroit at the present time include Jill Witherspoon, Naomi Madgett, Ahmed Alhamisi, and Frenchy Hodges. Don L. Lee, now living in Chicago, is originally from Detroit and four of his books have been brought out by Dudley Randall. Detroit is also the home of Peter DeVries and Harriette Arnod, the novelists. Joyce Carol Oates lives in the city and commutes to Canada where she teaches at the University of Windsor.

Joyce Carol Oates can write a powerful novel. *A Garden of Earthly Delights* is a woman's counterpart to Mailer's *Why Are We in Viet Nam*, but what Mailer approaches in terms of myth, Joyce Carol Oates details as common, harsh reality. It is the story of a woman who comes one day to accept the myth because the myth is simpler and more bearable than her own life.

> He was to keep coming for the rest of Clara's life, for many years, though she would sometimes not bother to look away from her television set when he appeared.
> She seemed to like best programs that showed men fighting, swinging from ropes, shooting guns and driving fast cars, killing the enemy again and again until the dying gasps of evil men were only a certain familiar rhythm away from the opening blasts of the commercials, which changed only gradually over the years.[52]

Clara is the kind of woman that young girls in America are warned not to be. She is also the kind of person that American women have often been told they are. Joyce Carol Oates realizes her fully from within. She places Clara in a land that sometimes seems to merge with the sky. Hills sweep up into clouds, erasing boundaries between heaven and earth. The land also seems to dissolve in another direction into vast systems of production, distribution, ownership, inheritance. Between the visionary landscape of desire and the hidden landscape of possession, there is very little place for anybody to live.

Three of the universities in the south of the state are centers for literary activities. At Western Michigan University, John Knapp edits the *Westegan Review* and John Woods, author of *The Deaths at Paragon, Indiana,* is a member of the staff. At Michigan State University, Linda Wagner, the Williams scholar, organizes a yearly conference on contemporary literature. In Ann Arbor, Donald Hall has sparked a healthy interest in creative writing and has been instrumental in organizing the Ann Arbor Poetry Circuit. Radcliff Squires is on the staff, as is Hall, of the University of Michigan, and Robert Hayden, born in Detroit and a graduate of the university, has returned there after many years on the faculty of Fisk University in Nashville.

The poet Theodore Roethke was a native of Michigan. He spent his boyhood in Saginaw where his father and uncle owned a greenhouse. The city is inland a little from Saginaw Bay which opens out into Lake Huron. Roethke comes back there to shape his knowledge of the small lives in the greenhouse, to bring order to what he sees as a primordial rage for life. He comes from his own word as a burly, loving man who yearns for peace, though he threatens always to shatter on the tips of his nerves. No one has desired tranquility more or has sought to avoid the possibility of oblivion with such anger, so fierce a denial of a final senselessness, or admitted so frankly the contrary urge to have done with the struggle:

> In this hour,
> In this first heaven of knowing,
> The flesh takes on the pure poise
>   of the spirit,
> Acquires, for a time, the sand-
>   piper's insouciance,

The hummingbird's surety, the
   kingfisher's cunning—
I shift on my rock, and I think:
Of the first trembling of a Michigan
   brook in April,
Over a lip of stone, the tiny rivulet;
And that wrist-thick cascade tumbling
   from a cleft rock,
Its spray holding a double rain-bow
   in early spring,
Small enough to be taken in, embraced,
   by two arms,—
Or the Tittebawasee, in the time
   between winter and spring,
When the ice melts along the edges
   in early afternoon.
And the midchannel begins creaking
   and heaving from the pressure
   beneath,
The ice piling high against the iron-
   bound spiles,
Gleaming, freezing hard again,
   creaking at midnight—
And I long for the blast of dynamite,
The sudden sucking roar as the culvert
   loosens its debris of branches
   and sticks,
Welter of tin cans, pails, old bird
   nests, a child's shoe riding a log,
As the piled ice breaks away from the
   battered spiles,
And the whole river begins to move forward, its bridges shaking.[53]

    Above Saginaw, Michigan becomes a fine place
for camping. There are miles of sand dunes, good
fishing lakes, some of them warm enough for swim-
ming, and counties of beech and evergreen forests.
There are good-sized, self-sustaining towns, summer colonies, clusters of homes of the affluent from
Cleveland, Cincinnati, Chicago, St. Louis, ore boats
on the lakes that can be seen from the windows of

shore houses, and to steep the land, a three-hundred year written history.

This is the country Hemingway's Nick Adams identifies as his own, but only the second growth woods, the cut-over wilderness, is reserved for Adams. Those items listed above are, for the most part, absent from the young man's mind as Hemingway presents him. *In Our Time* where the first of the Nick Adams stories occurs the society that is given—father, mother, school friend, a handful of Ojibways, a punch-drunk boxer, chance-met whores —seems more restricted than it is, perhaps because there is a silence and a loneliness in the mind of the boy who is registering what is going on around him. As Hemingway gives these stories to a reader, they are set against other stories that reveal the adult Adams in the Europe of the first world war.

His experience in that conflict wounds him physically and psychically, and he returns as a man to that Michigan country to make a retreat in the wilderness. Two Hearted River is in the Upper Peninsula. It flows north into Lake Superior. The country is scarcely inhabited, even today, what towns there are being set south in the county away from the lake. When Adams returns, all traces of civilization have vanished:

> The train went up the track out of sight, around one of the hills of burnt timber. Nick sat down on the bundle of canvas and bedding the baggage man had pitched out of the door of the baggage car. There was no town, nothing but the rails and the burned-over country. The thirteen saloons that had lined the one street of Seney had not left a trace. The foundations of the Mansion House hotel stuck up above the ground. The stone was chipped and split by the fire. It was all that was left of the town of Seney. Even the surface had been burned off the ground.[54]

This is the country Adams returns to, a scarred man in a scarred wilderness. Here he restores himself for a moment, preoccupied with small tasks of easy survival on his vacation. He is at home for a while trout fishing, enjoying life on a basic level that he can totally control. Whatever bothers his troubled mind can be set aside for review later, just as he can delay going into the swamp to fish:

> Nick did not want to go in there now. He felt a reaction against deep wading with the water deepening up under his armpits, to hook big trout in places impossible to land them. In the swamp the banks were bare, the big cedars came together overhead, the sun did not come through, except in patches; in the fast deep water, in the half light, the fishing would be tragic. In the swamp fishing was a tragic adventure. Nick did not want it. He did not want to go down the stream any further today.[55]

The review in "Father and Sons" comes when Nick Adams is fully grown, a man in conversation with his own small son whose questions remind Nick of his past and his relationship to his own father. Nick's father lived in that second-growth wilderness by a kind of natural right. He was a good hunter, a better marksman than his son. He had a sense of the value of the last primitive cultures of the region. He entered the cabins of the Objibway as a doctor, someone offering a necessary service. If he needed the wilderness, the wilderness needed him. If his relationship to the Objibways was paternalistic, it has to be said of him that he did not despise them. Nick Adams, however, is someone who has taken from the wilderness and who is unable to give anything back. He lives in his Indian Eden for just so long and then becomes suddenly a scalp hunter at the moment when in the continuity of the generations he should be a brother. His mind stops there, arrested, it would seem: "Long time ago good. Now no good."[56] He exists with a loneliness in his psyche. The shattering of the totality of justice destroys the unity of his personal history. But within "Fathers and Sons" Hemingway attempts some kind of balance, a hint at restoration. Nick's

119

son desires to pray at the grandfather's grave and promises to pray at Nick's grave, too, one day. However else this can be read, it is a gratuitous gesture and a benediction on the part of the boy, a show of honest sonship that is there whether it is deserved or not or whether it can do any good or not.

At the lower end of Lake Michigan, down from Benton Harbor and across the state border from Niles, is South Bend, Indiana. There were five poets on the faculty of Notre Dame University at approximately the same time in the middle-fifties: John Hardy, John Logan, John Frederick Nims, Paul Carroll, and Ernest Sandeen. The charismatic Frank O'Malley was holding classes there, a man who gave a generation of students cultural alternatives far removed from the noise of Saturday afternoon football games.

After Paul Carroll left Notre Dame he joined the staff of the *Chicago Review* and was one of the editors responsible for an entire issue of work by Beat poets and prose writers. A second issue had been planned but it was suppressed and Carroll then founded *Big Table*, printing that material as his first offering. *Big Table* became a primary publication for Beat generation work for a number of years.

John Logan began *Choice*, a magazine of poetry and photography, in the late fifties, getting out his first issue in the spring of sixty-one. Logan welcomed poets whatever their approach to the art. The magazine, in its early days, created a voice for those writers who wanted to mark their own time and who were restless in the universities. These institutions in the fifties were often the refuge for academic and fugitive theorists. They held key professorships and top editorial posts with the literary quarterlies, forming an interlocking literary directorate. *Choice* was a reaction to this dominance. It served to widen the breathing space for the dissidents.

Big Table and *Choice* (originally *Chicago Choice*) can be set, at least in the early sixties, within a modern literary tradition that extends back to the Chicago of the 1890s when Hamlin Garland and Henry

Blake Fuller were active in the city. Fuller's role is of particular importance because he was the first American novelist of stature to discern that the unholy axiom that money makes things run could be used as a theme for creating fictional works. Years later Dreiser would praise him as the man who pioneered the way to a real expression of American life.[57]

During the next twenty-five years so many writers came to the city, drawn by the opportunities available with the town's score of newspapers, that Chicago became the leading producer of young talented, rebellious authors. Dreiser, Dell, Hackett, Cook, the visiting Norris, Lardner, Masters, Lindsay, Sandburg, all contributed to the literary explosion that is now known as the Chicago Renaissance.

Although the main creative thrust of the Chicago Renaissance was over by 1921 with the publication of Dell's *Moon-Calf*, Sandburg's *Cornhuskers* and *Smoke and Steel*, and Anderson's *Poor White* and *The Triumph of the Egg*, there was an afterglow, a silver age. A new group of brilliant young newspapermen had gathered in Chicago. Harry Hansen, another Davenport friend of Floyd Dell's, took over the book section of the *Daily News*. *The Tribune* was represented by Burton Rasco and later by Fanny Butcher, both proponents of the new literature. The round table at Schlogl's was the meeting place for journalists and authors. One of the regulars there was James Weber Linn, the professor from the University of Chicago who encouraged James Farrell. This was also the era of Ben Hecht and the Dill Pickle Club, the roaring and cynical twenties.[58]

As the twenties came to an end, a group of writers appeared who served their literary apprenticeship and graduated into the Depression: James T. Farrell, Albert Halpen, Meyer Levin, Richard Wright and Nelson Algren. Their interest in the city links them to Dreiser, but where Dreiser wrote of individuals who lose their old identities in the activity and dream life of the city, these writers spoke of ethnic groups, children of the many ghettos that American urban life had created, and of class conflict. Their portrayal of American life was often violent. Marxism and the Depression gave them a radical and an explicit basis for their criticism of American society which they built on according to their particular needs.

In his *Studs Lonigan* trilogy, James T. Farrell pictured the lower-middle class, working Irish of South Side Chicago. Taking his subject from his own remembered youth, Farrell says that he deliberately avoided writing about a slum environment because his purpose in the trilogy was to show a "pervasive spiritual poverty" that stemmed from causes too profound for an economic justification.[59] Home, school, church, institutions that might offer cultural advantages, cannot enrich the consciousness of Studs; they are themselves lacking, unable to face into the times. The Lonigan home is filled with empty people:

> At supper they had a quarrel, as usual. And his mother asked him to pray so he could decide about his vocation. And the old man told him he ought to go to confession, because he hadn't been there since June. Then they kicked at Martin not having his fingernails cleaned and Loretta and Frances squabble. After supper, he went to sit by the parlor window. Frances sat down to do her homework. The old man asked him didn't he have homework. Studs said he had done it in a study period at school. The old man said it would be good to get ahead. Studs said he didn't know what homework they'd have ahead. Frances called in to ask him if he knew what declension "socius" belonged to. He said he didn't. The mother said she guessed the girls learned more rapidly than boys did, and they went ahead faster in their lessons. The old man put on his house slippers. He listened to *Uncle Josh Joins the Grangers* on the Vic. Then he opened his *Chicago Evening Journal.* Looking over the paper once, he said:
> "Well, Mary, now that the kids are coming along, we'll have to take more time to ourselves, and next summer we'll have to do a little gallivantin' of our

own, and go out and make a night of it at River-
view Park."
 Studs sat looking out of the parlor window, listening to night sounds, to the wind in the empty
tree outside. He told himself he felt like he was a
sad song. He sat there, and hummed over and over
to himself . . . *The Blue Ridge Mountains of
Virginia.*[60]

Farrell's book can be located within a tradition of
energetic masculinity that goes back to the tall tale
heroes who later become cowboys in the endlessly
proliferating myth of the West or who become tragic
figures such as Norris's McTeague. Both McTeague
and Lonigan are strong, aggressive men who falter
when they are faced with nonphysical barriers. The
prairie, as the avenue is called by the South Side
Irish, yields before Studs and his friends. It offers
no tangible resistence to them, but squanders their
manhood while catering to their conceits.
 Men and women in this book are strangers at best.
Sex is lonely, even when it is permissible. Most relationships seem to hover on the verge of some kind of
undirected violence. In this world Studs has the conviction that he is meant for something big. This conviction prevents him from enjoying even a minor
success in some ordinary way. It traps him, but it
also puts him at odds with his society, and though
he is no rebel, he is a threat to its stability and its
image of itself.
 Studs never understands what is happening to him.
As he moves through depression Chicago in the last
days of his life, he knows that his trouble is deeper
than the fact that his heart is bad and that he cannot find a job. But the ultimate commentaries are
made by Farrell. As fiercely committed to his man
as he is—and he has all the loyalty of an old line
Irish pastor—Farrell moves on a different plane
from Studs. The powerful description of the mara-
thon dance, the vignettes of social unrest on the left
and the right, the frenzy of the Armistice celebration, all have one meaning for Studs and another for

Farrell and the reader. It is through this ironic and often painful separation that the book reaches its fullness.

No such distances exist in Richard Wright's novel *Native Son*. In an introduction which is almost like a prologue to the novel itself, Wright talks about how the idea and person of Bigger Thomas haunted his childhood and how the character of the man was ratified and expanded in later years. Experiences such as Wright's work with the South Side Boys' Club, his conversion to communism, and his close study of events in Europe during the thirties all went into the making of *Native Son*.[61]

The book is deep in the tradition of classic American literature. It is not in irony alone that it is titled *Native Son*. Wright says in his introduction that "if Poe were alive, he would not have to invent horror; horror would invent him,"[62] a statement which reflects Wright's relationship to the world around him and which gives an indication of the tradition to which the novel belongs.

Bigger Thomas lives in and is born from the old American Gothic nightmare. He does not have the innocent freedom which sends Ishmael and Gordon Pym across the face of the earth to discover fear in the phenomenon of whiteness. He does not need such esoteric justification. His awareness is polarized, symbolic, and radical from his first awakening. Chicago, as Wright creates it and as Bigger moves in it, is a black-and-white film, photographed without props, but pulsating with the mysterious and the blatant meanings of these two noncolors. In Gothic fiction, particularly as it develops in America, the action is always to destroy, not so much through violence alone as through participation in horror, an easy innocence. It is this aspect of Mary Dalton that enrages Bigger Thomas, and it is this innocence on the part of readers that Wright seeks to terminate once and for all.

Another aspect of the classical tradition in *Native Son* is Bigger's effort to put an end to the split within himself:

124

> There was something he *knew* and something he *felt;* something the *world* gave him and something he *himself* had; something spread out in *front* of him and something spread out in *back;* and never in all his life, with this black skin of his, had the two worlds, thought and feeling, will and mind, aspiration and satisfaction been together; never had he felt a sense of wholeness.[63]

In Wright's hands this theme has a tendency to break down the categories of experience. It becomes political, metaphysical, psychological. He gathers within the narrow bounds of the plot the wide reach of the divided American psyche. He defines this divided American psyche in terms of one of its most radical components, its shackling racism.

The present Chicago scene is as active as ever. Peter Michaelson, Charles Newman, and Mary Ellmann are associated in various ways with Northwestern University. John Frederick Nims is back in the city after several years spent on the faculty of the University of Illinois in Urbana. Black writers include Don L. Lee, William Wandick, and Walter Sublett. Also, Cyrus Colter who won the Iowa Prize in short fiction last year. And Gwendolyn Brooks is running a lively workshop for youth on the South Side. Chicago is also a backyard for Lisel Mueller and Barbara Harr. Daryl Hyne, present editor of Harriet Monroe's *Poetry,* founded in 1912, is teaching at the University of Chicago. Bill Knott is a ghostly presence in the city. Donald Sheehan is at the University of Chicago. Eugene Wildman, experimental novelist, teaches at the University of Illinois, Chicago Circle, and John Schultz, editor of *F–1,* is at Columbia College. Philip D. Ortego, Chicano scholar and fiction writer, was born in the city. So was Harry Stephen Keeler, the eccentric pop lit author whose last eight bulky novels were all published in Spanish or Portuguese translations, but not in English.

Paul Carroll is one of those writers deeply committed to the city. He has spent a lifetime teaching, translating, publishing and editing, and constructing his odes. They reveal his sense of the extreme clutter and vitality of urban existence in contemporary America:

Over the forlorn holes of Orlando Wilson's
    jockey shorts,
    the skulls of mummies in museums,
    the truck fender twisted like the limbs
      of belly dancers
    in Greek Town down on Halsted
      Street
    blooming into mountains in the
      junkyards of Chicago,
    over the atomic toys of Fermi,
the keen prerecorded chorus of the
      whippoorwills of promise:
    you fly with rumors from our
      chimneys.
Over found objects scattered in the
    attics of the February moon,
    the cats of City Hall,
    the feudal system of our junkies
      and their fix,
    the magpies of misery and true love,
    the foreskins of the towers of
      Marina City,
    twin cyclones of cement,
and the Rockefeller Chapel organ of
    our anxieties: you come flying,
Claes, like a Christmas tree of
    Playboy bunny tails.[64]

Carolyn M. Rodgers, also native to the city, can give a strange universal dimension to a subject, mitigating an expected rage with pathos:

let uh revolution come. uh
state of peace is not known to me
anyway

since I grew uhround in chi town
where
howlin wolf howled in the tavern on
   47th st.
and muddy waters made u cry the
   salty nigger blues,
      where pee wee cut Lonnell fuh
      fuckin wid
   his sistuh and blood baptized the
   street
   at least twice ev'ry week and judy got
   kicked out grammar school fuh
      bein pregnant
   and died tryin to ungrow the seed
   we was all up in there and
   just livin was guerilla warfare,
      yeah
let uh revolution come.
couldn't be no action like what
   i dun already seen.[65]

North of Chicago and over the state line in Wisconsin, Bink Noll and Chad Walsh, the poets, teach
at Beloit College. Robert Gard coordinates the regional writing programs that are based at the University of Wisconsin. The poet Felix Pollak is there
in Madison, also the curator of rare books for the
university library. The library holds the largest collection of little magazines in the United States. Middle Wisconsin was the stomping ground for the late
August Derleth who may have been the most prolific
writer in the country. A younger group of poets is
now working in Milwaukee. Roger Mitchell is at
Marquette University and James Hazard at the state
university there. Kathy Weigner of this group is also
director of the Third Coast Poetry Center, the name
chosen because the opening of the St. Lawrence
Seaway has made the Great Lakes cities international ports. The late Loraine Niedecker was associated with the objectivist group of poets. And R. E.
Sebenthall is presently living in Mt. Horeb, Wisconsin. The novelist Thomas O'Malley is a resident of

Wausau, Wisconsin. There are several writers in the Green Bay area at the moment: Michael Culross, Warren Woessner, and Peter Cooley, poetry editor for the *North American Review.*

Wisconsin was home state for Glenway Wescott. Wescott is remembered for his novel *The Grand-mothers* which contains one of the most notable attacks written against what have been called the traditional values of the Midwest:

> Most of the new people, Saxons and Bavarians, had come there without a penny. Then they had hired out to the settlers and put by more of their earnings than any Anglo-Saxon could. Steadily they had bought fields, farms, and at last groups of farms. These determined fathers made their women and children work like serfs—the healthy young ones hurried into the fields, the unhealthy allowed to die, and more begotten. Their sons were not permitted to marry until their late twenties, or later still; then, broken to harness, they were put upon adjoining farms. There was no talk among them of letting the young go their own way.
> Meanwhile the original families seemed to be dying out. . . .
> The immigrants were glad to see them go. They believed that children should be envious of no one but their own elders; now there would be an end of the bad example of discontented Yankees going off to school or to town. And for their own com-fort, no more interference with their primitive habits, such as beating their wives, animals and children, or their amusements, such as Sunday dancing and drinking.[66]

Wescott is fascinated and repelled by life in rural Wisconsin:

> Peacock lakes of bronze weeds and vivid water, with steep shores; four or five of them to be seen at a time from certain hilltops. Fertility and wilder-ness in rapid succession along powdery highways: classic meadows where the cattle seem to walk and eat in their sleep, sandy slopes full of foxes, ledges

where there are still rattlesnakes. Sad forests full of springs; the springs have a feverish breath. There are metallic plants which burn your hand if you touch them. All summer the horizon trembles, hypnotically flickering over the full grain, the taffeta corn, and the labor in them of dark, overclothed men, singing women, awe-stricken children. These say nothing; their motionless jaws give an account of their self-pity, dignity, and endurance. Sheet-lightning at night, and they sleep in the grass, in hammocks, on folded blankets on the floor—the beds are too hot. They get up and work with strange, ardent motions and the obstinacies of ghosts in the heat; there is wealth in it. In the sky mocking marble palaces, an Eldorado of sterile cloud. Not sterile—down fall large black-and-blue rains, tied with electric ribbons; they never seem to be doing much good, but the crops are saved.[67]

Writing in the twenties, at a time when artists were preoccupied with being alienated members of society and America was lost once more and trying to rediscover itself, Wescott could assert that the country he returned to was beyond definition:

A place which has no fixed boundaries, no particular history; inhabited by no one race; always exhausted by its rich output of food, men, and manufactured articles; loyal to none of its many creeds, prohibitions, fads, hypocrisies; now letting itself be governed, now ungovernable . . . The Middle West is nowhere; an abstract nowhere. However earnestly writers proud of being natives of it may endeavor to give it form and character, it remains out of focus, amorphous, and a mystery. And by attempting to be specific as in these notes of my visit I have done, one over-particularizes, inevitably. What seems local is national, what seems national is universal, what seems Middle Western is in the commonest way human. And yet—there is the sluggish emotional atmosphere, the suavity of its tedium, the morbid grandeur of its meanest predicaments, or are these illusions of those who take flight, who return? It is a certain climate, a certain landscape; and beyond that, a state of mind of people born where they do not like to live. A certain landscape? All the landscapes, except the noblest: the desert, the alp, the giant seas. One of its climates, one of its anarchic aspects clings to every memory, and deforms or charges with excessive lyricism the plain facts; so the winter, dazzling and boring as it is, has brooded too much over this account. There are other aspects, other seasons. In recent years I have not been at home except in midwinter or midsummer; next time I shall try to come in the fall.[68]

West and above Wisconsin, Lake Superior rolls up agates on the stony beaches. Duluth is on the western extremity of the lake. Inland from there is Dylan country. He took T. S. Eliot's old themes and irregular lines and invented "Wasteland Rock," a rhythmic accompaniment for a generation of counterculture wanderers who know America and its regions intimately, as do the elderly couples who travel the country in their big, comfortable rigs and tell you that America is just too much to comprehend.

It is two hundred and thirty-seven miles from Minneapolis northwest to Moorhead, Minnesota, where the Red River keeps a course for the Bay of Winnipeg and the Arctic. Opposite Moorhead on the other side of the river is Fargo, North Dakota. There are two state universities and a Lutheran college in the immediate area. A clutch of poets for this locale publish work in *Dacotah Territory*—Richard Lyons, Marnie Walsh, Mary Pryor, Joe Sanders—and in *Poetry North*.

Thomas McGrath is native to this scene. Though he has traveled widely, working as a student in Louisiana when the Agrarians came to Baton Rouge and serving in the Army at Amchitka during World War II, he has always returned, sooner or later, to Fargo or Moorhead. Whatever his wanderings, he has had a constant vision, a proletarian dream, and his long continuing poem, *Letter to an Imaginary Friend,* is

an epic recounting of that dream on a personal and
social level in booming six stress lines. It is history
he remembers that most others have forgotten—
how, for example, it was at the close of the war
when so many thought that at long last the eagle on
the dollar really would fly:

Country full of strangers in their queer
    costumes . . .
And a hurrying fury clapperclawing their
    lack . . .
Bandits . . . murderers in medals hold-
    ing hands in the catch-as-can dark
With the carking, harked-back-to, marked-
    down virgins of the stark little towns
Where, once, their paper histories dropped
    on the thin lawns
And rocking porches of the dead-eye dons
    and the home-grown dream-daddies
Now still with their war-won monies.
        Bandits . . . gypsies—
Under the humped cloth of war . . .
    Those sad children . . .
Older than headlines, under their khaki
    print.
And mad for money, those guys: for the
    lost pre-war
Land locked virgin and the homespun
    moss of her historical North Forty.
        Aiee!
        Great God in a basket!
    Those famous men
All green with their green-backed hope!
Country of strangers . . .
Myself strange, under the corroding
    moon,
And the cold charity of the first, thin,
    early, snow.[69]

South from Moorhead about a hundred and fifty
miles on Route 75 is the town of Madison, mostly

Norwegian, where Robert Bly lives. By the middle fifties he had found his own voice and his own desire in a poem of deep intensity that was not confessional and which did not rely on intricate verbal surfaces for its effects. Many poets at that time were puzzling the use of the image and there were excellent and startling works being done by Robert Kelly and Jerome Rothenberg, among others. Bly, working with James Wright who was then teaching at the University of Minnesota, and William Duffy who was co-editor of the *The Fifties*, found a shadow-shape for this developing deep image poetry. The poem was bound in time or place by a pedestrian title and the riches of the images were set off by an ending felt as inevitable, but not drawn logically from the text. An excellent example is the Wright poem which leads off the first collection of such work by the three poets in *The Lion's Tail and Eyes*, "Lying in a Hammock at William Duffy's Farm in Pine Island, Minnesota":

> Over my head, I see the bronze butterfly,
> Asleep on the black trunk,
> Blowing like a leaf in green shadow.
> Down the ravine behind the empty house,
> The cowbells follow one another
> Into the distances of the afternoon.
> To my right
> In a field of sunlight between two pines,
> The droppings of last year's horses
> Blaze up into golden stones.
> I lean back, as the evening darkens and
>   comes on.
> A chicken-hawk floats over, looking for
>   home.
> I have wasted my life.[70]

Lines from "Late at Night During a Visit of Friends," one of Bly's offerings in the same collection, reveal a poetry of commitment as well as of place:

The human face shines as it speaks of
    things
Near itself, thoughts full of dreams.
The human face shines like a dark sky
As it speaks of those things that oppress
    the living.[71]

These poets were doing serious reading and translating from a number of Latin-American and European writers whose works speak in terms of whole
eras and cultures rather than the anguish of the individual ego or the excesses of urban artists as members of a peer group—Cesar Vallejo, Pablo Neruda,
Garcia-Lorca, Jimenez, Georg Trakl, Blas de Otero.
In Bly's poems there is a love of place and a rich
moral bias:

How strange to think of giving up all
    ambition!
Suddenly I see with such clear eyes
The white flake of snow
That has just fallen in the horse's mane![72]

His attentiveness to the overlooked detail and em-
pathy for things frail and weak kindled to a rage
with the deepening involvement of the United States
in the Vietnam War. In practical terms he began,
with David Ray, a writers' protest movement against
the war and has visited a multitude of campuses
over the country to argue for the change in national
spirit required to put an end to the war once and for
all. His attitudes are spelled out in his second book,
The Light Around the Body. "Counting Small-boned
Bodies" captures as perfectly as anything written in
recent times the horror of the language of overkill:

Let's count the bodies over again.
If we could only make the bodies smaller,
The size of skulls,
We could make a whole plain white with
    skulls in the moonlight!
If we could only make the bodies smaller,

Maybe we could get
A whole year's kill in front of us on a desk!
If we could only make the bodies smaller,
We could fit
A body into a finger-ring, for a keepsake
forever.[73]

The fruitfulness of Bly's effort is to be seen in dozens of magazines around the country. The pages are filled with the works of younger writers who can express where they are and who are conscious of the social ills both in their regions and in the society at large. It is only a score of miles further south from Madison to Pipestone, Minnesota. Just outside the town there are open pit quarries, some acreage of virgin prairie, a stream, falls, and massive rock formations. This site has been set aside as a national monument. Here the red catlinite was (and is) mined to be carved into ceremonial pipes which when fitted into stems became the calumets, symbols of faith and honesty, smoked in council when any decision of importance had to be made by an Indian band or tribe or nation.

George Catlin wrote the first account of the area after his visit in 1836:

> The Great Spirit, at an ancient period, here called the Indian nations together, and standing on the precipice of the red pipe stone rock, broke from its wall a piece, and made a huge pipe by turning it in his hand, which he smoked over them, to the North, the South, the East and the West; and told them that this stone was red—that it was their flesh—that they must use it for their pipes of peace—that it belonged to them all, and that the war-club and scalping knife must not be raised on its ground. At the last whiff of his pipe his head went into a great cloud, and the whole surface of the rock for several miles was melted and glazed; two great ovens were opened beneath, and two women (guardian spirits of the place), entered them in a blaze of fire; and they are heard

there yet (*Tso-mec-cos-tee* and *Tso-me-cos-te-won-dee*), answering to the invocations of the high-priests or medicine-men, who consult them when they are visitors to this sacred place.[74]

The quarries were protected by the Yankton Sioux, wardens of that sacred ground. An effective novel of Yankton life, centered as it was at Pipestone, has been written by Frederick Manfred, author of some six farm novels earlier under the pen name of Feike Feikema. *Conquering Horse* recounts the story of a chief's son who follows his spirit vision across the plains into Nebraska to capture a fabled white stallion. It is a story of regeneration; the fortunes of the tribe were dependent on spotted horses. The young man trails the stallion and its herd long nights and days, sleeping in the saddle, in an effort to wear down the stallion. Some of the sense of reverence for all things that is integral to the cosmic vision of the Sioux is caught in this night scene:

And waking, he saw them all as white shadows, white silences, of the other world. Both he and his sorrel and the white one and his bunch were spirit ghosts. They were all gods together in the night. They had now no need of either life or death. They had need now only of song, of vision, of long white wings.[75]

Manfred has worked to encourage American Indian writers. Of the novel, the Yankton have paid him a high compliment: They say that Manfred has told the truth about them.

Manfred lives near Luverne, his house built against a shelf of quartzite. The shelf is called the blue earth or the blue mounds because it appears that color in the evening. It is a surprise, this outcropping; the vast area around it is rolling hills and grassland and town planted in ash and elm. The quartzite is thought to be the top of an ancient mountain range that once towered in the center of the continent. The rocks are the oldest known in the

United States, some three and a half billion years.

Split Rock Creek, Sioux River, Sioux Falls, James River, Flandreau, Colton—these are the place names which locate the action of Ole Edvart Rolvaag's novel, *Giants in the Earth*. His Norwegian prairie settlers build a little town in that piece of the country just west of Minnesota and just north of Iowa and Nebraska in South Dakota. And here it is all plain, and to the west eight hundred miles. It is open country, open to raw weather, extremes of shattering beauty, and the violence of the seasons. The wind seems to be forever, gusting and unchanging, eroding rhythms in the mind, heard even when the wind is not there.

Rolvaag places the indomitable Per Hansa in this setting, a man with dreams great enough to capture the American will-o'-the-wisp, and his wife Beret who finds only an abode of evil in those western distances her husband has brought her to. The story of their relationship is tragic, but not in the classical sense of the term. The reader is left with a mood of disquiet when he puts the book down. The incomprehensible has not been given a satisfactory shape for him; rather, questions have been raised that demand the most intense confrontations, and a man is left heartsick with his own life when he sees the frozen body of Per Hansa with its glazed eyes staring into the west. Rolvaag is closer to the lithography of Edward Munch than he is to the vision of Sophocles.

The world Rolvaag has created, however, is much larger than the sod house of Per Hansa and Beret. It includes the love match of Hans Olsa and Sorine, the tempestuous but enduring relationship of Tonseten and Kjersti. It contains the compassionate and able minister whose presence radiates a grace that brings Beret out of her insanity. There are etched portraits of other pioneers, the forlorn man and his deranged wife who search in vain for the child they had to bury by a stone on the grasslands. On all these, spoken of with "magical objectivity"[76] by Rolvaag, the great plain watched breathlessly.[77]

In Cottonwood, Minnesota, Phil Dacey edits the magazine *Crazy Horse*. A drop down south takes the traveler to the well-kept towns of northwestern Iowa. Iowa has been fortunate in its state universities and private liberal arts colleges. As a result almost any town in the state can boast a writer of some stature, born there or resident there. A sample includes James Hearst, Cedar Falls; Robert Dana, Decorah; John Logan, Red Oak; Gary Gildner, Des Moines. Josephine Herbst was born in Sioux City, a town at the edge of the Missouri River bluffs, at the turn of the century. Sioux City is the resting place of Sergeant Charles Floyd who was lost to the Lewis and Clark expedition there in 1804. He is buried on the summit of a high bluff that overlooks the town.

Josephine Herbst has a keen sense of history. She writes of the decline of a mythical family, the Trexlers, in three novels: *Pity Is Not Enough, The Executioner Waits* and *Rope of Gold,* published in 1933, '34, and '39. The orientation of her trilogy is Marxist; the decline is chronicled in terms of the decay of middle-class values in America and the affirmation of the coming of a new consciousness, a group-centered society that will supplant the ego-centric world of survival of the fittest enterprise, and this despite the contemporary successes of totalitarian governments in the thirties.

She wrote with some impatience. She was an active woman. As a journalist, she was on the scene in the USSR in 1930; she covered the fierce Iowa farm strike in 1932; she was in Germany, observing the rise of Hitler in 1935 and present in Cuba when Batista put down the general strike in that year; she witnessed the automobile workers' strike in Flint, Michigan, in 1937; she saw the shelling of Madrid in Spain. She was short-tempered with cocktail ideologies. Years later she would remember the scene in New York City as a tempest in a pisspot, and recall that the communist press wrote a jargon there that meant nothing to farmers and laborers in the Midwest.[78]

For Josephine Herbst there was no looking back on the heroic virtues of the pioneer past. Men today were no better or worse than they ever were. If a man was wiped out, it was because of nature and of economic factors that he could not control:

> Stella thought of the last summer with grass-hoppers jumping into their very mouths, gumming up the radiators of the cars, stripping the foliage of the trees and vines, like hail. She tried to look back at the years, to count the good years and the bad, the lean and the fat. In the lean years when they had nothing to sell, then you got dollar wheat. When you had a full granary it went down to thirty cents. You couldn't hold on to wheat, it might as well be water. You had to store it and the Big Fellows owned the elevators. You had to get it to the granary, then there was the banker and the machinery people all nosing around, holding out their hands. Their palms were always itching and you had to oil them. They could clap a sheriff on your back; they could snake your good tools and your farm away. Men in towns got money for what they sold. Looked like the farmer was the only jackass, paying for the chance to get up early and work in the muck.[79]

This Sioux City novelist wrote of the waste of the land and of its human resources. She wrote, too, in *Rope of Gold* of the waste of love in those most committed to redressing the social ills of the day. Though the novel is flawed, not well paced and with some characters scarcely to be distinguished from others, that taste of ashes in the mouth which so characterizes the thirties is there for the reader today.

Below Sioux City there is Omaha, another river town, and below Omaha, Kansas City. The unruly Missouri is on a north-south course and these cities are almost on a line. To the west it is all distances. In Omaha, on a summer night, the town swelters with the intense heat of the plains. Omaha knows itself. Its history and the history of the westering nation is told in the halls of the Joslyn Memorial Art Museum, in a series of rich and thoughtfully mounted exhibits.

Omaha is the home of Michael Anania, literary editor of the Swallow Press in Chicago, and the city with its bluffs and land round about is the concern of his first book, *The Color of Dust.* The book has a headnote from Neruda whose speculations are so often congenial to the midwestern imagination: "when I try to explain my problems/I shall speak, not of self, but of geography." The note gives point to the poems of Anania, the vast land he knows subdues his voice:

> Let us consider the migration of trees,
> the birch seeds that drifted down
> from the forests of Minnesota,
> how they came upstream with the Platte.
>
> The trees are green, the prairies green
>   with corn;
> the waters of the Platte enter the brown
>   river
> in no great ecstacy.
> Bluff crests in Fontenelle are quiet,
> give no emblem, figured name.[80]

Several midcontinent poets have attempted variations on the relationship of geography and the self. They are concerned, as Kenneth Rothwell has it, with the outward journey, they seek "truth in the landscape of external nature."[81] John Neihardt in his *Cycle of the West* covers the history of the expansion westward from 1822 through the defeat of the Sioux at Wounded Knee. The Wichita poet, Bruce Cutler, in *A West Wind Rises* concentrates on a single episode in the bitter history of Kansas, a raid against Free State settlers by a party of slave-owners in 1858. Dan Jaffe of Kansas City, Missouri, recounts the career of Dan Freeman, the nation's first homesteader. Jaffe's work combines the theme of settlement with a quest for personal identity, and

sometimes attains eerie correspondences, as in this
episode during a river crossing:

> From the rear of the raft the boatman
>   hollered, "Friend,
> Before you reached this crossing, what
>   was your name?
> I list all the sad souls that the fates send."
> I shouted back at him through the rain,
>   "The same
>
> As it is! Same as it's likely to remain."
> He came out of the mist, knife in hand,
> In a cavernous voice repeated, "Your
>   name? Your name?"[82]

Among those who have tried to fashion native
material with an epic scope, among the "astoriads,"
to use Rothwell's term, is M. B. Tolson, author of
Harlem Gallery, born in Moberly, Missouri, and educated at Fisk, Lincoln, and Columbia Universities.
Tolson ended his days in Oklahoma where he held
office four terms as mayor of Langston, directed the
Dust Bowl Theatre and served as professor of creative literature at Langston University. Tolson must
have known that the history of the West was, despite
the white-washing of the myths, partially the story
of the black man. Black citizens were there from the
beginnings. There were black trappers, black fur
traders, black troopers, and black cowboys, the cowboys in numbers at least twenty-five percent of those
who took the herds out of Texas and up into Kansas
and Nebraska. But he seems to have anticipated
that black experience in America, when it came to
an age of sophisticated self-expression, would be
urban rather than rural or regional in its impulse.
Tolson writes of the settlement, according to Rothwell, of Harlem as the archetypal ghetto in the new
world.[83] Whatever his choice, Melvin B. Tolson
achieved a language of his own, taking an oral culture's habit of using dictionary words in contexts
that give them eccentric meanings, imitating this

but at the same time setting his own word choices in their exact context. His language is always tense, and controlled:

> With a dissonance
> from the Weird Sisters,
> the jazz diablerie
> boiled down and away
> in the vacuum pan
> of the Indigo Combo.[84]

Tolson describes the odyssey of a people increasingly urbanized in the New World. Gordon Parks tells of that community in its rural setting, his own birthright, and of the boy Newt growing up in a placed called Cherokee Flats that is located somewhere in the southeastern corner of Kansas, proximate to Chanute, Parsons, Pittsburg, and Cherryvale. Newt's mother defines the place for him as best she is able. She is a woman who tries to live a decent life, a woman of deep faith, though her faith is troubled by memories of outrage done to her own family in its secret history. She tells Newt:

> Cherokee Flats is sorta like a fruit tree. Some of the people are good and some of them are bad—just like the fruit on the tree.[85]

Cherokee Flats becomes the learning tree for the young Newt. The novel that Parks writes is about the fruit of that tree, so much of it bitter as the young man experiences it and comes to his own knowledge of good and evil.

In Moberly, Missouri, or just outside of the town, there was a coal mine known as the Monkey Nest. Jack Conroy, founder of the *Anvil* which later merged with the *Partisan Review,* was born in the mining camp. His novel, *The Disinherited,* recounts the life of Larry Donovan, a boy who lives to see his father and three older brothers killed in the mine and who escapes into a succession of jobs, crumbs for the laboring man during the years of prosperity and crash as the twenties came to an end. Donovan finds work in a railroad switch yard, but loses his job when scabs break the workers' strike. He works in a steel mill, a rubber factory, he goes to Detroit and works on an assemblyline, he is wiped out with everyone when the plants cut back in '29, he starts home again, lives in a Hooverville, works with a gang laying pipe, and finally on a crew that builds a road up from the south through his hometown. *The Disinherited* is a believable novel. There is a folk honesty about it, and the descriptions of hard labor that ruined men have the authenticity of personal observation:

> Men stripped to the waist were tending the steam presses which melt the raw biscuit-shaped heel into the cured one. Their skins were flushed as with fever, their lips parched. Sweat blinded their red-rimmed eyes, but they were too busy to wipe it away. They jiggled tiny washers, inserted to keep the nails from pulling through the brittle rubber, on to pegs set in the cavities of heavy steel molds. Heat-puffed fingers fumbled the washers. The raw heels were imposed upon the pegs, and the molds were closed and shoved into the press. As fast as a new mold was elevated to the steam chamber, a cured batch was ready. Hastily drawing on asbestos gloves, the pressmen pried open the sizzling molds and tore out the heels.
>
> Hans was not at a press, but sitting on a stock pan, holding his head in his hands. He told Jasper he had got a ringing in his head and stopped sweating, and that his eyes blurred so he couldn't see the molds. So he sat down to blow for a spell. To stop sweating is dangerous.[86]

The Disinherited avoids the sententiousness and angry righteousness that signatures so much of the proletarian fiction of the thirties; it comes across now as a fresh item in a catalog that has grown musty over the years.

Moberly is in the north central part of Missouri. Some miles south is Columbia and the University of Missouri where Conroy went to school. Several writers have been on the staff at the university for many years. John Neihardt, teaching there in his eighties, was an awe-inspiring presence. It was reported that he could speak to the birds and the flowers. William Peden, short-fiction writer, served at one time as head of the English Department. Donald Drummond is on the staff, an old compatriot of Alan Swallow. And the poet and novelist Thomas McAfee. Drummond and McAfee have helped in the progress of a number of younger talents, including David G. Smith, Charles L. Willig, James Taylor, and R. P. Dickey, for many years editor of *The Poetry Bag*.

This is in the center of the state. Jefferson City lies a few miles south on a limestone bluff overlooking the Missouri River. The river cuts the state in half on an east-west axis. It is somewhat tamed now with straightened banks and wing dams to keep it honest, a hawk under a hood. In the old days it took eight days to move upstream from its mouth above St. Louis to the Kansas City area. Francis Parkman made the trip in 1846:

> . . . the boat struggled upward for seven or eight days against the rapid current of the Missouri, grating upon snags, and hanging for two or three hours at a time upon sand-bars. We entered the mouth of the Missouri in a drizzling rain, but the weather soon became clear, and showed distinctly the broad and turbid river, with its eddies, its sand-bars, its ragged islands and forest covered shores. The Missouri is constantly changing its course; wearing away its banks on one side, while it forms new ones on the other. Its channel is continually shifting. Islands are formed, and then washed away, and while the old forests on one side are undermined and swept off, a young growth springs up from the new soil on the other. With all these changes, the water is so charged with mud and sand that, in spring, it is perfectly opaque, and in a few minutes deposits a sediment an inch thick in the bottom of a tumbler. The river was now high; but when we descended in the autumn it was

fallen very low, and all the secrets of its treacherous shallows were exposed to view. It was frightful to see the dead and broken trees, thick-set as a military abattis, firmly embedded in the sand, and all pointing down stream, ready to impale any unhappy steamboat that at high water should pass over them.[87]

Washington Irving had made his visit to the West earlier in 1832. His party dropped down from Independence, Missouri, and camped near Harmony:

> Leave Harmony at three o'clock—cavalcade—four waggons—horsemen lead horses—we hire a half-breed called Broken Hoof—Mr. Chouteau hires another—crossing the Osage River—group of Indians on a knoll looking on.
>
> Camp after sunset in a beautiful grove at the foot of immense trees—by a brook opposite a prairie—moonlight—owl hoots—prairie wolf howls—barking of dogs—bells of our horses among the trees—supper—beef, roast ducks, and prairie hens—others boiled. Fine effect of half moon among lofty trees—fire of camp with guides, Indians and others around it—dogs lying on grass—waggons—tents by fire light—groups of attendants lying at foot of trees and round fires.[88]

Why did they come west, Parkman and Irving? For Parkman the reason is clear enough. He was twenty-two. His journey along the Oregon Trail into the Black Hills and Sioux country was a rite of passage, a confirmation of his manhood, and when he left the inland continent, he did not have to return again. He gave his favorite rifle to his guide, Henry Chatillon. The gesture is symbolic, told in the last paragraph of his account. Some extension of his life would always remain in the West even when he turned east and "saw once more the familiar features of home."[89] For Irving the journey is a coming home, strangely, for a cultivated easterner who had spent his recent time abroad on a grand tour. It was, according to John Francis McDermott:

. . . a voyage of discovery made by a man who had been long absent from his home and who wanted now to see and feel and smell and hear his own country, who ardently desired to realize it for himself.[90]

And what did they find? A place of terror and delight, a vast and lonely land filled at one moment in history with an extraordinarily varied life, both in its animal and its human nature, a place of solitude and companionship that could test the spirit until it was honed to its sharpest edge.

The frontier still flavored the area around Neosho, Missouri, when Thomas Hart Benton was a boy. The Nations inhabited the country just west over the border in what is now Oklahoma. Benton's father was a congressman and the young Benton knew as much about back country politics as Caleb Bingham from Arrow Rock. Benton went on to art school in Chicago and did his stint in the bohemias of New York and of Paris, but he had that certain generosity toward the folk that distinguished many artists during the thirties—James Agee, Charles Ives and his plains compatriots, Grant Wood, and John Curry, among others. For Benton the return to Missouri is always to the known, a fulfillment to the hankering of a restless life:

There is a high rugged bluff above the Missouri River a few miles from Kansas City. I drive out when I get bored and sit on that bluff. The river makes a great curve in the valley below and you can see for miles up and down the running yellow water. Although I was born and raised in the hill country of southwest Missouri, the great river valley appeals to me. I feel very much at home looking down upon it. Either I am just a slobbery sentimentalist or there is something to this stuff about your native land, for when I sit above the waters of the Missouri, I feel they belong to me, and I to them.[91]

145

Benton wrote this paragraph in the spring of 1937. In 1969 Missouri-born Josephine W. Johnson approaches the land with a very felt need. She speaks of a small acreage outside of Cincinnati where she lives with her husband who edits *The Farm Quarterly*, a skillfully done magazine of rural life. The title of her recent work is suggestive: *The Inland Island*. She comes to the land to hold and to protect it, and at a time when attention to the media and technology threatens to obliterate all local distinctions, this turning to a particular place is significant. Men have to live with their contradictions. In the future the careful husbanding of a half acre may generate the justice and charity the earth demands and provide the basic culture that will make a third world possible:

> This beautiful slice of land is all that's left. It's my lifeblood. The old house is abandoned down in the valley where the mammoth bones were found in the quarry. We are on this side the ridge from that valley now. The children are gone. The horses gone. The old house gone. What's left? A world of trees, wild birds, wild seeds—a world of singular briary beauty that will last my life. The land— my *alderliefest*—the most beloved, that which has held the longest possession of the heart.
>
> I was born of Franklins on my mother's side, and the Franklin was a landowner, a freeman, in the Anglo-Saxon days. I have had a love for the land all my life, and today when all life is a life against nature, against man's whole being, there is a sense of urgency, a need to record and cherish, and to share this love before it is too late. Time passes— mine and the land's.[92]

Today in Kansas City the scene is productive. Dan Jaffe teaches at the University of Missouri there and David Ray has recently joined the staff as editor of the old *University Review*, now called *New Letters*. Joan Yeagley, John Popko, and Virginia Scott Miner are poets working in the area. The Kansas City Poetry Contest helps to contribute to the liveliness of the scene. James Tate, although he roams the country, comes home to get himself together at periodic intervals. He can say everything in two lines: "Nobody goes to visit the insane anymore/nobody goes to visit the graveyards."[93]

Kansas City is also a mythical town for Edward Dahlberg, his spiritual city, but his attitude is complex, as ambiguous as a primitive tale-teller's toward the culture hero or the tribe's totem:

> Kansas City is a vast inland city, and its marvelous river, the Missouri, heats the sense; the maple, alder, elm and cherry trees with which the town abounds are songs of desire, and only the almonds of ancient Palestine can awaken the hungry pores more deeply. It is a wild, concupiscent city, and few there are troubled about death until they age or are sick. Only those who know the ocean ponder death as they behold it, whereas those bound closely to the ground are more sensual.
>
> Kansas City was my Tarsus; the Kaw and the Missouri Rivers were the washpots of joyous Dianas from St. Joseph and Joplin. It was a young, seminal town and the seed of its men was strong. Homer sang of many sacred towns in Hellas which were no better than Kansas City.[94]

But he does not want to return. This antitranscendentalist knows too well how ungovernable the desire is for a man in his age to recover the images of those he broke bread with in his youth, how he becomes Everyman and kindred creeps into his soul. He wants to be a rational man, though the isolation is painful:

> Ay, go to your native city, but why? It is buried deep down in the loamy cairn of identity in which one can plant everything without going anywhere. Socrates said it was foolish to travel since one always took oneself along anyway. He also said that one mountain, one vale, and one sea divulges everything. One Kansas City, my Mother City, her Tomb, for all her defeats are interred there, and my own; we mourn for our memories and hate

them. I need never go back, for my mother lies in the hurt and open sepulchre of my soul, and another return to her could only be a tough and barren pain that I do not require either for a book, or for my life, or for my Mother.[95]

It is strange that this man who has written so lovingly of the cities of the earth should conclude that in America "whatever we do is vast, unconscious geography" and that "we cannot bear each other because we are immense territory."[96] Perhaps he takes this position because the cities of America are, like taxes, designed for the movement of goods, and not for the comfort of people in their social and festive nature, so that they long for a courtesy in space that they do not find in the street and the boulevard.

Kansas is a long state. On the eastern edge there are places that could be mistaken for college towns in New England, but west in the state it is another land. Below Dodge City a traveler can stand and turn full circle. He will see nothing but the horizon, a flat deception, where for all appearances no man has ever lived. Such an experience is hard to contain, an exaltation of the spirit, a diminution of the ego that is almost total. This twofold response has been noted by plains writers. William Inge describes a sunset in the voice of a boy from the southeastern part of the state who is west for the first time:

> At sunset we all became quiet. The sky now dominated everything, the earth itself appearing humble and poor, its grass and foliage already seared by the burning sun, the soil dry and hard, not knowing when it would ever receive again the blessing of rain. As we looked to the west, there was nothing of man's creation between us and the horizon. Occasionally, a ramshackle farm or shed. Nothing on earth seemed of the slightest consequence; but in the sky, something important was happening. Day was being destroyed by coming night, and the burst of orange in the sky was like

a final flush of blood in the body's system before a being passes away. I have seen many prairie sunsets since that time, and they have always moved me to believe that there is something going on in the sky much bigger than man himself; that man's presence upon the earth is an incidental gift that we must make the most of while it lasts, even though our strivings, our creations, our sins and our virtues are all lost in infinity.[97]

This sense of slow progression, a man spaced out in his long time, infuses much of William Inge's work, and makes bearable the vicious racial violence in a novel such as *Good Luck, Miss Wyckoff* where the psyche in its flesh survives outrage and takes a lonely comfort in the knowledge that other human beings are anxious for its days, its safe passage.

The plains so treeless and so sparsely settled, even today, expose those who live on them to extremes of weather, to wind, heat, hail, snow. Living as they do so close to the unchecked elements, they often talk in terms of survival and sometimes the tales they tell extend the limit of belief. Mari Sandoz recounts the story of a young school teacher lost in the blizzard of 1949, the teacher and eight small children cut off without provisions for eight days while the snow piled to fifty inches and the temperature stood at thirty-eight below zero. She harried the children, kept them alive with her memory of native Indian and pioneer experience in killing snows:

> The teacher squinted back along the line, moving like some long snowy winter-logged animal, the segmented back bowed before the sharpening blizzard wind. Just the momentary turn into the storm took her breath and frightened her for these children hunched into themselves, half of them crying softly, hopelessly, as though already lost. They must hurry. With not a rock anywhere and not a tree within miles to show the directions, they had to seek out the landmark of the ranch country—the wire fence. So the girl started downwind again, breaking the new drifts as she searched for valley ground where fences were most likely, barbed-wire

fences that might lead to a ranch, or nowhere except around some hay meadow. But it was their only chance the girl from the sand hills knew. Stumbling, floundering through the snow, she kept the awkward string moving, the eyes of the older ones straining through frozen lashes for even the top of one fence post, those of the small ones turned in upon their fear as the snow caked on the mufflers over their faces and they stumbled blindly to the pull from ahead.[98]

Western Nebraska, the Dakotas, Kansas are dry wheat and open range. It is difficult to distinguish west from middle west here; perhaps by occupation —wheat farmers middlewestern, ranchers western, a slim difference for men who drink coffee together in the town cafes, all equally weathered and the dust of the region etched into their faces, hands, the roots of their hair. If a man thinks cattle, though, surely his cast of mind drops south, say, from Medora, North Dakota, into west Texas or turns with the sunset into eastern Montana and Wyoming. Andy Adams rode trail through that general area after the Civil War. His modest *The Log of a Cowboy* describes the journey as a herd of cattle was brought out of Mexico and taken to Montana as a gift from the government to the Blackfoot Nation. At one stage of the journey the cowhands drove the herd across the North Platte near old Fort Laramie:

> I had one of the best swimming horses in our outfit, and Flood put me in the lead on the point. As my horse came out on the farther bank, I am certain I never have seen a herd of cattle, before or since, which presented a prettier sight when swimming than ours did that day. There was fully four hundred yards of water on the angle by which we crossed, nearly half of which was swimming, but with the two islands which gave them a breathing spell, our Circle Dots were taking the water as steadily as a herd leaving their bed ground. Scholar and his men were feeding them in, while half a dozen of our men on each island were keeping them moving. Honeyman and I pointed

them out of the river; and as they grazed away from the shore, they spread out fan-like, many of them kicking up their heels after they left the water in healthy enjoyment of their bath. Long before they were half over, the usual shouting had ceased, and we simply sat in our saddles and waited for the long train of cattle to come up and cross. Within less than half an hour from the time our saddle horses entered the North Platte, the tail end of our herd had landed safely on the farther bank.[99]

The plains were known early. Coronado and thirty men searched mid-Kansas for cities of gold in 1541. They found a tough, short prairie grass that injured the hoofs of their horses, round ponds of salty water; they found themselves surrounded by the sky, a whirlwind (old timers called them cyclones—tornadoes now) driving hail that dented their helmets and broke their pots, all this on the way twenty-five hundred miles out of Mexico. They reached very likely a village of the Wichitas—sapling huts woven with bunches of prairie grass, waterproof, and cured golden, no doubt—and out on the plains buffalo in numbers that staggered the imagination, and little else to tempt a Spaniard any further.[100]

N. Scott Momaday tells how the plains struck awe into the heart of the Kiowa:

> The first man among them to stand on the edge of the Great Plains saw farther over land than he had ever seen before. There is something about the heart of the continent that resides always in the end of vision, some essence of the sun and wind. That man knew the possible quest. There was nothing to prevent his going out; he could enter upon the land and be alive, could bear at once the great hot weight of its silence. In a sense the question of survival had never been more imminent, for no land is more the measure of human strength. But neither had wonder been more accessible to the mind nor destiny to the will.[101]

What held for the Kiowa holds as well for the traveler today, once off the great main highways, of course, for these carry according to their own traditions and customs the truckers, salesmen, hitch-hikers, kids, and the formidable American family on the move. Off these roads there is that other world of the wide plains, a world seemingly but a moment's remove from the eyes of the first hunters who came on to them. Those back roads are lonesome; a day's drive encounters sometimes maybe five or six other vehicles. That drive can be all night in a lightning storm from Rapid City to Medora, great sudden reaches of light and silhouettes of high buttes caught for a moment and gone again into darkness as if they had never been there at all. Or it can take a person a long way through the Nebraska sand hills from Valentine to North Platte where he will see almost what Parkman saw and learn from his own thirst how priceless the water is on the high plains. Parkman's description is classic:

> A low, undulating line of sand-hills bounded the horizon before us. That day we rode ten hours, and it was dusk before we entered the hollows and gorges of these gloomy little hills. At length we gained the summit, and the long-expected valley of the Platte lay before us. We all drew rein, and sat joyfully looking down upon the prospect. It was right welcome; strange, too, and striking to the imagination, and yet it had not one picturesque or beautiful feature; nor had it any of the features of grandeur, other than its vast extent, its solitude, and its wildness. For league after league, a plain as level as a lake was outspread beneath us; here and there the Platte, divided into a dozen thread-like sluices, was traversing it, and an occasional clump of wood, rising in the midst like a shadowy island, relieved the monotony of the waste. No living thing was moving throughout the vast landscape, except the lizards that darted over the sand and through the rank grass and prickly pears at our feet.[102]

For the native peoples, though there was plenty, they too had to cope with the caprice of wind and weather. They lived on a subsistence economy and

152

their tales and legends reflect this. They reflect also that sense of man alone with himself in an endless world. There are stories of lost children, of magical appeasement of hunger, of individual bravery, of cruelty. The Pawnee told George Bird Grinnell what they remembered, that was in 1888, for the nation had been decimated by wars with the Sioux, the Crows, the Kiowas, the Cheyennes, the Arapahoes, the Comanches, the Osages, and the Kansas, and their earth lodge villages on the Loup rivers above North Platte, Nebraska, had stood in the way of the advance of the settlers moving west. This is the story of Yellow Fox:

A long time ago, while the Pawnees were on their winter hunt, a young boy, *Kiwuk-u lahkahta* (Yellow Fox), went out alone to hunt, to see if he could kill a deer. When he left the camp in the morning, it was warm and pleasant, but in the middle of the day a great storm of wind and snow came up, and the flying snow hid everything, and it grew very cold. By and by the ground was covered with snow, and the whole look of the prairie was changed, and the boy became lost, and did not know where he was, nor what way to go to get to the camp. All day he walked, but saw nothing of the camp, nor of any trail, and as it became colder and colder, he thought that he would surely freeze to death. He thought that he must die, and that there was no hope of his ever seeing his people again. As he was wandering along, numbed and stiffened by the cold, and stumbling through the deep snow, he heard behind him a curious singing sound, and in time with the singing was the noise made by some heavy animal, running. The sounds came nearer, and at last, close by the boy, ran a great big buffalo bull. As he ran near the boy, he sang a song, and as he sang, the sound of his hoofs on the ground kept time to the measure of the song. This is what he sang:

A-t-us	ti-wa-ko	Ru-ru!	Teh-
My Father	says,	Go on!	He
	wah-hwá-ko		
	keeps saying,		

Ru-ru-hwá-hwá. Wi-ruh-re.
Keep going on. It will be well.

The boy's heart became strong when he heard that the Father had sent the bull, and he followed him, and the bull led him straight to the camp.[103]

George Bird Grinnell knew the Blackfoot, also, and they were the fierce watchmen of the northwestern plains. The loss of the patrimony was a shattering of the soul:

> In later times once, *Nápi* said, "Here I will mark you off a piece of ground," and he did so. Then he said: "There is your land, and it is full of all kinds of animals, and many things grow in this land. Let no other people come into it. This is for you five tribes (Blackfeet, Bloods, Piegans, Gros Ventres, Sarcees). When people come to cross the line, take your bows and arrows, your lances and your battle axes, and give them battle and keep them out. If they gain a footing, trouble will come to you."
>
> Our forefathers gave battle to all people who came to cross these lines, and kept them out. Of late years we have let our friends, the white people, come in, and you know the result. We, his children, have failed to obey his laws.[104]

For a while the bitter changes became the stuff of drama, available to everyone in the Wild West show, a crazy business. But José Martí, the Cuban writer and revolutionary, read a shameful dimension in such theatricals after watching Buffalo Bill's extravaganza in July of 1884:

> The Indians fire from between the ears of their horses and under their bellies; they are wraiths through whom bullets seem to pass without effect; the white man, who is Buffalo Bill, is now out of ammunition; he reels, and he seems mortally wounded; the Indians close in, like vultures around the dying eagle; he embraces the neck of his horse, whose body has served to protect him, and dies.
>
> The war whoops become ear-splitting shrieks of victory; it is as if the Indians had killed not one, but all white men; they enact the scene in the

circus for the entertainment of Easterners; but it is so rooted in their souls that the show takes on the aspect of reality. Now they pick up the corpse; now they sling it across the saddle of a brave who fell in the skirmish; and now they are riding off, happy and shouting, when to the jingle of harness bells, shouts, and the crack of the whip, in comes a stagecoach filled with white men. To the fray! . . . The public breaks into wild applause, for in this they have improved on Rome: the applause was formerly for the gladiator that slew, now it is for the one that rescues. The whip cracks; the band strikes up; music fills the air and the stagecoach disappears in a cloud of dust.[105]

In 1890 Chief Big Foot came down from the Badlands with his band and died in the slaughter at Wounded Knee, and after that there was no more counter-culture. In 1931 Black Elk of the Pine Ridge Oglala Sioux would tell his vision to John Neihardt, taking care that the invocation would be right:

So I know that it is a good thing I am going to do; and because no good thing can be done by any man alone, I will first make an offering and send a voice to the Spirit of the World, that it may help me to be true. See, I fill this sacred pipe with the bark of the red willow; but before we smoke it, you must see how it is made and what it means. These four ribbons hanging here on the stem are the four quarters of the universe. The black one is for the west where the thunder beings live to send us rain; the white one for the north, whence comes the great white cleansing wind; the red one for the east, whence springs the light and where the morning star lives to give men wisdom; the yellow for the south, whence comes summer and the power to grow.[106]

Black Elk would say that Wounded Knee broke the hoop of the Sioux nation and scattered it, and that the center was gone.[107]

There have been recently a number of books and several good motion pictures which recapture these last days, Thomas Berger's *Little Big Man* among

155

these. These are important because they work toward the truth of things as they were and the films have represented a certain honesty of landscape, but they also carry in them a white wish-fulfilment: The old chief whose wisdom is a compound of symbolic medicine and St. John at Patmos cares for the white child, identifies his unique state, and delivers him somehow from the unoriginal sin of survival of the strongest on the plains. The earlier choice, white child and black father, cannot be taken any more now that the black community has developed its own identity. The lone child still cries, and it will not be long, perhaps, before the native Indian and Chicano writers project societies that will shut out that cry. The writing may or may not be militant, it will make no difference. In Montana among a covey of good poets—Richard Hugo, Earl Ganz, and Ken McCullough—the amiable James Welch, can speak for the Blackfoot experience:

> When tribes are broke and holdings gone,
> legislators plan relief: Gros Ventres
>   owned
> this land, pay up. Children yelp
> against sour milk, half-price, plan
> to be happy stuffed with rice and rage
> Sometimes in three day ceremonies, fancy
>   dancers
> jingle meat home to pot. Drums restore
> wine to rightful owners when rain is right.
>
> Forget the ceremony and this land belongs
> to stone. Too often clouds sweep north,
>   stealing
> rain from tarred barrels and sloughs
>   stuffed
> with bugs. The bugs will live,
> hungry where weeds are thick with stink.
> Where Indians used to live, cabins are
>   padlocked
> and white men choose alfalfa, water rights
> penciled in wives' names, still enrolled
>   though white.[108]

156

That experience of its nature cannot ease a white conscience. . .

On the reservations today in South Dakota, Pine Ridge and Rose Bud, there are teachers who are writers or writers who have visited in and taught for awhile, so that there is a body of work that attempts to come to terms with life as it is among the Sioux and which describes the complex relationship that has to exist today among the races. Jay Janda, "Luke," Michael Flecky, and W. E. Ryan, and others, have contributed to this body of work. A poem by Flecky hones the edge of this painful knowledge:

> in the dark
> a black angus
> outside a hole in the fence
> eats goldenrod
> its butt hanging over
> your side of the road
> like truth
> it looks up for a second
> as you swerve by at 95
> you sweat
> and the bright copper eyes
> hypnotized by the headlights
> haunt
> and make you see
> steers over every rise
> in the moonlit road
> up ahead.[109]

And at the Porcupine Day School on Pine Ridge the children learn to write and to be photographers. They are children, they talk about the things they know—cats, trees, horses, open windows, winter, grandmothers, loneliness, death. David Bears Heart writes this about death:

> A sad and lonely time.
> A church filled with sad
> and crying people.
> a cold deep hole
> filled with quietness.[110]

Faith Two Eagle wrote this about the nature of the Sioux: "Water reaches toward light/at the end of the deep darkness."[111]

Some of these writers may be able to establish a distinctive voice and measure up to their adult counterparts among the capable Sioux artists: Claymore, Trimble, Freeman, Amiotte, Penn, Eder, Rave, Lafferty, Monyileaux, Red Elk, Howe, Larvie, Standing Soldier, White Buffalo Man, Two Bull, Bad Heart Bull, Herman, and Broken Rope.

Meanwhile there is Wounded Knee. It is a place near the center of a triangle formed by Porcupine, Pine Ridge, and Batesland a score of miles above the Nebraska border in South Dakota. There is a stone marker for the mass grave and a building which contains photographs of the dead. There are no trinkets sold there, nothing is sold there.

It is a two day drive back east on the plains to Lawrence, Kansas, or to Lincoln, Nebraska, for anyone who does not want to set a record or die of heat exhaustion. Lawrence is a magnet for a number of writers, some associated with the University of Kansas. John Maritz edits the little magazine, *Tansy.* Harley Elliott has recently published a book of poems, *The Dark Country,* which contains a long work on hunting rattlesnakes in Kansas. And Victor Contoski and Al Dewey are both poets working in Lawrence at the moment. In Lincoln Greg Cuzma edits *Pebble,* Roy Sheele, *Three Sheets.* Ted Kooser, Barry McDonald, and Mordecai Marcus are all publishing poets centered in Lincoln. William Kloefkorn teaches there, also, at Nebraska Wesleyan University, and not far away Donovan Welch teaches at Kearney State. Jon Milton edits the *South Dakota Review* in Vermillion, South Dakota.

These are the contemporaries; Willa Cather is the classical author of the plains. *My Antonia* is a prose pastoral, a Virgilian eclogue of pioneer life and its seasons, the raw spring, the heroic summer, the fruitful autumn. Jim Burden returns to visit Antonia and to find in her an amplitude and generosity that is consonant with the promise of completion that the land offered them as children. This is enough for him, a confirmation that helps him cope in a world of railroad and empire, a world of acquisitive and competitive time that makes a necessity of greed. The scene on the farm at the end of the novel is a tableau. Antonia's husband is there as well as Jim Burden, and he, too, has recently returned. He has no mystical feelings about the landscape, except that he farms it well. His return from Chicago is a return to his family and home.

My Antonia is Willa Cather's most affirmative statement. In other novels she continues to work the theme of the land and its histories, but often her characters who have the deepest sense of these things end up the most isolated from their fellow human beings or from any way of realizing their most profound interior experiences.

It is not easy to keep the plains in balance. There is a feeling of temporality about the outer Midwest. When Parkman made his 1847 adventure he met Shawnee, military commanders, Kickapoo, French mountain men, Mormons, Baltimore travelers for California, Mexican team drivers from Santa Fe, families, English agents, Canadian traders, Delaware, Pawnee, fur traders, trappers, American government couriers, missionaries, volunteer militia, and most of them in Westport, Missouri, at the beginning of his travels, and his survival has to be given to luck or providence, a dangerous journey. In the early 1860s Mark Twain makes that journey, too, but on a bumpy stagecoach, a monotonous ride a passenger enjoyed with a flask or a bottle. Almost all gone, almost unrecorded. That condition of shift and change is still there. The landscape covets a broken windmill, reminder that a few years ago a farm family lived and worked in this corner of the nation, or a concrete step seemingly dropped into an open field, a place where three hundred people came for church ten years ago. And with this, too, so much of the past had to be discarded, like so much excess furniture abandoned along the routes of the wagon trains, because the institutions of the East and of

Europe had to be adjusted radically to the sheer limitless horizon of the West.[112]

The desire to rescue fragments of life from immediate history is strong in William Stafford, born in Hutchinson, Kansas. He is preoccupied with remembrance:

> When they mention your name,
> our houses out there in the wind
> creak again in the storm;
> and I lean from our play, wherever I am,
> to you, quiet at the edge of that town:
> "All the world is blowing away."
> "It is almost daylight."
> "Are you warm?"[113]

What to do with a past of broken continuities, with events that move so quickly that men are encased in their history, bees in amber, while they are still living? Wright Morris is concerned with these problems. *Ceremony in Lone Tree* embraces Nebraska as a geographical entity from Chadron to Lincoln and the action is set along the graceful southering curve the Platte River channels across the state. Lone Tree is a ghost town still existing only because the eighty-nine year old Scanlon continues to live there. He is the past locked in on itself,[114] his vision as blemished as his window:

> Scanlon's eyes, a cloudy phlegm color, let in more light than they gave out. What he sees are the scenic props of his own mind. His eye to the window, the flaw in the pane, such light as there is illuminates Scanlon, his face like that of a gobbler in the drayman's hat. What he sees is his own business, but the stranger might find the view familiar. A man accustomed to the ruins of war might even feel at home. In the blowouts on the rise are flint arrowheads, and pieces of farm machinery, half buried in sand, resemble nothing so much as artillery equipment, abandoned when the dust began to blow. The tidal shift of the sand reveals one ruin in order to conceal another. It is

all there to be seen, but little evidence that Tom Scanlon sees it. Not through the clouded eye he puts to the glass. The emptiness of the plain generates illusions that require little moisture, and grow better, like tall stories, where the mind is dry. The tall corn may flower or burn in the wind, but the plain is a metaphysical landscape and the bumper crop is the one Scanlon sees through the flaw in the glass.[115]

The birthday celebration for the old man during a day and a night of family squabbling, illusion and disillusion, incongruous distortion, ends with the death of Scanlon and the beginning of his funeral journey, the body placed in the Conestoga wagon he was born in (for lack of anything else), driven by the grandson Calvin who perhaps will be able to shuck the past; and carrying McKee the mercantile man who speaks in clichés of the manifest destiny of growing towns in Nebraska; and the artist Boyd, a man who has tried to find his place in the scheme of things by commanding the eccentric gesture and little else, who falls asleep while McKee is talking.

A sense of the ongoing life of the outer plains is caught in Warren Fine's novel *The Artificial Traveler,* a preoccupation with baseball as played by local townsmen in the widely flung leagues of western Kansas, games played in the intense heat of a treeless country:

> It was then that Martin found the blue oval of cloud running at the sun, a sun that grew like bread dough in the bowl of his skull, and he wished he had not forgotten his hat. Robert Hernandez leaned on the dugout roof, staring at Martin. The blue cloud guarded the mouth of the yellow sun and turned green, like fire or like grass, and it burned fiercely like either one. Martin wanted to swallow the oval cloud whole or wash it in his mouth and let it get big in his head with the sun. He wished he had not somewhere forgotten his hat. The Sheridan team took the field in the top of the seventh and Martin watched, eyes blasted

and hollowed by the sun; the players swarmed
before him and unfolded as if they were their own
shadows. He wished he could put the cloud on as
though it were a hat and the sun a medallion on
its crown.[116]

The presence of Hernandez in Fine's novel is a
witness to the presence of the Chicano in the Middle
West and the decision of Hernandez at a moment of
crisis in the novel never to speak in English again
can be taken perhaps as a sign of the Mexican-
American turning away from the Anglo world and
back into itself and its own ancient traditions. The
Chicano has known the Midwest intimately. As a
migrant he has traveled the roads from one end of it
to the other and he knows where the old man is
buried and the child in unmarked graves at the edge
of the highways. But he is not always a migrant; he
has settled his own communities and lived in them
for generations in Illinois and Michigan as well as
in Kansas and Nebraska. And he is tired of being
treated with contempt, or worse, ignored as if he did
not exist at all.

Rodolfo Gonzales in *I Am Joaquin* has written
that he will withdraw into the safety within the circle of his own people, into *mi raza*. There, among all
those experiences that touch upon the existence of
the Chicano and among the names of those so special to the Chicano soul—Cuauhtemoc, Hidalgo,
Zapata, Espinozas—he gives a place to those who
say nothing:

> I am in the eyes of woman, sheltered
>   beneath
> her shawl of black,
>   deep and sorrowful eyes,
> That bear the pain of sons long buried or
>   dying,
>   Dead
> on the battlefield or on the barbwire of
>   social strife.

162

Her rosary she prays and fingers
endlessly
like the family
working down a row of beets
to turn around
and work
and work
There is no end.[117]

The movement for Chicano self-expression has
centers of activity in the far West and the Southwest,
but Denver, backed on the mountains on the very
western edge of the plains, has its press and book-
shop, also. The Migrant Workers Press and Barrio
Publications are located in the city. And Rodolfo
Gonzales is a native of Denver.

The history of the plains, so recent in terms of
settlement, has been caught in rich detail by Laura
Ingalls Wilder. Her stories retrace the fortunes of
the Ingalls family during a series of journeys from
Wisconsin to Oklahoma Territory and northward
again through Kansas and Minnesota to the Dakota
Territory where the family homesteaded in the
1880s. Her books for children spell out with thor-
oughness and depth the pioneer confrontation of
the land and the ideals of the independent farm
families in the homesteading era. The values that
release the pioneering impulse endure to shape the
ethos of settled families working their own land.
The old agrarian belief that farm life is more
healthy, more moral, more independent, and more
American than life in the city pervades Laura
Wilder's work.

Her heroine, Laura, is her own remembered self,
a sensitive child reclaimed by an honest writer.
What Laura could have known is put in the books, a
strange sense of loss when the tribes leave the territory, the haggling over the price of wheat at a time
when most of the settlers are going hungry, the town
itself is like a scab on the landscape, the destruction
of corporate property by farmers who argue that the
railroad is cheating on rates, a woman driven to

suicidal depression because she cannot stand the life on the prairie.

As Laura grows older she absorbs the folk and genteel culture of the town. She enjoys this, the chance for social life, for earning money, but she misses the wild prairie of her childhood. She needs challenge, not safety, and chooses the lot of a farmer's life to satisfy this need. The man she will marry, Almanzo Wilder, speaking to his brother, makes a distinction between two kinds of life that is a crucial one to the values Laura Ingalls Wilder upholds in these books: "Oh well, you're a shopkeeper, Roy. A farmer takes chances. He has to."[118]

For Laura, and in a sense for the nation, too, at one moment in time she gains the best of both worlds. She keeps the things of civilization which she must have, the social ties, the responsibilities, the education, the poems of Tennyson, but she maintains her contact with the earth with a commitment that is worthy of her love for it. After the turn of the century, however, for many on the plains, it became more difficult to keep these two worlds in balance. Plagues, dust storms, depression, foreclosure, these destroyed the will of the farmers and there was a mass exodus from the Midwest, a drift of the defeated into California. The nostalgia they felt and the values they coveted, the old populist hope and fear, produced in the work of L. Frank Baum the one, indigenous American fairytale. *The Wizard of Oz* is based on harsh reality. The cyclone that brings Dorothy to that fabulous place destroys the farm of Aunty Em and Uncle Henry, a terrifying Kansas wind, and Dorothy's anger when she confronts the wizard has an added edge—he is a good Nebraska man succeeding in the city by taking the easy way out and becoming a trickster.[119]

The myth of the farm family is still potent, but the farms themselves are now a vast submerged reality on the midwestern landscape. The Second World War ended the midwestern rural revolution. The postwar years witnessed an astonishing enclosure movement by corporations, so that vast reaches of farm land are now under corporate title and part of that system. This happened almost without people being aware of it, except for those directly concerned, another disturbed environment. What will happen politically and economically is open to question now that citizens are beginning to struggle against the concept of corporate supremacy. The counter-movement back to the land, the establishment of social and religious communes, the demand for organic produce, these are forces that must be reckoned with also. Whatever develops, it seems sure that we are heading for a new confrontation with the earth we get our food from, and this means a radical confrontation with ourselves and all that we believe in.

Statements about the Midwest as a region have to be made with caution. Preconceptions about the frontier have to be abandoned. The mind wants to entertain the notion that the farther west the frontier the more primitive the life. But this is not so, and this is why the Midwest is so puzzling. The imagination sees the logging industry as an important element of frontier enterprise, and yet, early as logging was in Minnesota, there were German settlements on the frontier three decades before the origin of tales of Paul Bunyan and the great blue ox, and these communities were enjoying their concerts of Mozart and Bach. And great rafts of hardwood timber were being floated down the Ohio to Cincinnati and Louisville as late as the First World War. Rafts out of the Missouri are still seen occasionally today on the Mississippi below Granite City, Illinois. Nor was the movement of the frontier a movement of steady expansion westward. Salem, that village where the young Lincoln came of age, place of split rail and chinked cabin on the Illinois prairie, existed side by side in time with the urban commercial and educational center of St. Louis ninety miles to the south and west of the Sangamon valley.

The Midwest is expressed in many literatures and

many cultures. There is room for a native literature in German that remains to be translated, for the somber statement of Rolvaag, for the reclaimed homeland of Dahlberg, for a classic American exploration of freedom and identity in Richard Wright's *Native Son*, for a longstanding tradition of homemade histories that result from the experience of literate families settling down on the frontier, a tradition that is manifest in the work of Edward Eggleston, Glenway Wescott, and Josephine Herbst. Furthermore, cultures that are supposedly dormant or provincial have a way of flickering into life and proving themselves dynamically related to the contemporary mind. Kate Chopin's *The Awakening* comes in the late 1890s and remains a stunning statement in regard to the dilemma and nature of womanhood, and yet it is clearly a product of the French influence in the Mississippi Valley, written by an author who was very much aware of her French and living heritage. Flaubert and de Maupassant influenced the style and outlook of this author; Louisiana Creole background became the evocative source of action and imagery.

Another characteristic of the mid-continental mind is its own very hazy sense of itself. This is a problem that seems to be indigenous. Distances have to be taken into account. Midwestern cities are like hubs in wheels of space. From St. Louis it is 650 miles to Minneapolis, 295 to Chicago, 230 to Indianapolis, 350 to Cincinnati, 270 to Louisville, 280 to Memphis, 350 to Little Rock, 500 to Oklahoma City, 250 to Kansas City, 450 to Omaha. Because the centers of culture manufacture are on the West and East Coasts, the interior cities may be more aware of San Francisco and New York than of one another. But their very distances one from another help them to maintain life styles that are distinct. Omaha is not Kansas City, Minneapolis is not Detroit. They cannot be assimilated into the stereotype of big midwestern town. In the early twentieth century the writers in revolt demonstrated how to write about the cities. Today it may be the urban blacks and Chicanos realizing their own home towns will prove that these particularities have relevance to the creating imagination.

Space and distance are obliterated in the national myth of the outlaw West. Where is Dodge City? Where are Ogallala, Rose Bud, Deadwood, Leavenworth, Scotts Bluff, St. Joseph, Glendive, Northfield, Medora? Not since the Middle Ages when knights were able in the romances to fly by magic from one country to another have distances been dealt with with such appalling ease. The motion pictures have been the great purveyors of the western myth, and the tendency of directors has been to find an easily available or spectacular backdrop for the scene of action rather than to work for a true sense of place. This fosters one aspect of the myth, that America is an infinite and timeless reality, but it has sadly impaired our ability to account for ourselves. In *True Grit* a girl attempting to revenge the death of her father moves from Arkansas into the snow-capped mountains and alpine meadows of Oklahoma. In *How the West Was Won* a fur trapper steps into a birchbark canoe somewhere in the Rockies and is next seen paddling up the Ohio to Cave-in-Rock in what is now the state of Illinois, a daring and incomprehensible journey.

The concentration on certain narrow aspects of the settlement of the broad Midwest at the expense of so much lived reality has blurred and denied many relationships. One of the most important is the interplay between the region's lived and artistic experience. There is little popular awareness of the many religious sects that came into the Middle West and how they took root and developed. And yet the art of a Dahlberg, the theology of a Reinhold Niebuhr, the social commitments of a Bly or the Berrigan brothers cannot be fully understood or appreciated without this context. In the memory of the nation there does not seem to be a place in the way west for Mormon pioneers taking turns dragging their two-wheeled carts over the plains, or for the many utopian communities and religious communes that were established on the prairies.

The nation's fables about itself tend to polarize what is often linked by multiple secret and fruitful intimacies. There is a midwestern ragtime that cannot be explained except in terms of German right-hand piano technique and black left-hand chord arrangements. At the same time, a failure to accept our own past leads to the creation of cultural and regional stereotypes which blot out longstanding conflicts that have formed both the region and its literature. An example of this is the determination to see the Midwest as the phlegmatic homeland of Middle-American normalcy. This denies an active spirit of dissent which has been abroad in the region from its settlement to the present day. Socialism in the German Turner Halls, the illusions and disillusionments following on passage of the Homestead Act, the Granger Movement, populism, the IWW, the Knights of Labor, the revolt of farmers in the thirties, the SDS, the unrest of the hard-hat and the blue-collar worker that challenges the rationale of mass production—these are movements, organizations, events that have shaped the thought of the Midwest and given direction to its art. Because this aspect of the region's history is seldom given its full weight, writers and artists who are most representative of the region are consistently lauded as fugitives.

At the present time, in the terror of the moment, when one way or another limits have been set on manifest destinies and imperial expansions, a person turns in an act of introspection toward the interior of the continent. There is fear in this, the idea that the past and the region are dead issues which will lead only to a constrictive isolation or some kind of sick chauvinism. But instead of a dead center, he finds an energetic multiplicity of relationships, human and formal, that extends far beyond the imagined boundaries of the region, and has from the beginning. The contemporary writer about his business in the Midwest is concerned to express these things. And there are so many it is not possible to

168

mention them all, but among them there is Robert Sward who knows that in this country no one talks about anything except America, and Ray Bradbury, and Jerome Mazzaro who writes of an Italian ethnic background in Detroit, and John Gardner re-creating *The Beowulf* in Carbondale. These will have to stand for the many.

Finally, to bring this article to a close, it is necessary to come back all the way east to Pittsburgh. This is where the Midwest begins, the place of the Golden Triangle. Sam Hazo, consciously Lebanese, directs the International Poetry Forum. Sarah Henderson Hay, Jerry Costanzo, Ed Roberson, Richard O'Keef, Edward Orchester are writers active in the area. And then there is Paul Zimmer, editor of the University of Pittsburgh Press. The title of his book of poems can serve as a good description of the spirit of the region, and although, given the nature of the times, not everyone can be quite comfortable with it, surely the Midwest is in its widest reach a "republic of many voices."

Notes

[1] James Wright, "Stages on a Journey Westward," *The Branch Will Not Break* (Middletown, Conn.: Wesleyan Univ. Pr., 1963), p. 21.

[2] *Ibid.*, "Miners," p. 24.

[3] Lisel Mueller, "Midwestern Poetry: Goodbye to All That," *Voyages to the Inland Sea: Essays and Poems by Lisel Mueller, John Knoepfle, David Etter*, John Judson, ed. (La Crosse: Wisconsin State Univ., 1971), p. 8.

[4] James Wright, "The Jewel," *The Branch Will Not Break*, p. 17.

[5] Lafcadio Hearn, *Children of the Levee*, O. W. Frost, ed. (Lexington: Univ. of Kentucky Pr., 1957), p. 25.

[6] William H. Gass, *Omensetter's Luck* (New York: New World Library, 1967), p. 67.

[7] William J. Harris, "For Bill Hawkins, a Black Militant," *Natural Process: An Anthology of New Black Poetry*, Ted Wilentz and Tom Weatherly, eds. (New York: Hill and Wang, 1970), p. 48.

[8] Dale Kramer, *Chicago Renaissance: The Literary Life in the Midwest 1900–1930* (New York: Appleton-Century, 1966), pp. 30–31, 34–35.

[9] Larzer Ziff, *The American 1890s: Life and Times of a Lost Generation* (New York: Viking, 1966), pp. 339–340.

[10] "Buckeye Jim," *Folksong: U.S.A.*, John A. and Alan Lomax, eds. (New York: Duell, Sloan & Pearce, 1947), pp. 36–37. (Text slightly reset.)

[11] Kurt Vonnegut, Jr., *The Sirens of Titan* (New York: Dell, 1959), pp. 314–15.

[12] Kurt Vonnegut, Jr., *Mother Night* (New York: Delacorte, 1961), p. 190.

[13] Kurt Vonnegut, Jr., *God Bless You, Mr. Rosewater: Or Pearls before Swine* (New York: Dell, 1968), pp. 55–56.

[14] Warren Fine, *In the Animal Kingdom* (New York: Knopf, 1971), p. 51.

[15] *Ibid.*, p. 123.

[16] Quoted in *Mississippi Panorama*, Perry T. Rathbone, ed. (St. Louis, Mo.: City Art Museum of St. Louis, 1950), p. 34.

[17] Timothy Flint, *Recollections of the Last Ten Years in the Valley of the Mississippi*, George R. Brooks, ed. (Carbondale: Southern Illinois Univ. Pr., 1968), p. 76.

[18] *Ibid.*, pp. 162–163.

[19] Vance Randolph, *The Talking Turtle and Other Ozark Folk Tales* (New York: Columbia Univ. Pr., 1957), p. 118.

[20] Stanley Elkin, *A Bad Man* (New York: Random House, 1967), p. 42.

[21] Robert Coover, "Cat in the Hat," *New American Review*, no. 4, Theodore Solotaroff, ed. (New York: New American Library, 1968), pp. 41–42.

[22] Walter J. Ong, "Burnt Norton in St. Louis," *American Literature* (Jan. 1962), pp. 522–26.

[23] Mona Van Duyn, *To See, To Take* (New York: Atheneum, 1970), p. 37.

[24] Constance Urdang, *Natural History* (New York: Harper & Row, 1969), p. 173.

[25] Eugene Redmond, "Rush City—The Hole," *Today's Negro Voices*, Beatrice M. Murphy, ed. (New York: Messner, 1970), pp. 100–101.

[26] Henry Dumas, *Ark of Bones and Other Stories*, Hale Chatfield and Eugene Redmond, eds. (Carbondale: Southern Illinois Univ. Pr., 1970), p. 43.

[27] Quoted in John Bakeless, *The Eyes of Discovery* (New York: Dover, 1961), p. 337.

[28] Samuel Langhorne Clemens, *The Adventures of Huckleberry Finn* (New York: Norton, 1962), p. 20.

[29] Vachel Lindsay, "Adventures While Preaching Hieroglyphic Sermons," *Collected Poems* (New York: Macmillan, 1941), xlvii.

[30] *Black Hawk: An Autobiography*, Donald Jackson, ed. (Urbana: Univ. of Illinois Pr., 1964), pp. 88–89.

[31] For background material, see Dale Kramer, *Chicago*

Renaissance (New York: Hawthorn, 1966) and Arthur E. Waterman, *Susan Glaspell* (New York: Twayne, 1966).

[32] W. D. Snodgrass, *Heart's Needle* (New York: Knopf, 1960), pp. 59–60.

[33] Ray Young Bear, "One Chip of Human Bone," *Pembroke Magazine*, no. 2 (1971), p. 5.

[34] *Heartland: Poets of the Middle West*, Lucien Stryk, ed. (DeKalb: Northern Illinois Univ. Pr., 1967).

[35] David Etter, "Moonflowers," *Go Read the River* (Lincoln: Univ. of Nebraska Pr., 1966), p. 58.

[36] Charles Edward Russell, *A-Rafting on the Mississip* (New York: Century, 1928), p. 82.

[37] Richard Bissell, *High Water* (Boston: Little, 1954), pp. 103–104.

[38] Raymond Roseliep, from "Tour, In Rain," *The Small Rain* (Westminster, Md.: Newman Pr., 1963), p. 69.

[39] Dennis Schmitz, from "Eclogues," *We Weep for Our Strangeness* (Chicago: Big Table, 1969), pp. 17–18.

[40] Hamlin Garland, "The Return of a Private," *Main Traveled Roads: Six Mississippi Valley Stories*, Thomas A. Bledsoe, ed. (New York: Holt, 1963), pp. 138–39.

[41] Larzer Ziff, *The American 1890s*, pp. 94, 106.

[42] F. Scott Fitzgerald, *The Great Gatsby* (New York: Scribner, 1925), p. 177.

[43] John Berryman, *77 Dream Songs* (New York: Farrar, 1965), p. 84.

[44] Alvin Greenberg, *Going Nowhere* (New York: Simon & Schuster, 1971), pp. 123–24.

[45] Sinclair Lewis, *Main Street* (New York: Harcourt, 1920), p. 124.

[46] J. F. Powers, *Morte D'Urban* (New York: Popular Library, 1963), p. 116.

[47] Frances Densmore, "Chippewa Music," Bulletin 45, Bureau of American Ethnology.

[48] Edward Dahlberg, *Alms for Oblivion* (Minneapolis: University of Minnesota Pr., 1964), p. 58.

[49] *The Edward Dahlberg Reader*, Paul Carroll, ed. (New York: New Directions, 1967), pp. 82–83.

[50] Langston Hughes, "Personal," *American Negro Poetry*, Arna Bontemps, ed. (New York: Hill & Wang, 1963), p. 66.

[51] Sherwood Anderson, *Winesburg, Ohio: A Group of Tales of Ohio Small-Town Life* (New York: Modern Library, n. d.), p. 251.

[52] Joyce Carol Oates, *A Garden of Earthly Delights* (New York: Vanguard, 1967), p. 440.

[53] Theodore Roethke, "Meditation at Oyster River," *The Far Field* (Garden City, N.Y.: Doubleday, 1964), pp. 17–18.

[54] *The Viking Portable Hemingway*, Malcolm Cowley, ed. (New York: Viking, 1949), p. 466.

[55] *Ibid.*, pp. 439–90.

[56] Ernest Hemingway, *The Fifth Column and the First Forty-nine Stories* (New York: Scribner, 1938), p. 596.

[57] Larzer Ziff, *The American 1890s*, p. 111.

[58] Dale Kramer, *Chicago Renaissance*, pp. 331–34.

[59] James T. Farrell, *Studs Lonigan* (New York: Modern Library, 1938), p. xii.

[60] *Ibid.*, pp. 200–201.

[61] Richard Wright, *Native Son* (New York: Harper & Row, 1966), p. viii–xxvii.

[62] *Ibid.*, p. xxxiv.

[63] *Ibid.*, p. 225.

[64] Paul Carrol, "This Ode . . . for Claes Oldenburg on His Visit to Chicago in the Snows of 1963," *Odes* (Chicago: Big Table, 1969), p. 25.

[65] Carolyn M. Rodgers, "U Name This One," *Natural Process*, Ted Wilentz and Tom Weatherly, eds. (New York: Hill & Wang, 1970), pp. 117–118.

[66] Glenway Wescott, *The Grandmothers: A Family Portrait* (New York: Harper, 1927), pp. 350–51.

[67] Glenway Wescott, *Good-Bye Wisconsin* (New York: Harper, 1928), pp. 9–10.

[68] *Ibid.*, pp. 38–40.

[69] Thomas McGrath, *Letter to an Imaginary Friend* (Denver: Alan Swallow, 1962), pp. 94–95.

[70] *The Lion's Tail and Eyes: Poems Written Out of Laziness and Silence* (Madison, Minn.: Sixties Pr., 1962), p. 11.

[71] *Ibid.*, p. 37.

[72] Robert Bly, *Silence in the Snowy Fields* (Middletown, Conn.: Wesleyan Univ. Pr., 1962), p. 46.

[73] Robert Bly, *The Light Around the Body* (New York: Harper, 1967), p. 32.

[74] Quoted in Harold McCracken, *George Catlin and the Old Frontier* (New York: Dial, 1959), pp. 175–76.

[75] Frederick Manfred, *Conquering Horse* (New York: McDowell, Obolensky, 1959), p. 259.

[76] Phrase borrowed from an application to the art of Munch; Wilhelm Weber, *A History of Lithography* (New York: McGraw-Hill, 1966), p. 104.

[77] Ole Edvart Rolvaag, *Giants in the Earth* (New York: Harper, 1929), p. 61.

[78] David Madden, ed., *Proletarian Writers of the Thirties* (Carbondale and Edwardsville: Southern Illinois Univ. Pr., 1968), p. xxii.

[79] Josephine Herbst, *Rope of Gold* (New York: Harcourt, 1939), pp. 105–106.

[80] Michael Anania, from "Missouri among Rivers," *The Color of Dust* (Chicago: Swallow, 1970), pp. 7–8.

[81] Kenneth S. Rothwell, "In Search of a Western Epic: Neihardt, Sandburg, and Jaffe as Regionalists and 'Astoriadists,'" *Kansas Quarterly*, 2, no. 2: 53–63 (Spring 1970).

[82] Dan Jaffe, from "The Crossing," *Dan Freeman* (Lincoln: Univ. of Nebraska Pr., 1967), p. 22.

[83] Kenneth Rothwell, "In Search of a Western Epic," *Kansas Quarterly*, 2, no. 2: 70 (Spring 1970).

[84] M. B. Tolson, *Harlem Gallery: Book I, The Curator* (New York: Twayne, 1965), p. 76.

[85] Gordon Parks, *The Learning Tree* (New York: Harper & Row, 1963), p. 38.

[86] Jack Conroy, *The Disinherited* (New York: Covici-Friede, 1933), pp. 162–63.

[87] Francis Parkman, *The Oregon Trail* (New York: New American Library, 1950), p. 14.

[88] William P. Trent and George S. Hellman, eds., *The Journals of Washington Irving* (Boston: Bibliophile Society, 1919), vol. 3, p. 121.

[89] Francis Parkman, *The Oregon Trail*, p. 286.

[90] Washington Irving, *A Tour of the Prairies*, John Francis McDermott, ed. (Norman: Univ. of Oklahoma Pr., 1956), p. xv.

[91] Thomas Hart Benton, *An Artist in America* (Columbia: Univ. of Missouri Pr., 1968), 3rd ed. rev., p. 275.

[92] Josephine W. Johnson, *The Inland Island* (New York: Simon & Schuster, 1969), p. 8.

[93] James Tate, from "Nobody Goes to Visit the Insane Anymore" (Cambridge: Halty-Ferguson, 1971), p. 92.

[94] Edward Dahlberg, *Because I Was Flesh* (New York: New Directions, 1963), p. 1.

[95] Edward Dahlberg, *The Leafless American* (Austin: Roger Beacham, 1967), p. 26.

[96] *Ibid.*, p. 2.

[97] William Inge, *My Son Is a Splendid Driver* (Boston: Little, 1971), pp. 44–45.

[98] Mari Sandoz, *Winter Thunder* (Philadelphia: Westminster Pr., 1954), p. 15.

[99] Andy Adams, *The Log of a Cowboy* (Garden City, N.Y.: Doubleday, 1960), pp. 181–82.

[100] John Bakeless, *Eyes of Discovery*, pp. 95–101.

[101] N. Scott Momaday, *House Made of Dawn* (New York: New American Library, 1969), p. 121.

[102] Francis Parkman, *The Oregon Trail*, pp. 55–56.

[103] George Bird Grinnell, *Pawnee Hero Stories and Folk-Tales* (Lincoln: Univ. of Nebraska Pr., 1961), pp. 206–207.

[104] George Bird Grinnell, *Blackfoot Lodge Tales: The Story of a Prairie People* (Lincoln: Univ. of Nebraska Pr., 1962), pp. 143–144.

[105] José Martí, *The America of José Martí: Selected Writings*, Juan de Onís, trans. (New York: Minerva Pr., 1968), pp. 99–100.

[106] John G. Neihardt, *Black Elk Speaks: Being the Life Story of a Holy Man of the Oglala Sioux* (Lincoln: Univ. of Nebraska Pr., 1961), p. 2.

[107] *Ibid.*, p. 276.

[108] James Welch, from "Wolf Story, The Rain," *The Young American Poets* Paul Carroll, ed. (Chicago: Follett, 1968), p. 501.

[109] Michael Flecky, "12:30 AM near Murdo, S.D.," *Saint Louis University Magazine* (April 1970), p. 8.

[110] *Photographs and Poems by Sioux Children* (Rapid City: Indian Arts and Crafts Board of the U.S. Department of the Interior, 1971), p. 38.

[111] *Ibid.*, p. 52.

[112] See Carl Frederick Kraenzel, *The Great Plains in Transition* (Norman: Univ. of Oklahoma Pr., 1955).

[113] William Stafford, from "Before the Big Storm," *Traveling Through the Dark* (New York: Harper & Row, 1962), p. 47.

[114] David Madden, *Wright Morris* (New York: Twayne, 1964), p. 133ff.

[115] Wright Morris, *Ceremony in Lone Tree* (New York: Atheneum, 1960), pp. 4–5.

[116] Warren Fine, *The Artificial Traveler* (New York: Coward-McCann, 1968), p. 133.

[117] Rodolfo Gonzales, *I Am Joaquin* (Denver: Crusade for Justice, 1967), pp. 17–19.

[118] Laura Ingalls Wilder, *The Long Winter* (New York: Harper & Row, 1971), p. 258.

[119] Jordan Brotman, "A Late Wanderer in Oz," *Chicago Review* (1965), pp. 63–73.

frontier myth and southwestern literature

Larry Goodwyn

Photograph by William Wittliff

The southwestern United States is a land suffused with the legacy of a rich, tormented history. In contrast, the literary heritage is strikingly thin. The two statements describe more than a mere cultural phenomenom: their entwined relationship is central to the analysis of modern southwestern writing.

Somehow, the very complexity of the region's past —grandeur interlaced with plunder and horror— has seemed to overwhelm those southwestern writers who have tried to extract meaningful literary materials from their region's tangled heritage. A great many have become captivated by the very myths they were trying to penetrate; others have attempted to cope with the past by explaining it away. Both approaches have failed to produce a body of literature that transcends the romantic or regional, and the knowledge of that failure weighs heavily on modern southwestern artists who are attempting to surmount those aspects of the received heritage that defeated their predecessors. The substance, direction and tone of the new effort—and its difficulty—are not easily described. Neither are the literary attempts of the past and the violent, elusive history that accompanied them and, as it happened, predestined them to failure.

Larry Goodwyn is with the Center for Southern Studies, Duke University.

The history is by no means simple to sort out. This is at least partly traceable to the fact that a ruthlessly candid account of the southwestern past would paint the Anglo-Saxon American in a considerably less heroic mold than public school textbook committees are likely to appreciate. For example, to Mexican scholars, the Texas war for independence from Mexico in 1836 had more to do with the land grabbing expectations of frontier speculators than it did with constitutional ideals. Nor are our neighbors to the South the only skeptics about the traditional version of "how the West was won." The repeatedly confirmed Anglo-Saxon habit of abrogating solemn treaties with Indians to get at more of the frontier landscape is cited as a further illustration of the crude acquisitiveness that persisted behind the rhetorical facade of "manifest destiny."

The point here is not that southwestern Americans were, or are, less noble than their own folk epics paint—the same could be said of most histories that various peoples write about themselves. Among historians the axiom exists, lamented but incontrovertible, that winners write the history books, not losers. The Southwest is not unique in this respect. Rather, the difficulty lies in more subtle ramifications imbedded in "the frontier legend" itself. It is a rendering of history that bequeaths in the first instance an assured aura of triumph, answering the question, "how the West was won," with narrowly focused, self-serving epics about forthright, courageous men building civilization in a prairie wilderness. The legend is pastoral: the courageous men conquered nature, but at the same time were "at one" with nature. The legend is inherently masculine: women are not so much without "courage" as missing altogether; cowgirls did not ride up the Chisholm Trail. The legend is primitively racialistic; it provides no mystique of triumph for Mexicans, Negroes, or Indians. .

Thus stands the historical inheritance, as it exists on the first level of communication, as a tale of one's ancestors. On a deeper level, the frontier legend provides each new generation with a model of conduct that merges manners into "manliness" in a way that defines the prerogatives of the sexes in terms of a hunter society. On a deeper level still, the legend— through its inherent processes of exclusion (women, Mexicans, Negroes, Indians, the noncourageous, and urbanites out of tune with nature)—encourages a moral code that is remarkably narrow in its application: a "manly" man, being Christian, is ethical, but in a competitive world, one is ethical first of all with those within the pale.

The power of the frontier legend has been, and is, enormous. It hovers over the people of the southern frontier, shapes the way they act publicly and privately, and defines the style of their politics, including the politics of protest. It is, in essence, the fountain from which southwestern culture has flowed.

In its primitively celebratory form, the legend is self-evidently a constricting literary legacy. Southwestern writers in thrall to its narrow, nativistic assumptions have left a mountain of trivial and heartily chauvinistic manuscripts in their wake.

However, in defining both the legend and the scope of its impact, a precise distinction should be made. It is not correct to say that the legend, though massively influential culturally, is inherently inadequate as a literary source. It is the *unexamined* legend—the propagandistic Anglo-Saxon folk myth —that has proven to be such a debilitating literary frame of reference. Moreover, even in this sense, the legend cannot be described as an all-pervasive blight. In the first place, the many categories of people who are excluded from sharing in its reflected emotional glow obviously should find its blandishments easy to resist. Secondly, southwestern writers may avail themselves of perspectives offered by other, non-frontier traditions. As shall become clear, a few have done this. They, too, do not have to cope directly with the legend's mystique. Finally, there is the possibility—not yet realized—that the legend itself can, through skillful and creative examination, be utilized as a source of meaningful dramatic statement.

Yet, even with these potentially large qualifications as to its scope, the literary impact of the frontier legend in the southwest has been huge. The simple fact is that most southwestern writers have been unable to resist the pull of the unexamined legend and have, as a result, unconsciously reflected pastoral, "manly" and nativist presumptions; this, indeed, explains why southwestern writing is still best described as a "frontier" literature. The writers have viewed their region, its way of life, its people, and their folkways, as rustic triumphant, Anglo-Saxon phenomena.

Leaving aside, for the moment, the appeal of the unexamined legend, a remarkable misreading of the nature of the region's heritage is also required to achieve this narrow focus. In thought, deed, manner of dress, custom, and even in vocabulary, place-names and fashions of folk festivals, the Southwest is Mexican-American and Spanish-American as well as Anglo-American. The one thousand mile sweep of land from the Texas gulf coast to the arid plateaus of New Mexico encompasses not only a vast amount of space but also all the recorded history of America. This is a decisive fact: the states of the southern frontier find their beginnings not in the relatively recent westward movement of Anglo-Saxons but in the colonial explorations of sixteenth-century Spain.

Here, on the southern frontier, the soldiers of Spain fought and died before the Pilgrims landed at Plymouth Rock. Here, Santa Fe and San Antonio had begun to take on their unique aspects while the rest of colonial America remained rooted along the Atlantic Coast. Here, Santa Anna's hardy armies of Mexican revolutionaries perished at the hands of a mixed Texas-Mexican army of even stouter revolutionaries in 1836. Here, the Indians of the southern plains raised their last ensign of revolt against the white man in the 1870s and '80s. Here, too, black slaves came in the first half of the nineteenth century and black freedom came in the aftermath of the social upheaval that accompanied the Civil War. The result, today, is a multiracial and multicultural civilization. The modern southwesterner, whether of

European, African, or Mexican descent, is, like his sundry nineteenth-century precedessors, a child of this unique regional inheritance. A writer need not use this heritage, of course; but should he make the attempt (and most southwestern writers have) the unexamined legend severely diminishes the richness of the dramatic sources that a fuller use of the past would make available.

For example, a substantial proportion of southwestern literature indirectly reflects or directly expresses the values and life-style that have come to be associated with that legendary American, the cowboy. Yet, one cannot speak accurately of the Texas cowboy as a cultural figure without conceding his almost completely Mexican origins. The mounted herdsman could be white or black, anglo or mexicano, but his very way of life was a fundamental assertion of his Mexican, not American, origin. "La reata" he used to rope his longhorns became "lariat" and the "chaparejos" he wore to protect his legs in mesquite country became "chaps," but the anglicizing of the words concealed only from the unknowing the seminal nature of the Mexican influence. The longhorns he marketed, the mustangs he rode, the sombrero and bandanna he wore, all came from south of the Rio Grande. In consequence, Texas cowboys, white and black, were bearers of a Mexican cultural inheritance, just as mexicano cowboys were. More importantly, Texas cowboys were *conscious* bearers of this inheritance and—most important of all—they purported to be proud of it; it was what distinguished them from the urbanites and tenderfeet, the men afoot, who lived north and east of Texas. (Why they felt the need to stress their differentness from other Americans is another question, and one to which we shall return.)

The cowboy example is instructive. As a literary figure, he has been skinned and dressed down, and his bones left to bleach in the stultifying rays of a sunny myth that diminished him as a memory even as it whitened his corpse.

It is curious that the cowboy should have been the

central victim because the cowboy is but one of many actors who have moved through the cultural crossroads that is the Southwest. Frontiersmen of all kinds, from Spanish conquistadoes and Franciscan friars to buffalo hunters and Texas Rangers, have rivaled the mounted drover for attention—and some for longer and more meaningful periods of time. But the cowboy has risen to symbolic dominance because he stands center stage in a drama far larger than himself; the Legend of the American West. And in this setting, the lack of focus on the cowboy's true origin and nature has led to caricature. In the process, the Legend of the West has become elevated to an emotional plane that transcends not only the southwestern but the American experience as well. The triumph of the good frontiersman over his enemies is more than an expression of America's view of the beneficence of its own continental development. It answers longings in men everywhere. The worldwide appeal of the drama of the white hats versus the black hats rests on its stark simplicity as a primitive morality play. No cliché can really blunt its power: evil can be ferreted out, identified, and dropped in the streets at high noon. Indeed, because of the universality of its appeal, the struggle between the bad gunslinger and the sheriff has made the transition from legend into myth. From that standing it is not likely to be dislodged, for a myth is impervious to rational arguments.

The cowboy is essential to this American morality play because it is through him that all the stage props necessary for drama can be harnessed. Without the cowboy there could have been no Chisholm Trail and no roundups, no rustlers, stampedes, or rodeos. Wyatt Earp could not have become marshal of Dodge City; there would have been no Dodge City. The cowboy is indeed the center of the legend's universe. Railroads were built to transport his cattle, and water and land customs evolved in response to his needs. He pioneered the bleak "dry-drive" trails across the western desert and it was he who cussed those intruders from civilization, the nesters. Lurking in the background is the benign father figure, cut in the image of the drover: the cattle baron. The latter, while perhaps useful as a reminder of the Horatio Alger aspects of the legend, has proven less useful dramatically than the nameless protagonist who drove the longhorns up the trail. As a mythic figure, the cowboy remains a plebe, not a prince.

Yet in providing insight into the true nature of the southern frontier, the cowboy—when handled according to the dictates of the legend of which he forms the centerpiece—is a singularly indicisive fellow. He is not only nameless but seemingly without provable traits of character. He sits on his Spanish mustang, alone in the vastness of the frontier, amid his longhorns, his chuck wagon, and his remuda of horses, certain in his innocence to be fleeced by sharpsters in the town at the end of the trail. His only fixed reference seems to come from the land itself. The range sustains him and his enemies alike and thus nurtures his style of life. His saga is fleeting—he defeats all his foes and then abruptly finds himself hopelessly obsolescent. Soon thereafter, he becomes a baffled foil for popular exploiters.

It need not necessarily have been so. From a literary standpoint, the cowboy would seem to have left a useful legacy—certainly one rich enough symbolically to be arrayed alongside the decayed landed gentry who have served hundreds of southern novelists.

Yet an examination of southwestern writing reveals that nothing of the sort has happened.

The literature of the Southwest may be divided into a number of categories or periods. The first of these would encompass all the literature, including promotional writing, that reflected a Spanish point of view. For reasons that will presently become clear, this work has had little impact. A second and parallel style embraced the utilitarian and brazenly promotional literature of the first Americans who came to the southern frontier—largely to engage in land speculation. The third and final type of early southwestern literary forms encompasses the evolving oral tradition that described frontier life as high adventure. The oral tradition materialized in stories of Big Foot Wallace and Sam Houston and produced a tradition both heroic and romantic. These tales have all the essential savor of a folk heritage; as they were polished at scores of camp meetings and over thousands of camp fires, they justified life on the barren plains, reassured the people who lived such a life, and grew popular because they enhanced both the tale-teller and his listeners. In all its varied forms—treasure stories, bad man stories, hero stories, and accounts of Indian-white relations (invariably described as Indian "depredations"), the tales formed the basis of an emerging folk literature, achieved rather simply by the process of "writing down the oral tradition." John C. Duval's *The Adventures of Big Foot Wallace* represents a classic illustration of this development.

These early literary forms served the function of documenting the uniqueness of the region, geographically and culturally, and had the effect of laying a foundation for the more reflective literary inquiries that followed. It is pertinent to note that these relative primitive forms of regional writing occupied southwesterners for the better part of four centuries. It was not until early in the twentieth century that novelists and poets along the southern frontier matured to a point of view and a prose style beyond the language of celebration.

The event that may be taken as a milestone marking a distinct change in literary tone was the closing of the frontier around 1890. It is almost impossible to exaggerate the psychological importance of this event: it has profoundly affected the modern literature of the Southwest.

Southwesterners were by no means alone among Americans in reacting to the closing of the frontier. A kind of nationalistic optimism had been the hallmark of American writing at least since James Fenimore Cooper and, in 1890, this approach was still very much in full view in the poetry of Walt

Whitman. But to many thoughtful Americans, North and East, as well as South and West, the closing of the frontier stirred an uneasy intimation that made Whitman's affirmations seem oddly timed. To such observers, the closing of the frontier marked the end of the time, bountiful but regrettably brief, when God's special grace had blessed the United States. For the better part of three hundred years, the frontier had stood as more than visible proof of America's gift of virgin land; more even than the promise of a new start for Europe's impoverished and monarchy-ridden millions. The frontier was not only the gleaming nugget in the national treasury, it represented an unending flow of credit to benefit the body politic itself—a "safety valve" that siphoned off the discontented from the increasingly crowded eastern cities. By its simple presence, the frontier had for generations fortified and made believable Jefferson's dream of a "nation of freehold yeomen" and justified the robust Fourth of July oratory that self-consciously depicted an egalitarian culture rooted soundly in land ownership by the masses.

Given the psychological hold the frontier had obtained on American intellectuals, from the earliest colonists through the founding fathers of the eighteenth century and their grandchildren in the nineteenth century, it is understandable that its closing seemed to mark the passing of America's uniquely favored status among the nations of the world. Though it would be a number of years before this intuition began to permeate the whole of American society, the West as living symbol was finished. Its meaning might perhaps now be investigated and debated, but its values could no longer be invoked by the simple incantation of the phrase, "western frontier." A symbol should evoke some glimmer of reality and the western frontier was, quite finally, no more.

At this critical juncture in the nation's intellectual history appeared Frederick Jackson Turner, a young and obscure historian who had grown to maturity in the West. Turner was to have enormous impact on

America's view of itself and became the single most dominant literary influence on the Southwest down to the present.

Frederick Jackson Turner resuscitated the frontier, as a symbolic value, at the moment it ceased to be a part of the life of the nation. His famous "frontier thesis," spelled out in 1893, asserted simply and grandly that "the existence of an area of free land, its continuous recession, and the advance of American settlement westward, explain American development." The sweep of Turner's meaning lay in those last three words, for he meant to suggest nothing less than that the frontier was the explanatory key to the entire American experience. To the frontier went the credit for shaping American political institutions, for on the frontier European immigrants became "Americanized, liberated, and fused into a mixed race."

To trace Turner's impact is to follow not only the literary development of southwestern writing in this century, but also to probe the deepest and most rigidly held presumptions of its artists and scholars. Not only were southwesterners in thrall to Turner's vision, but also it is not too much to say that, from a literary standpoint, they were imprisoned by it. For generations, almost no southwestern writers were able, consciously, to break through the boundaries defined by Turner. In hundreds of books, poems, and histories that emerged from publishing houses in the Southwest—and from not a few located in Manhattan—the region and its people, including its symbolic person, the trail driving cowboy, emerged as *the very essence of American democracy*. The themes rarely varied from this Turnerian format. Just behind the Frontiersman as democrat stood the Frontiersman as Possessor of the Old Virtues: Faithful, Unassuming, Honorable, Courageous, Generous, and above all, Individualistic.

But not quite "above all." At the center of this literature, so secure as to be frequently left unstated, was a thunderously provincial belief: the southwesterner was the Purest American.

This presumption is evident even when different writers defined in slightly varying ways just who the southwesterner was and what he represented. Whatever the minor modifications, the essential agreement lay in what he was not. He was not corrupted by commercialism; his style, therefore, reflected the country, not the city. Further, he had an unarticulated but nevertheless indisputable identification with the folk. The latter, however, were invariably (and almost always unconsciously) defined so that *the* folk and *his* folk were one. By this process, an unspoken agreement was reached and soon became a regional literary tradition: the folk were not black and not Mexican. (Among southwestern Turnerians, Turner's "mixed race" has somehow gotten dropped out, though no one seemed to notice.)

With those unconscious echoes sounding through twentieth-century southwestern writing, the prose had been diffuse indeed—far more so than many of its practitioners were aware. For devotion to humanistic impulses, few Texans merit more respect than the venerable folklorist and chronicler, J. Frank Dobie. Yet, captivated by the post-Turnerian cultural environment of his region, Dobie could write that his native state of Texas was settled principally by "the go-ahead Crockett kind of backwoodsman." Dobie knew the people of his native state, and knew them sometimes critically, but his vision was often narrowly focused. Writing of a land of intricate racial and cultural diversity, he could describe the code of conduct of Texans as essentially southern, rural, and white: "the riding, the shooting tradition, the eagerness to stand up and fight for one's rights, the readiness to back one's judgement with a gun, a bowie knife, money, life itself."

The thought processes at work here are complex: Dobie unconsciously saw the authentic Texan as a frontiersman and illustrated this stereotype through recourse to another stereotype, the southerner. In both instances, he was highly selective in his definitions, though little in his writing indicates he was aware of the other available alternatives. The

"Southerner" he instinctively embraced parallelled the specimen described (with considerable more irony) by W. J. Cash as a rustic, fun-loving "hell of a fellow." Cash went on to define the "fellows" as pelagra-ridden peckerwoods who were intimidated by the "Great Captains" who derived their style from the landed gentry. Dobie's idea of "the South" and the "Southern code of conduct" was considerably less diverse and at the same time less precise. Instinctively hostile to aristocracies, landed or otherwise, Dobie nevertheless borrowed the gentry's "code of honor" in order to graft it onto his Texas frontiersmen. In the process, the latter also received the "hell of a fellow" attributes of southern yeomen. It is possible that Dobie considered the frontiersman as embodying the best of both these different southern worlds, though he never specifically said so. Dobie was equally selective in his characterization of "the Texan." The authentic "Texican" was a frontiersman —all other Texans were simply not authentic in the same way his outdoorsman was.

The redeeming feature of Dobie's influential work in southwestern folklore is that the vigor and range of his interest in people periodically transcended the narrow symbolism that governed his definitions of the regional heritage. In homage to a Turnerian view of the frontiersman as the primary conveyor of American democratic ideals, Dobie nevertheless found much to admire in those of his comrades from the South Texas brush country who were of Mexican descent. More than most of the southwestern writers of his generation, he accepted the enormous Spanish-Mexican influence on the life-style and techniques of the cattle kingdom, though Dobie, like his colleagues, described the resulting frontier inheritance essentially as an Anglo-Saxon gift to an Anglo-Saxon nation. Nevertheless, one learns from Dobie that black cowboys, as well as Mexican vaqueros, rode up the Chisholm Trail. If all this sounds unfocused, that is not an inaccurate way to sum up Dobie's work. In *Coronado's Children, Tongues of the Monte, The Longhorns, The Mustangs,* and in literally scores of other books and essays, he attempted to recapture the flavor of that part of his region that fascinated him. He saw some special significance in the struggle of the Texas frontiersman, though he never wrote the great "luminous" book he wanted to write that might have imparted a broader substance to the distinctive regional experience. In short, he described the way of life without ever finding a way to describe its meaning.

J. Frank Dobie has been the most significant of what might be described as the interpreters of the oral tradition. Animated by the knowledge that the old cultural forms were disintegrating under the impact of twentieth-century urbanization, the writers who joined Dobie in the effort to interpret the received oral tradition expended much of their energies, as Dobie put it, "in getting it all down before it went away on the wind." These men, including, in addition to Dobie, John Lomax, Mody Boatwright, Wilson Hudson, Stith Thompson, and B. A. Botkin, thus concentrated rather less on interpretation than on the gathering of materials—though, of course, the selection of materials to gather was itself a form of unconscious interpretation. In any event, these folk chronicles succeeded, by and large, in replacing the tall tales with a somewhat more authentic expression of the folk experience.

Lomax's exhaustive gathering of folk ballads occupied his productive lifetime. Born in Bosque County, Texas, in 1867, he watched the passing of the cattle trail at first hand and began his search for the songs of the dying era. *Cowboy Songs and Other Frontier Ballads*, published in 1910, was followed by *Songs of the Cattle Trail and Cow Camp* in 1918. He ranged widely, going where his singers went—to camp meetings, back alleys, bordellos, and jails. It was Lomax who encountered an unheralded black guitarist in a Louisiana prison during the depression and gave American a vital addition to its folk culture in the songs of "Lead Belly." Lomax's collection, *Negro Folk Songs as Sung by Lead Belly* is deservedly a classic.

Stith Thompson, along with Dobie, Boatwright, and Hudson, was active in the Texas Folklore Society and edited some of the organization's collections. B. A. Botkin was another southwestern folk chronicler, concentrating primarily on Oklahoma.

Taken as a piece, the impact of this diverse body of work is difficult to measure. We can be grateful that much of the flavor of a simpler agrarian age has been preserved. Lomax's ballad collections are of inherent value as are the accumulated productions of the Texas Folklore Society. Yet, in another sense, the three-generation inquiry into the life and times of the folk frontiersman may have fortified the one cultural bastion J. Frank Dobie was most determined to conquer—the Legend of the West, itself. Dobie believed—and spent a lifetime trying to prove—that the real experiences of the southern frontier were more meaningful, more "authentic," than the simplistic and misleading portraits by popular exploiters of the legend in romantic novels and Hollywood films. But by some curious process of inversion, he and his fellow chroniclers seem to have been overwhelmed by the spirit of the legend, even as they attempted to correct its specific details. In the hands of these southwesterners, the frontiersman is hardly less true-blue as a social type than in Zane Grey's pot-boilers or in numberless Grade B westerns. Neither the authors of romantic cow-novels nor Hollywood directors had ever heard of Frederick Jackson Turner, but the southwestern chroniclers who tried to correct the former seem to have been impeded by their allegiance to the latter. Shining through this massive compilation of folk history is the aura of the frontiersman as somehow more incorruptible, and democratic, than those Americans who had the misfortune of being either urban or eastern. In this literary tradition, now in its maturity, the cowboy had his moments of loneliness, and suffered incursions of knavery from various quarters, but in the end both he and his values prevailed. The tragedy of the frontier—the narrowness, the ruthlessness, the mindless racial violence, the empty

lives lived in so many unlamented empty places—
remains as a subdued minor theme or is missing
altogether. In this manner, the "authenticity" that
has been recaptured by the folklorists is laced with
the mythology it was meant to replace. There are
young writers in the Southwest today who feel as
entrapped by this celebratory, self-serving folk literature as Dobie felt diminished by Zane Grey.

Meanwhile, as the interpreters attempted to cope
with the received oral tradition, another and not
wholly unrelated literary form began to take shape
in the twentieth century. It may be described, quite
loosely, as a "literature of nostalgia." The range of
works fitting this description is broad and includes,
at its best, a sensitive literature that reflects considerably more introspection than characterized the
folk literature that developed chronologically at the
time. Perhaps the phrase, "literature of nostalgia,"
is an unfair description of the works of men such as
John Graves and Tom Lea, for both writers are
capable of cold realism in facing the passage of the
agrarian virtues. Graves' *Goodbye to a River* is a
pungent lament for a boyhood stream doomed by
the demands of modern society. In Graves' hands,
the Brazos is more than a river condemned—by a
high dam—to the loss of its pastoral tranquility;
Graves' loss is a specific Texas emotion, rooted in
the history of a particular place and the people it
has sheltered. In taking one last trip with his dog
down the river, and writing of both its history and
his own memories enroute, Graves seems to be engaged in a private emotional severance from a private frontier of his past, as if the river, itself, were
the connection that made the history surrounding it
endure. The sense of loss is immense, and Graves is
a good enough writer to make his readers share it.
But the specific loss, as apart from the sense of loss,
is less clear, and this, perhaps, is the elusive ingredient that keeps this lovely work from being a
truly great book. One wishes Graves would write
more, and perhaps, risk more.

Tom Lea is an artist turned writer. His paintings of southwestern life reached millions through *Life* magazine before his novel of bull-fighting, *The Brave Bulls*, became a prize-winning best seller in 1949. *The Wonderful Country, The Primal Yoke,* and *The Hands of Cantu* followed. In 1957, Lea completed a two-volume study of that symbol of the Texas cattle kingdom, *The King Ranch*, a massive historical work that was tellingly illustrated by the author's paintings.

Lea has a fine story-telling gift—as warming as a campfire on a cold night in the Paso Del Norte country he knows so well. He can reconstruct the action of a frontier fight with the Apaches and relate the fine points as well as the drama of a bull-fight in a style that goes impressively beyond the Hemingway precedent.

But Lea has drunk deeply at the fount of the frontier myth. *The Brave Bulls* climaxes with an epic fight, well-told, but flawed with sentimentality. Fortunately, there is a leanness about Lea's work that frequently spares him from the excesses one suspects he is consciously guarding himself against. For the most part, he is successful, but the effort seems to deflect him from exploring far deeper nuances in the clash of cultures that is his recurring topic.

Of all the novelists to emerge from the Southwest in recent years, two of the best known are William Humphrey and Paul Horgan. Both draw on traditions that are outside the framework of Turnerian affirmation. Humphrey's literary architecture is Southern Gothic, relieved from time to time by a bit of deadpan Yankee plainness. His novels reveal the strong influence of William Faulkner and, to a lesser extent and in a less fundamental way, of Mark Twain. On the other hand, Horgan's quiet, graceful prose is an expression of his deeply rooted Catholic faith. He is, in the best sense, a Catholic writer, and probably the best one at work in America today.

In a sustained literary effort of almost forty years, Horgan has produced more than a dozen novels. A novelette, *Devil in the Desert,* written midway through this long career, isolates much of the thematic material, technique and atmosphere that has characterized Horgan's work: "Remarkable for its poetically vivid re-creation of the New Mexican scene, its appealing portrait of the gallant old missioner and the almost mystical ferver of its climactic vision, this is . . . for those who delight in an exquisitely worked literary miniature." *Devil in the Desert,* the story of an old priest who meets death while visiting parishioners in the lonely Rio Grande country, was one of the few works Horgan published during a thirteen-year period when he was laboring on a massive historical study of his native land. *Great River: The Rio Grande in North American History* was widely acclaimed when it finally appeared in the mid-1950s. Painstaking, diligent, controlled—these are the adjectives Horgan's work elicits. He knows the southern frontier well and writes of it with a sustained serenity. If his deep personal faith has insulated him from feeling the need to probe for that elusive regional quality that co-exists so easily with violence, his work nevertheless is a monument of craft as well as a generosity of spirit.

William Humphrey's reputation rests on two novels and a collection of stories. His first novel, published in 1958, was the promising *Home from the Hill,* followed in 1965 by the best-selling *The Ordways* and in 1968 by the short-story collection *A Time and a Place. The Ordways* opens with a beautiful set-piece—"graveyard working day" in a small southern village in East Texas. The West is present, just beyond the town, "out there," but the village itself, as well as the private geography of William Humphrey's inner being, is firmly located in the American South, not on the frontier.

Critic Elizabeth Janeway has said Humphrey "is not a primary writer." What Humphrey does "is accept the vision that Faulkner and others have bequeathed to their heirs, and built on it. His books are less original than those of his masters', smaller and more constructed, and with a touch of conscious synthesis about them." Nevertheless, Miss Janeway, like most American critics, finds Humphrey's art to be "terribly good." Other people's writing may be built into Humphrey's southern vision, "but they are the best people, and the echoes are worthy of them." Miss Janeway's criticism seems too sweeping and prematurely final for a novelist still in the process of testing his full powers. William Humphrey is at work in a very rich mine and it seems too early to announce the value of his findings.

There is another aspect of Humphrey's writing that is, we may hope, a portent of an increasingly healthy literary environment in the region—if only outside the framework of the unexamined frontier legend. This is the extraordinary range in mood evident in his first three published works. *Home from the Hill* was a doom-filled first novel of southern apocalypse. Whatever its merit in terms of originality, it was nevertheless told with the precision of a writer who knows what he is about. If it left lingering suspicions that Humphrey's scope was as narrow as it was derivative, these doubts were set at rest by *The Ordways,* an expansive and at times comic treatment of the rhythms of life that bubble through the southern ethos. Even more impressive is the fact that Humphrey's control of the mock epic is as sure as his handling of tragedy. Beyond these evidences of craftmanship and range is Humphrey's undeniable capacity to describe the southwestern land in an original and compelling style.

Of these novelists—Graves, Lea, Horgan, and Humphrey—the first two draw on the frontier tradition directly while the latter two avoid it altogether in favor of older traditions—Horgan, his Catholic faith, Humphrey, the literary heritage of the Old South.

There is, however, one kind of southwestern literature that has managed to exist wholly outside the framework of frontier affirmation while at the same time exploiting the materials of the frontier itself. It is a literature not of optimism but of despair, and reflects not a received heritage of triumph but the daily recurrences of personal agony and defeat. One of the earliest of those works—and certainly one of the most suggestive—was *The Wind*, written in 1925 by Dorothy Scarbrough. In Miss Scarbrough's hands, the frontier itself is the villain—the stark, bleak land defining a stultifying emptiness that is symbolized by the endless, unengageable prairie wind. *The Wind*, is the story of Letty Mason, a sensitive Virginia girl driven to despair, murder, and suicide on a West Texas ranch. Not for Miss Scarbrough a story of triumphant frontier men and women finding personal liberation and fulfillment through a casual conquest of nature. Letty Mason does not conquer. The cause is geographical; she would not have died in Virginia. "The wind was the cause of it all," writes Miss Scarbrough. "The sand too had a part in it and human beings were involved, but the wind was the primal force." Personal oppression, rushing on haunting winds, fills the vacumn of the great plains. The land does not liberate, it maddens.

Miss Scarbrough has not been alone in her dissent against the regional propaganda of triumph. It is striking, and instructive, to note that among her companions in skepticism are two of the finest draftsmen ever to write of the dehumanizing aspects of the plains environment—and both of them are women: Katherine Anne Porter and Willa Cather.

Katherine Anne Porter is justly regarded as the *grande dame* of American fiction. Such short stories as *Old Mortality, Noon Wine,* and *Pale Horse, Pale Rider* are classics of the form and, with her celebrated novel *Ship of Fools*, are evidence of the unrelenting intensity that has characterized her work. The lean tragedies that buffet her characters are as stark and elusive as the plains wind itself. Life scars their sensibilities like gritty sand, eroding strong men into petty tyrants and weak ones into drifting residues of human futility.

Very early in her career, Miss Porter attained that level of cultural assurance, bordering on arrogance, necessary to the act of seeing one's land for what it is. The grim, constricting environment of her Texas youth is not to be judiciously edited and romanticized. Rather, its meaning is searched for in whatever hidden arroyos of the past she can discover. When she writes of innocence, the trait is far more likely to be fatal for its possessor than an illustration of the virginal purity of the common heritage. Both the starkness of the land and the stridency of its people come through in Miss Porter's fiction not as pluses or minuses on some frontier checklist but as a function of the paucity of alternatives her characters have been able to perceive. The lonely struggle with the resisting land is seldom enlarging or elevating. The silences that come up out of this isolation punctuate dreams that disappear on the wind and ideas that are never born. Boredom vies with futility and foolishness. Passion, intruding suddenly upon the weariness, is a desperate assertion of the possibilities of life; rather more violent than loving, it becomes symbolic of possibilities unredeemed.

One searches Miss Porter's fiction in vain for evidence that the experience of the American frontier has somehow produced an ennobling individualism that fortifies confidence with generosity. Insularity spawns ignorance and sudden violence, self-destructive and often pathetic. Miss Porter's westerners bring no special facility to bear on the imponderables of the human spirit, denied to other Americans or to Europeans.

It should be noted that, as a woman, Miss Porter represents one of the categories of people who have been excluded from the frontier legend. She has thus not had to cope with the implicit presumptions, including the thunderously masculine ones, buried there. Holding no appeal for her, the legend also has not had the effect of constricting the range of her perspectives. For generations, the representative style of the people of the southern frontier has been a kind of hearty, primitive innocence. The expression of this innocence in confident terms has in turn been an expression of their own reading of their frontier past. From her own intuitions, Miss Porter has come to suspect both the pose of confidence and the value of the innocence it shelters. Through the widest possible use of the received regional inheritance, supplemented by her own intuitions as to what has been left out by the chroniclers and the historians, Miss Porter has armed herself with a vision of life that is at once humane and tragic. The result is finely sculptured fiction that cries out in compassion and apprehension about the fate of man.

Willa Cather's struggle with the implications of her regional materials took a radically different form. In her earliest writing, Miss Cather focused on the debilitating effect of a land without definition:

> Across the river stretched the level land like to the top of an oven. It was a country flat and featureless, without tones or shadows, without accent or emphasis of any kind to break its vast monotony. . . . The flat plains rolled to the unbroken horizon vacant and void, forever reaching in empty yearning toward something never attained. ["El Dorado: A Kansas Recessional"]

Another description, also taken from her early work:

> He knew by heart every individual clump of bunchgrass in the miles of red shaggy prairie that stretched before his cabin. He knew it in all the bitter barrenness of its autumn. He had seen it smitten by all the plagues of Egypt. He had seen it parched by drought, and sogged by rain, beaten by hail, and swept by fire, and in the grasshopper years, he had seen it eaten as bare and clean as bones that vultures have left. After the great fires, he had seen it stretch for miles and miles, black and smoking as the floors of hell. ["On the Divide"]

Though what is perhaps her finest novel, *Death Comes to the Archbishop,* is set in New Mexico, Willa Cather was not herself a child of the southern frontier. The barren plains she recoiled from, and ultimately fled, were the plains of Nebraska. But her curiousily truncated inquiry into her own cultural roots in the West is strikingly illustrative of the problems that have afflicted most novelists of the southern plains.

The passages quoted above from Miss Cather's early work are "naturalistic"—a word almost never applied to her later work. She was, in fact, psychologically and physically defeated by the plains. Her girlhood, in a farming region fatally located west of the thirty-inch rainfall line near Red Cloud, Nebraska, was suffused with the end-of-the-century despair that drove thousands back from the frontier and inculcated in those who remained—from the Dakotas to Texas—a revolutionary anger that took the political form of Populism. But Willa Cather was no agrarian radical. Rather, she soon fled to the East where she soon began to move in circles of artistic sensibility and social gentility. The result was disastrous in terms of her relationship, as a creative artist, to her sources. As the critic Robert Edson Lee has put it: "She chose the rosy tints of romanticism, which inhibit all of her later writings about the West. She chose to write an idyll or a pastorale. Beautiful as it may be, it hasn't the strength or the vigor or the reality of the history itself. She has polished and tamed a land and its people out of all recognition. She did this, she had to do this, in self-defense; who cared, after all, about Nebraska? She had come . . . to write from the point of view of the East, substituting artifice for truth."

Cather's fate can be linked to that of the writers who celebrated the West in Turnerian terms. Seeing the hostile plains environment more clearly than they, she fled to the East and grafted on to her bleak western consciousness the artificial sensibility of a passing eastern literary fashion. So armed, she could then write romantically of the West—not unlike the practitioners of frontier romanticism in the Southwest. Unable to bear the loneliness of her land, she departed before making the effort to probe it for the materials necessary for literary statement; her colleagues on the southern plains, suffering the same loneliness of spirit, attempted to deny its force by celebrating its causes.

But, as noted, women have not been the only group of writers free of the more stifling influences of the frontier myth. Negroes, too, were excluded from its constricting embrace. Indeed, the exclusion was pervasive. Far more so than women, Mexicans, or urbanites, Negroes were almost invisible as historical actors in the frontier drama. In *Invisible Man*, Oklahoma's Ralph Ellison probed the bitter fruit of this cultural legacy, establishing himself in the process as one of the great literary talents to emerge from the southern frontier. As with Humphrey, Horgan, and Porter, the triumphant frontiersman is not to be found on Ellison's pages.

Interestingly, Ellison's stark portraits—so sharply at odds with the malaise of innocent optimism that suffused the frontier mystique—has not made him a pariah in his homeland. Ellison's angry, prize-winning novel of the 1950s included a shocking scene evoking the racist attitudes of whites in the narrator's boyhood hometown. Yet, in the 1960s, Ellison was invited back to Oklahoma to receive an engraved state medal as one of Oklahoma's most "distinguished" sons.

Three other southwestern writers, George Sessions Perry, Hart Stilwell, and Oliver LaFarge are representatives of a slowly evolving regional literary attitude resting on materials that, like Ellison's, reflect the outside or "underside" of the frontier struggle— from the casualties of the competition: Mexicans, Indians, poor whites. In *Hold Autumn in Your Hand*, Perry examines the inherited suffering and casual despair of the southern tenant farmer. In *Border Town*, Stilwell touches the struggle for dignity by Mexican-Americans in a town run by Anglos. In *Laughing Boy* and in *Enemy Gods*, LaFarge wrestles with the problems of red men in a white world. All written between 1929 and 1945, these novels are not in themselves impressive; they are noted because they are examples of an emerging skepticism about the universal beneficience of the frontier experience.

In the newest generation of southwestern writers, this skepticism is rampant. It is also, for the most part, without focus. Beyond these generalizations, the emerging new literary attitude is difficult to describe with precision. Like every other part of America, the southern frontier is being absorbed, for better or worse, into an increasingly amalgamated urban society that is supported by an impersonal technology and symbolized by the instance culture of television. Meanwhile, the twilight of puritanism casts ever fainter rays across the land. The literary ramifications of these influences are everywhere evident—in the comic pornography and drug-infested escapades of Terry Southern, the homosexual novels of John Rechy, the urban traumas of Donald Barthelme. The authors' grip is rarely very firm in these works, though a high sense of irony sometimes enlivens the frantic quests through which the new generation is acting out its questions. What is common to most of this prose is a sharp immediacy, an impulse for instant realization and instant verification that is far removed from the accepted loneliness and "manliness" of the old literary frontier. Some of these younger writers consider their literary predecessors passé—Southern has said as much of Katherine Anne Porter in a review of *Ship of Fools*—and for the most part they ignore their elders. The reason is evident enough—the new writers are asking radically different questions both about the nature of human experience and the functions of a received heritage in informing that experience.

The impact of television in shattering regional modes of thought, particularly among those who have literally grown to maturity under its influence, is self-evident as a basic element in the transformation of values and expectations among the young. It is not necessary to define this nascent "culture"—indeed, that would be impossible since it is still in the process of discovering its own dimensions—but it probably should be noted that its limits already have been extended far beyond the specific definition provided by Theodore Roszak (the "counter-culture").

The broad brush strokes beginning to crowd upon the southwestern literary canvas have, as yet, provided little in the way of additional specific definition. By no standard could the work of Southern or Rechy, for example, be considered "major." Their themes are conventional—modern man at bay, seeking identity (or escape) in an impersonal machine age. The angle of approach is, however, distinctive: a veneer of irreverence fails to camouflage the spectacular good will and longing that pervade much of the literature from the underground of the counter-culture. Also present, unacknowledged but visible, are vestiges of the frontier legend, outlined by the negatives that surround it. To many younger southwestern writers, the values implicit in the frontier myth are regarded as being co-extensive with the values of the "establishment." This is, of course, simplistic. The frontier, for all its exploitation by self-serving writers and self-identified frontiersmen, was a unique human experience and one that produced, when freed from the clutches of romanticism, enduring values. Perhaps because the new bohemians are preoccupied with their quest for fresh frontiers of sensibility, the prose emanating from that quarter is not yet distinguished by intellectual precision.

One of the most interesting young novelists in the Southwest—and certainly the most embattled in terms of the frontier heritage—is Larry McMurtry. He should be examined in some detail for a review of his literary inquiry serves to summarize both the uses and dangers of the frontier inheritance as it affects the newest generation of southwestern writers to toil under its shadow.

McMurtry's first two novels, *Horseman, Pass By* and *Leaving Cheyenne,* were promising efforts to put the materials of frontier culture to serious literary use. Descended from West Texas ranchers with the mystique of the frontiersman surrounding him through all the years of his youth, McMurtry has consciously attempted to avoid the language of celebration. Both his two earliest works are in-the-grain novels of people striving to live by the cultural values of the legend. An authentic mood is further heightened by the voice of the narrator. McMurtry speaks through a narrator who is frontiersman enough to move with ease through the tall-in-the-saddle milieu, but sensitive enough to note the ritualized energy and directionless fury surrounding him. In these two novels, one sees a writer laboring, desperately laboring, to transcend his heritage by finding something in it beyond the limits of the unexamined legend. There are values to be admired: a code of generosity in personal conduct, an intact ability to act. But (McMurtry gives us occasional reason to believe), there is something disturbing at the center of the world. The generosity is applied only to certain kinds of people, and the ability to act —untempered by reflection and introspection—can easily degenerate into mindless tyranny. McMurtry does not consciously underline this critical response, but it is clearly present within his material. A kind of unwilled drawing back from the frontier mystique on McMurtry's part can, for example, be read into the struggle of young Hud Bannon to shape his life outside the limits laid down by the authoritarian frontier patriarch whose presence dominates *Horseman, Pass By*.

His third novel, *The Last Picture Show*, represents a turning away from this kind of questioning, and his latest novel, the recently published *Moving On*, accelerates this movement. *The Last Picture Show* is about the transitional generation of frontier people who were raised in town. The novel avoids the obvious pitfalls: it is no panting pastoral lament for a lost wilderness, no brooding documentation of the disarray of misplaced agrarians baffled by the corrupting metropolis. Rather, what is missing is a sense of narrative control, as if the characters are "at home" but the author is not. The first person nar-

201

rative voice is gone, and with it vanishes much of the power that characterized McMurtry's first two books.

The feeling is therefore induced that we are in the presence of a skilled craftsman who is uncertain what he is trying to portray. Is the legacy from the past too powerful to bear investigation? In the privacy of the author's mind, in what is *not* written in *The Last Picture Show* as well as what is, the frontier seems clearly to be winning the test of wills.

Moving On vastly increases the suspicion that McMurtry—like so many of his literary forebears in the Southwest—has turned from the effort to employ the frontier heritage in a way that, for example, William Humphrey utilizes the "Old South." Eight hundred pages long, *Moving On* is a repetitious book about a young couple bickering away their lives. The narrative voice is again missing, and, again, the loss of dramatic power is evident. The conjuction of these two facts may point to McMurtry's dilemma. Relying, in his first two novels, on the literary device of the provincial narrator, McMurtry found a voice that seemed to serve well as a strengthening connection between himself and his sources. In turning to new sources (which, of course, he has every right to do) McMurtry departs from a proven technique in a way that seems to have cost him a sense of literary focus as well.

In a book of intensely personal essays revealingly entitled *In a Narrow Grave*, McMurtry provides an absorbing insight into his own sense of dilemma as a writer and as a Southwesterner. One of these essays, entitled "Take My Saddle from the Wall: A Valediction," purports to be Larry McMurtry's personal declaration of independence from the frontier mystique. Describing a family reunion on the ranch of the patriarch of the McMurtry clan, he weaves a collage of family stories and tall tales into a fine portrait of stern, obsessive striving by tight-lipped people determined to conquer a resistant land. The emotional cost of this life-style is hinted at by McMurtry though never pursued with measured strokes; in fact, McMurtry seems to be vaguely taken by some undefined part of the legend by which the other McMurtry's have lived. In an essay meant to erect a highly visible personal milestone and to signal new departures therefrom, this ambuigity serves to remove bricks as fast as they are set in place. One comes away with the feeling that, despite its title, "Take My Saddle from the Wall" is not a work of apostasy at all. What is ominous is the beguiling simplicity with which McMurtry takes down his saddle in his mind while his heart immediately replaces it. He can do one or the other, and put either to dramatic use, but one would suppose he would have the distinctions well in hand; a writer simply cannot afford such innocence in respect to his own point of view, at least not in an essay entitled with such precision. One senses the same ambiguity at work in his last two novels: the frontier ethos, removed from the center of his work, continues to hover around the edges—it surfaces in minor characters who move with purpose through novels that do not.

Literary critics of the future will, when pausing to focus on the Southwest, probably bless Larry McMurtry for his presence. Far more than Katherine Anne Porter, Larry McMurtry's literary life reveals the forces at work in the dominant culture patterns of the Southwest: the anguish of those of its artists who are searching for firm ground upon which to stand within the ethos of the western legend, and the difficulty of their psychological effort to break through the limitations of frontier affirmation in order to achieve a critical focus on their material.

The creative agony of Larry McMurtry is, in its own complex way, a benchmark in the literary evolution of the southern frontier. His disarray is more visible than most of his predecessors because he is sufficiently armed, in a skeptical age, to ask questions that intimidated them.

In the second half of the twentieth century, then, the power of the frontier legend remains substantially intact, offering much, stifling much. For women, the legend did neither, and it is instructive to note that Katherine Anne Porter, utterly free of the frontier mystique, has been the region's most acclaimed writer. Others such as William Humphrey and Paul Horgan have avoided the debilitating effects of the legend by drawing on other sources. But, for many generations, most southwestern writers have worked within the cultural confines of the western ethos in a way that revealed them to be wholly intimidated by its power. Consciously or unconsciously reflecting the pastoral, masculine, and triumphantly nativistic presumptions of the unexamined frontier legend, they scarcely dared to question its limits, much less assess its intrinsic meaning. In the space of one man's lifetime—J. Frank Dobie's—the literature of the region has moved from a simplistic rendering of the oral tradition, through the first attempts to interpret that tradition, to the present inquiry into the value and meaning of the heritage itself. Dobie's life spanned those of Andy Adams, whose *Log of a Cowboy* is the most authentic account of the trail-driving experience, and Larry McMurtry, whose *Horseman, Pass By* describes much of the cultural legacy of that experience. To ask that this transition be achieved on the highest level of literary performance may be, perhaps, too much to ask of one lifetime. Certainly, in Dobie's own case, it is clear that he achieved much greater artistry in the simple act of living his own life than he did in writing about the common heritage. It is fitting that Dobie's best book should have been his posthumously published autobiography, *Some Part of Myself;* after a lifetime of "chronicling" the frontier heritage without subjecting it to searching interpretation, he found, in himself, his own best subject. The irony is extreme. Dobie—the generous, no-nonsense frontiersman who, not only as a boy, could employ cobwebs to staunch the flow of blood from a cut, but, as a man, could quote from *Midsummer Night's Dream* to justify the practice— lived out his life as a free man in the best frontier tradition. But he lived his last years separated from his beloved University of Texas because his individualistic capacity for political indignation got him fired by a board of regents composed of oilman and ranchers who prided themselves on their allegiance to the precepts of frontier individualism. In Dobie's lifetime, as on the original frontier, conformity was one of the prices of survival. Dobie, in living a free life and being punished for it by his peers, defined the limits of the heritage more accurately than all of his books.

The intuition that is here apparent could lead to a new and massively liberating literary perspective. In John Graves and Larry McMurtry, one senses something new struggling for life against the direct pull of the received heritage. But, as yet, the mainsprings of the frontier legacy remain as unexamined as in the long ago time before the appearance of Frederick Jackson Turner's frontier thesis. It is, in fact, a testament to the enormous psychological power the frontier mystique has obtained over so many of its artists and scholars that this ambiguity has been allowed to persist—for these mainsprings are obvious and require no subtlety of interpretation to fathom: the southern frontier is not "individualistic" but, rather, is one of the most rigidly conformist parts of America; the attributes of the frontier heritage—heartiness, generosity, and an unselfish openness of spirit—are qualities that are extended, in their truest sense, only to those who willingly participate in the common conformity. Violence or, at least, ostracism is visited upon these who do not. And the list of those who are excluded is broad: women, Mexicans, Negroes, Indians, the unmanly, urbanites, and like Dobie, any number of free men. Chroniclers and folklorists would do well to remember that the demonstrably valuable aspect of frontier culture will continue to masquerade as mere propaganda unless and until they are set alongside this darker legacy. And on the available evidence, novelists might do as Porter, Humphrey, and Horgan have done, and as McMurtry may be trying to do—forsake the legend for broader ground.

The southern frontier, then, has yet to produce a body of literature worthy either of its heritage or its victims. It cannot, one suspects, describe one without measuring the value of the other. Should this happen, the legend would, of course, be transformed. A painful experience for a prideful people, this—but a literary outpouring of high quality might well be one of the results. In the meantime, the legend continues to stifle more than it succors: the region's finest writers have had to find their materials in frontiers of the spirit far beyond the received heritage of the Southwest.

archetype west

William Everson

Photograph by Frank J. Thomas

Author's note: In this essay I have attempted to delineate the western archetype by examining one of its most salient features: the creative writer. Abstracting from his personal achievement I treat him as a distinct species, a phenomenon spanning several generations of western experience, to arrive as a late but authentic symbol in the pantheon of American images we have developed over our two centuries of national existence. I have sought to isolate this image in order to grasp the focus of energy which it actually represents, so that we will have a clearer understanding of how to cope when we seek to appraise the western attempt and the western achievement. My probe, therefore, is back and down, a recovery of tap root, a quest for the mysterious force that makes a region recognizable as a distinct cultural entity: the mystery of place.

I have approached the subject of western writing from this archetypal point of view because I am not able to make sense of regionalism from any other perspective. Too many writers exist who use the materials of a locale without partaking of its ethos. On the other hand I am well aware that the liability of the archetypal approach is the evasion of the issue of quality, the factor of excellence. The most archetypal writer of any region may by no means be its best one. But that is a symptom of cultural immaturity, and if a region remains vital, its archetype will continue to throw up figures of sharpening definition in the context of its subsistent regional ethos, until quality achieves parity with content—something Robert Frost appears to have accomplished in the case of New England.

Of course, regionalism has had a bad press since the ad-

William Everson, the West Coast poet, lives in Davenport, California.

vent of the Modernist movement early in this century. That movement was international in its outlook and regarded the regional accent as provincial and myopic, emphasizing content at the expense of quality, and hence constituting a threat to both culture and art. Over against this perspective I believe that the impress of place on man's artifacts is something not only authentic but absolutely ineradicable, and in affirming it I have sought to isolate the energy shaping the specific western experience. We have to make bare the basic power below the mere decorative details usually attributed to regionalism considered as an influence in art. In reaching for this source of power I have had recourse to the uses of depth psychology as it applies to collective factors, and have employed its technique to grasp the root forces with which we are dealing; chief among these is the concept of the archetype.

This concept, I take it, has been sufficiently assimilated into critical perspectives since World War II to make another attempt at definition here superfluous. Carl Jung himself was none too explicit about the matter; he suggested that the archetypes are to be known rather than defined, experienced rather than understood. Intangible psychic forces in unconscious collective life, they work as motifs that shape the substance of our responses, and become, through the accumulation of experience, repository images, established symbolic forms, figures in our consciousness to be recognized principally through their effects. It follows, therefore, that I pursue the archetype of the western writer as a recurrent motif shaping the course of the literature actually produced here, a motif evolving out of West Coast experience, and manifesting itself through local attitudes, a habit of mind resulting in practices, procedures, and approaches which eventually result in the emergence of a composite image. Consequently the question "What is the image of the western writer, and how did it get that way?" while representing a considerable oversimplification, probably states the theme of this paper in a way the non-specialist can best understand.

The problem of defining the American West as a literary region is complicated by two factors: the lateness of its development and the prevalence of secondary characteristics stemming from extraneous influences. Hollywood has both attracted and obscured the attention of the nation in a way that confuses any attempt to understand what actually constitutes the western ethos, for it has accommodated many talented writers who have created serious works even as they earned a living from the production of its scenarios. The same holds true for the academy. The great universities play host to remarkable men who produce remarkable books; but their work is usually without any relevance to underlying regional determinants whatsoever.

Of the attempts to appraise writing in the West, Edmund Wilson's *The Boys in the Back Room*[1] is best known and therefore the most serviceable, though it does not escape the temptation to divide its attention between Hollywood and the rest of purely Californian achievement. But despite this distraction his summary does typify the abiding East Coast critical feeling about West Coast writing, and in listing it I do so both to avail myself of its entry into the western spirit, and to try to show how the effects he instances are capable of an interpretation differing from the one that he, and other critics, have chosen to put upon them. Wilson summarizes:

> But, as I say, it is not merely in Los Angeles that the purposes and passion of humanity have the appearance of playing their roles in a great open-air amphitheater which lacks not only acoustics to heighten and clarify the speeches but even an attentive audience at whom they may be directed. The paisanos of Tortilla Flat also eat, love and die in a golden and boundless sunlight that never becomes charged with their energies; and the rhapsodies of William Saroyan, diffused in this non-vibrant air, pass without repercussions. Even the monstrous, the would-be elemental, the would-be barbaric tragedies which Robinson Jeffers heaps up are all a little like amorphous cloud-dramas that eventually fade out to sea, leaving only on our faces a slight moisture and in our ears an echo of hissing. It is probably a good deal too easy to be a nihilist on the coast at Carmel: your very negation is a negation of nothing.[2]

On the contrary it is a good deal too easy for even the best critic to dismiss as irrelevant that for which he happens to have little affinity. The objection here is not lack of quality, though it is implied; but, specifically, lack of content, of substance. What is this "nothing" the Californian is supposed to be the nihilist of? Why does he return to it so persistently, seeking to hew it out, give shape to it, mold it into definition? These are questions this essay will seek to answer.

Though Wilson in conclusion does try to mitigate his harshness of verdict, he cannot conceal his antipathies:

> In describing their special mentality, I do not, of course, in the least, mean to belittle their interest or value. The writing on the coast, as I say, may seem difficult to bring into focus with the writing that we know in the East. But California, since we took it from the Mexicans, has always presented itself to Americans as one of the strangest and most exotic of their exploits; and it is the function of the literary artist to struggle with new phases of experience, and to try to give them beauty and sense.[3]

The westerner will agree that his writing is more often than not out of focus with that of the East; but that California is little more than an American exploit, something taken from the Mexicans, and that strangeness and the exotic between them sum up its relevance to the national experience, can never constitute the way he sees himself.

Rather he feels that his situation as *term* of the westward migration places him at the center, rather than on the periphery, of the American experience. It is no accident that the first book of the Coast's foremost philosopher, Josiah Royce, "the most influential American philosopher of his day," is titled *California—A Study of American Character*. The Californian knows that the expansiveness of attitude in the West is simply the well-known national expansiveness carried to its ultimate. As the typical American characteristic it has always alarmed commentators of formalist persuasion, who have regarded it at best as an awkward phase of the national development, hopefully outgrown.

The westerner knows better. He knows that "The American," in the words of the late Perry Miller of Harvard, "or at least the American artist, cherishes in his inmost being the impulse to reject completely the gospel of civilization, in order to guard with resolution the savagery of his heart."[4] If the result on the Coast has been, as Royce concedes, that "the Californian has too often come to love mere fullness of life and to lack reverence for the relations of life,"[5] that is hardly surprising, given a nation that struck up for a new world precisely because the relations of life elsewhere were being cultivated to the stultification of its fullness.

And the centrality of the West to the total American experience, with its melodramatic emphasis on "fullness of life," is incontestably evident in the national preoccupation with the popular "western." A powerful nostalgic need for a great American epic conceived around the model is deeply felt. Many years ago T. K. Whipple, a classmate of Wilson's at Princeton, called for precisely such an attempt. In an essay "The Myth of the Old West" he rebuked American writers for hankering after European refinements and declared, "To date the western story has not done all it might for us, because it has never received adequate representation. And no symbol can exert much force unless it is somehow objectified and worthily embodied." The story of the West, he avows, should be "the Great American Epic— does not everyone agree? Yet does not everyone doubt that the epic is still unsung? A strange situation, surely, when the United States is full of able writers, and when these writers are unanimous in their neglect of what is called the greatest of themes." And he goes on to ask for an in-depth depiction of frontier life cast in the heroic mold:

> What really happened to these men? All America lies at the end of the wilderness road, and our past is not a dead past but still lives in us; thus the question is momentous. But it has not been answered. Our forbears had civilization inside them-

selves, the wild outside. We live in the civilization they created, but within us the wilderness still lingers. What they dreamed, we live, and what they lived, we dream.[6]

This is true. But precisely because it is true the "momentous question" is met in realization rather than in recovery. The Epic of the Old West will not be written by a westerner. Every significant writer of the West wrestles with the here and now. He can do no other. It is the signature of his truth that he has been compelled to register the impact of its power on his own time.

"I am struck in California," wrote George Santayana in 1911, "by the deep and almost religious affection which people have for nature and by the sensitiveness they show for its influence . . . It is their spontaneous substitute for articulate art and articulate religion."[7] These words, written by yet another eminent philosopher when the century was still young, will serve as a first probe into the archetype of the peculiarly western literary attitude. The Californian himself, however, tends to think of formal art and formal religion as themselves the substitutes, surrogates for their root-force in the human soul, stand-ins for the primal and more deeply authentic impulse of these things that live behind and support their formalizations. Furthermore, he feels that this pantheism is not only the basic Californian or western point of view, but is essentially American, is indeed *the* characteristic American religious and aesthetic feeling. Whipple confirmed it as the prime ingredient in our national religious attitude, but he placed it as deriving from European romanticism, where it was masked under a "love of nature" craze:

> The experience is accompanied by a heightening of consciousness, a sense of freedom and enlargement; it is an ecstasy. Those in whom it is frequent tend to become mystics and pantheists, to develop a religion of nature worship. This type of

213

religious experience, common everywhere in the nineteenth century, is almost the only kind to find expression in American literature. If one judged by our literature alone, that is, one would say that the only genuine religion the United States has had has been nature worship.[8]

But de Tocqueville, with his customary penetration, pointed to a political attribution. Back at the beginning of the nature craze he identified it with the idea of democracy, so that both the craze and the philosophical theory emerge as adjuncts of the egalitarian attitude itself:

> In the democracies the idea of unity so possesses man and is sought by him so generally that if he thinks he has found it, he readily yields himself to that belief. Not content with the discovery that there is nothing in the world but a creation and a Creator, he is still embarrassed by this primary division of things and seeks to expand and simplify his conception by including God and the universe in one great whole.[9]

The East Coast provinces, however, did not begin as democracies; they began as colonies of European derivation, and to this day manifest a residual hierarchical disposition, however diffused by its American transplantation. But after the establishment of our independent constitutional democracy the shift westward proceeded without such underlying suppositions, so that the westerner emerges, in this regard at least, a cut above his East Coast counterpart. Not only so but this unconscious attitude put him more in line with the perspectives of the American Indian and hence closer to the roots of the land. Certainly the frontiersman's familiar adoption of Indian garb was no mere romantic imitation, but sprang directly from a life-style conforming to the aboriginal's democratic state of existence, which in spirit and practice ran far deeper than that of the citizens who supplanted him. A recent commentator has noted:

But quite aside from the novelty interest that their discovery had generated, the more advanced Indian tribes could hand out lessons in democracy to both the European and American continents in the sixteenth and seventeenth centuries. The Chief Kings of the East Coast tribes did not govern by any hereditary or divine right. They were elected to their positions only after they had demonstrated their fitness to rule. "They were kings by the will of the people—not by the Grace of God." It was this that inspired the ideals of "government by the consent of the governed," first put into words by Locke, and later incorporated, in modified form, by Jefferson in the Declaration of Independence.[10]

Modified indeed. Mari Sandoz shows how adulterated in spirit the white man's version was to prove in direct encounter with native practice. In their dealings with the Plains Indians the white administrators:

> . . . came to the Big Council and asked that the Indians make one head chief for the Lakotas, as the Great Father was head of the whites, so the two men could talk together for all their people.
> The Indians held their eagle-wing fans between their faces and the one speaking, not wishing to hear these words. It was not so easy to do this thing that was asked. The Lakotas were not the men to follow like pack mares as it seemed the whites did. Today they might listen to this one, tomorrow to that, or to none at all, for they were free men.[11]

The frontiersman, then, came by his buckskins naturally. Symbolically speaking leather is assimilable to blood, and its wearing to immolation, apocalyptic intensity. Fringes are assimilable to hair, and abundant hair, worn long and free, is assimilable to spontaneity, an unstructured approach to reality. For while structure always emphasizes relationships, the lack of structure emphasizes "fullness of life," in Royce's phrase, an increase in existential intensity culminating in apotheosis, the supreme accent of signification. Thus the Indian's "happy hunting ground" is not simply a place where game is of blissfully easy access. Rather it is an existentially situated *event* where the apotheosis of the kill is prolonged without diminution, something like the Christian's predication of heaven as a continuous rapture in the beatific vision of God.*

This brings us to the situation of the western writer. The European artist responded to universal crisis by interiorizing apotheosis and securing liberation through alienation, as we see in Baudelaire. The western writer, following the lead of the frontiersman, who, as conformism rigidified behind him was impelled into a deepening penetration of the wilderness, responded by transmuting the apotheotic quest into correspondingly elemental literary forms. This was a radically different recourse than that utilized by the hyper-sophistication of European art, and provides an alternative to the endemic crisis of consciousness not available to the Old World; and Whitman, who was from European perspectives a true

---

* It follows that after the concept of the archetype, the concept of apotheosis is the most decisive idea in this essay. By it I mean that point in an evolving process at which its intrinsic potentiality achieves not only actuation but transcendence—radical realization manifested in an instant of quintessential truth. All processes, be they never so horizontal, are destined to sometime, somehow, achieve a vertical accent, and this accent is the nucleus of apotheosis. For the vertical factor is ineradicable; it provides the point of stress that endows horizontal continuity with definition and hence with meaning.

Now it is apparent that whereas hierarchical cultures tend to structure out the vertical element against the unremitting deferral of apotheosis, democracies constantly seek to precipitate apotheosis in the here and now. They were born of the rigidification of hierarchy, and they are compelled constantly to precipitate new apotheoses to recharge their extreme horizontally with meaning. In American politics the party conventions are essentially enthusiastic attempts to precipitate apotheosis. Like primitive fertility orgies they are meant to liberate from the guts of the constituency the new being, the candidate who, as hero and redeemer, can deliver the nation from its leveling inertia.

man of the West, became its epitome. This solution, so viable and so "natural," explains why European critics to this day sing the praises of autochthonous American writers like Jack London while disdaining the supreme efforts of American stylists to equal French or German or Italian subtlety.

Now it is apparent that any strong preoccupation with apotheosis means that violence is bound to emerge as a positive, if unconscious, value. Its unparalleled effectiveness in precipitating a kind of paroxysm of sentient consciousness decrees that this be so. From such presuppositions it can be no surprise that death, maiming, and sexual anguish emerge as the foremost precipitators. As our journalism and our literature attest, they continue to occupy the forefront of our consciousness. A simulated violence becomes the benign agency through which transcendence is first offered and finally effected.

For this displacement from the level of action to that of contemplation does not denote a diminution or substitution. It pertains rather to a kind of

---

Historical Christianity, born of the impasse of Judaism under the Roman repression, retained its democratic, essentially anarchistic, character so long as the Parousia was expected imminently; but when that hope diminished was compelled to develop an hierarchial structure to preserve value against the winnowing onslaught of time. Revivalistic Protestantism reintroduced the primacy of apotheosis as central to Christian life.

But with the birth of industrialism in the modern world the social structure narrowed and grew more mechanical. It produced first the industrial masses and then the middle class millions, horizontally imposing an unreflecting conformism on all phases of collective endeavor. Then it was that the mantle of heroic consciousness passed to the artist, enabling him to achieve, through the transcendence of aesthetic form, the apotheosis that delivers the somnolent soul of modern man from the fixity of its inertia. What the political hero found less and less available in the mechanical density of modern politics, the artist maverick of the bourgeoisie found more and more possible in the phantasizing role of the imagination, and the illimitable university of aesthetic form.

strategic increase. Conventional morality decries the presence of violence in art because it is unable to grasp it in its quality of contemplative fitness. It is seen solely as a stimulus to action. The artist, however, knows that firmly situated in the domain of the aesthetic, violence elevates fragmentation from chaos into transcendence, subsumes the rupture of material forms into a wholeness. The American Indian himself clearly understood this relationship between two levels of reality. In his recourse to spontaneous poetry before episodes of great moment, he accommodated all the liability of the sentient condition into a teleology of symbolic truth.

For example, when Old Torino, a Navajo priest, was about to relate the story of creation, he made the following pronouncement, addressing as it were his own conscience, solemnly affirming that he was going to tell the truth as he understood it. And he said:

> I am ashamed before the earth;
> I am ashamed before the heavens;
> I am ashamed before the dawn;
> I am ashamed before the evening twilight;
> I am ashamed before the blue sky;
> I am ashamed before the sun.
> *I am ashamed before that standing within*
> *me which speaks with me.*
> Some of these things are always looking at
> me.
> I am never out of sight.
> Therefore I must tell the truth.
> *I hold my word tight in my breast.*

Margot Astrov, who quotes him in her introduction to *The Winged Serpent,* a collection of American Indian prose and poetry, observes:

> This declaration is nothing but a succinct statement of the Indian's relation to the "word" as the directing agency that stands powerfully behind every "doing," as the reality above all tangible

reality. It is the thought and the word that stand face to face with the conscience of the native, not the deed.[12]

Now these sentiments are clearly the credo of the western writer, intoxicated by his obsession with violence, and searching within its matrix for the clue to liberation from it. In the words of Old Torino he recognizes his own creative ordeal as the route to apotheosis.

Old Torino's spontaneous poem has for its support the awesome authority of a true shaman, but it is the ancestor of many an anonymous Beat poem tacked up in the coffeehouses of San Francisco. The visiting Ivy League professor quite understandably smiles at these naïve efforts, for from the hierarchial point of view their formlessness is fatal. In hierarchy, structure is all. But hierarchy plays very little place in the field of composition from which such poems spring. The onslaught of intensity has taken the place of structure as a normative value.

But can intensity without structure ever produce apotheosis? A generation of New Critics has denied it, and this denial is the force behind Edmund Wilson's jeer of a "California vacuum." It would be simple to retort that the quarrel has to do with an anterior question: What constitutes structure? But such challenges, once so vital, have become, in our world of social revolution, painfully academic. For the attempt to outstrip structure in the quest for apotheosis goes on, and will go on, despite all denials. It is actually the secret quest, the inner impulse, of democracy itself. Its urge is not negative, the simple denial of the uses of restriction, but positive, the effort to subsume the contour of structure in each constitutive law-of-existence that underlies a given phenomenon, whether object or event, entity or experience. What is being celebrated today is not disillusionment with law, only the law that completes and distinguishes, "finalizes." But the law that conceives and originates, this law is craved, and when found, is honored. Of course all creativity

219

utilizes both emphases, but it is where the accent is placed, or rather where the unconscious obsessions are rooted, that constitutes the ongoing struggle in the history of art.

At any rate this is the basic element that provides the relevance of writing in the West, and constitutes its deepest challenge to the nation as a whole. Two decades after Wilson's observation Allen Ginsberg's poem *Howl,* written in San Francisco, was likened to "a scream from a paddy wagon." Even a scream has structure, as the depth psychologists show; but it is a structure relating to the onslaught of incipience rather than to the finality of cloture. Old Torino's verse is not without its own kind of finality, but that is not what we go to it for. Rather it gives us the jet or spurt of precipitate energy in its act of spontaneous emergence. In both poems incipience is all.

We received our native pantheism, then, if de Tocqueville is correct, with our coming of age, our constitutional democracy. But even before that ordination another potent source can be seen in our Puritan religious heritage. This we received with our mother's milk. Perry Miller writes:

> What is persistent, from the covenant theology (and from the heretics against the covenant) to Edwards and to Emerson is the Puritan's effort to confront, face to face, the image of a blinding divinity in the physical universe, and to look upon that universe without the intermediacy of ritual . . . Edwards sought the "images or shadows of divine things" in nature, but could not trust his discoveries because he knew man to be cut off from full communion with the created order because of his inherent depravity. But Emerson, having decided that man is unfallen (except as his sensibilities have been blunted by civilization), announced that there is no inherent separation between the mind and the thing, that in reality they leap to embrace each other. Yes, that will do for the textbooks, or for students' note-

books. Yet true though it be, such an account leaves out the basic continuance: the incessant drive of the Puritan to learn how, and how most ecstatically, he can hold any sort of communion with the environing wilderness.[13]

Emerson wrote before the Gold Rush, but he might well be its true instigator. It has been suggested that Fremont's bold expedition to the Coast in the 1840s began a movement that was the material component to Transcendentalism's expansive tenets. This burgeoning spirit had been precipitated by the densening of civilization in the East, and the compensatory liberation offered by nature. With our environmental problems today it sobers us to recall that already at Walden Thoreau felt threatened. At any rate it is certain that the charge of such ideas, carried West, found in the staggering immensity of the landscape a heightened appropriateness.

For the West was not just unpopulated, it was, and remains, geographically vast. Quite apart from the civilization factor, the prospective western situation differs in scale, is essentially panoramic. This is not a mere literary property, something stimulated in western writers by an occasional visit to Yosemite. Royce, writing from Cambridge forty years after Fremont's trek, could still attest to it:

> In the gently mountainous regions of even the more rugged of our Eastern states one may wander for many days, and see many picturesque or imposing landscapes, without getting any clear notion of the complex water system of the country through which he journeys. In most such hilly regions, if he climbs to some promising summit, hoping to command therefrom a general view of the land about him, he often sees in the end nothing but a collection of gracefully curving hills similar to the one that he has chosen. Winding valleys divide these hills with their endlessly complex and often broken lines. He gets no sense of the ground plan of the region. It seems a mass of hills, and that is all. Painfully, with the aid of

his map, he identifies this or that landmark and so at last comprehends his surroundings, which, after all, he never really sees.

The distinction between this and the point of observation in the West is pronounced:

> But in the typical central Californian landscape, as viewed from any commanding summit, the noble frankness of nature shows one at a glance the vast plan of the country. From hills only eighteen hundred or two thousand feet high, on the Contra Costa side of San Francisco Bay, you may on any clear day see, to the westward, the blue line of the ocean, the narrow Golden Gate, the bay itself at your feet, the rugged hills of Marin County beyond, and the smoky outlines of San Francisco south of the Gate; you may follow with the eye, to the southward, the far-reaching lower arm of the great bay, and may easily find the distant range of the Santa Cruz Mountains; while to the eastward and northward you may look over the vast plains of the interior valley and dwell upon the great blue masses of the Sierra Nevada rising far beyond them and culminating in the snowy summits that all summer long would gleam across to you through the hot valley haze.[14]

All things taken together, therefore, it is not remarkable that in the West, during the second half of the century, what was being prepared was a pantheistic spirit of unprecedented scale, nor that, as a consequence of this rupturing of normative consciousness, what was emerging was an equally specific adjunct—the infusion of an awesome and illimitable violence. For here the unconscious transcendentalism of the newcomers experienced Nature not as refuge, as Thoreau experienced it at Walden, but as *encounter*. We see it first in *Two Years Before the Mast*. Dana starts the long voyage home from California and rounding the Horn encounters the sea as terrible. D. H. Lawrence puts his finger on the essence:

It is the story of a man pitted in conflict against the sea, the vast, almost omnipotent element. In contest with this cosmic enemy, man finds his further ratification, his further ideal vindication. He comes out victorious, but not till the sea has tortured his living, integral body, and made him pay something for his triumph in consciousness.[15]

The scale of conflict in the West is made evident here, as is its character of mystic encounter, but nevertheless we are in the presence of an important distinction. Dana, writing before Emerson, remains, as Lawrence points out, critical and conscious before the magnitude of the natural fact. The hierarchical point of view prevails. And this would be true of many notable writers in the West over the century to follow, right up to the present day. But it is a characteristic that sets them apart in probing the archetype which is the subject of this study.

What would have to jell, evidently, before the true Californian, the true westerner, could emerge was recognition and identification. These converge in the key term *participation,* which conforms to the factor of "fullness." For the westerner, regardless how universal his scope, truly belongs to his region, and celebrates it as he celebrates himself. Of course this attitude displaces the normative critical one of *discrimination,* which conforms to "relationship," i.e., measure and structure, but it is a mistake to dismiss such fullness as sentimental. Somewhere in his journals Thoreau observes that: "Nature is reported not by him who goes forth consciously as an observer, but in the fullness of life. To such a one she rushes to make her report." For in heightened participation there is no relapse of the critical faculty. It is simply that this faculty is suffused by the presence of the Other, and operates beyond its objectivity as a state of transfigured possession. No narrowly Californian susceptibility induced by a sun-drenched lassitude, as Wilson infers, this is a universal correlate. Lionel Trilling writes:

223

The men of the anti-rationalist tradition mock the mind's pretensions and denounce its restrictiveness; but they are themselves the agents of the most powerful thought. They do not of course really reject mind at all, but only mind as it is conceived by respectable society. "I learned the Torah from all the limbs of my teacher," said one of the Hasidim. They think with their sensations, their emotions, and, some of them, with their sex. While denouncing intellect, they shine forth in a mental blaze of energy which manifests itself in syntax, epigram, and true discovery.[16]

Such illumination at its highest is religious mysticism, but before it could achieve that perfection in the West the artist had to work through the more obvious and superficial mental adjuncts that accrete around it, and which complicate its substance in the generally derided cult of mindlessness. Certain solutions were already worked out by the American Indians across their long continental habituation, but their example, while adopted by resourceful frontiersmen, was spurned by the hoard of immigrants plunging West. The cultural overcharge from European sources was by then so thick as to enforce a real myopia in the encountering mind. Mari Sandoz writes:

> In the 1820s the 1840s the buffalo Indians were considered the most romantic of peoples, drawing visitors from everywhere. Such men as Prince Paul of Wurttenberg, Prince Maximilan, Sir William Drummond Stewart, Catlin, Parkman, and hundreds of others came to ride in the surrounds, to eat roast hump ribs, to study and become one with this great Red Hunter.
> But that was before the white man wanted these Indian's lands. The discovery of gold and the rise of economic and political unrest over much of the civilized world, with millions of men hungry for a new start, changed that, and suddenly the romantic Red Hunter was a dirty, treacherous, bloodthirsty savage standing in the way of progress, in the path of manifest destiny.[17]

As a consequence, those writers who were earliest explorers of the western milieu operated under the critical predispositions of the East and were interested mainly in interpreting the singularities of frontier life to the folk back home. Bret Harte and Mark Twain will serve for many lesser talents. Bret Harte is credited with beginning a new American fiction in 1868, ushering in "the wild humor and the wilder poetry of California."[18] He was a most able storyteller but not a major writer. Mark Twain was both, but he could not do for the West what he was ultimately capable of because he was destined to become the voice of another regional archetype altogether: the Mississippi. For the gods withhold their favors till the moment of apotheosis arises. And when it does, when the moment for a *Huckleberry Finn* at last occurs, their gifts are lavish.

For in literature as in war the spirit, the daimon, the archetype, whatever its point of orientation, is always trying to find its vehicle, its voice. Thus in the Civil War the Northern Army ran through commander after commander ineffectually until a Grant emerged to focus its vast energies into an invincible weapon. Early America had spawned its various writers, but it was not until the mid-nineteenth century that she found her Melville and her Whitman. The evidence is there for the world to see in *Moby Dick* and *Leaves of Grass*. It took a half century more for the process to crystallize out on the Coast, and then only tentatively. *The Octopus* of Frank Norris gave us our *Moby Dick;* but in poetry no artifact comparable to Whitman's *Leaves* at that time emerged.

This is puzzling because it is poetry rather than prose which is the natural vehicle of pantheism. Clearly the impact of *Moby Dick* is closer to epic poetry than to narrative fiction. This is not true of *The Octopus*. The *scale* of epic is there, and other powerful factors associated with it. But Norris's achievement as a writer is far greater in the delineation of graphic episode than in his poetic overreach. Some of the incidents of direct action in *The Octo-*

pus are unsurpassed in American literature—the shoot-out at the irrigation canal, for instance. But the same cannot be said of his attempts to register the transcendental implications of the regional base of that action. For all Norris's achievement (and for so young a man it is impressive) when he died in 1904, the West was still waiting for its poet. Certainly the birth ordeal was begun, but somewhere along the line gestation has miscarried.

In tracking the course of an archetype, however, a miscarriage is as instructive as an authentic birth. The following passage from Louis Untermeyer's survey of American poetry points to the western ethos and underscores its frustration in the paucity of talent available to it for expression:

> To the loose swagger of the West, two other men added their diverse contributions. Edward Rowland Sill, cut short just as his work was gaining headway and strength, brought to it a gentle radicalism, a calm and cultured honesty; Joaquin Miller, rushing to the other extreme, theatricalized and exaggerated all he touched. He shouted platitudes at the top of his voice. His lines boomed with the pomposity of a brass band; floods, fires, hurricanes, extravagantly blazing sunsets, Amazonian women, the thunder of a herd of buffaloes —all were unmercifully piled up. And yet, even in its most blatant *fortissimos,* Miller's poetry occasionally captured the grandeur of his surroundings, the spread of the Sierras, the lavish energy of the Western World.[19]

One opines that the cultural matrix was not yet dense enough to form a compression sufficient to canalize and focus the maundering archetypal spirit.

More important for our purpose is the evidence that the archetype has in fact emerged, and we had better not overlook it, for in the analysis of archetypal configuration the factor of inception is crucial. Every inception holds within it the potentiality of an ultimate, which requires only time to attain. Thus

Miller's low place in American poetry (and for that matter in Californian poetry) cannot permit us to ignore the fact of his emergence, for he introduces what we are seeking to identify in everything but talent. And the history of literature cautions us to be very careful in denying him even that. Too many poets have been written off because of reaction to their personalities or their réclame only to stand up from their graves and reassert themselves after their detractors are no more. Still, from the point of view of our present perspectives, Miller can be accredited with hardly a single achieved poem. Rather for us his claim is confirmed in his career alone:

> His first book (*Specimens*) appears in 1868, his second (*Joaquin et al.*) . . . from which he took his name, in 1869. No response—not even from "the bards of San Francisco Bay" to whom he had dedicated the latter volume. He resolves to quit America, to go to the land that has always been the nursing ground of poets. "Three months later, September 1, 1870, I was kneeling at the grave of Burns. I really expected to die there in the land of my fathers." He arrives in London, unheralded, unknown. He takes his manuscripts to one publisher after another with the same negative results. Finally, with a pioneer desperation, he prints privately one hundred copies of his *Pacific Poems,* sending them out for review. Sensation! The reversal of Miller's fortunes is one of the most startling in all literature. The reviews are a series of superlatives, the personal tributes still more fervid. He becomes famous overnight. He is feted, lauded, lionized; he is ranked as an equal of Browning, given a dinner by the Pre-Raphaelites, acclaimed as "the great interpreter of America," the "Byron of Oregon!"

Untermeyer then seeks to explain how this astonishing reversal of fortune could happen, and finds no difficulty in it:

> His dramatic success in England is easily explained. He brought to the calm air of literary

227

London a breath of the great winds of the plain. The more he exaggerated his crashing effects, the louder he roared, the better the English public liked it. When he entered Victorian parlours in his velvet jacket, hip-boots and flowing hair, childhood visions of the "wild and wooley Westerner" were realized and the very bombast of his work was glorified as "typically American."[20]

Perhaps. But Stuart P. Sherman does not see it in so harsh a light. Having conceded that Miller had indeed "caught the fancy of the London literary tasters, who are always hospitably inclined to real curiosities from overseas, and welcome a degree of crudity in a trans-Atlantic writer as evidence that he is genuinely American," Sherman nevertheless appraises the notices themselves more soberly:

> The reviewers, in general, touch lightly upon his obvious inequalities, blemishes, slips in grammar, and faults in metre; some of them apologize slightly for his frontier culture, more recognize it boldly as the source of his power, and proceed to speak in glowing terms of his freshness of theme and treatment, of his tropical color, his myth-making power, his fluent, rapid, and melodious verse, and "the supreme independence, the spontaneity, the all-pervading passion, the unresting energy, and the prodigal wealth of imagery which stamp the poetry before us."[21]

Truly, the archetype is speaking here, and Miller, in serving its embodiment, is reaping its rewards. Reading the last quotation one wonders: Is this reviewer talking about Joaquin Miller or Walt Whitman? At the time, both were anathema in America, for William Rossetti, brother of the poet, had just introduced the poems of Whitman to Englishmen with equal superlatives, and when Miller got back home he paid for it. Sherman writes:

> The traditional superciliousness of the East towards the West and a resentful unwillingness to have this uncouth frontiersman accepted abroad

as a leading or even a significant representative of American letters—these not altogether lovely notes are strident in a review in the New York *Nation* in 1871: "It is the 'sombereros' and 'serapes' and 'gulches,' we suppose, and the other Californian and Arizonian properties, which have caused our English friends to find in Mr. Miller a truly American poet. He is Mr. William Rossetti's latest discovery. We trust, however, that we have no monopoly of ignorance and presumption and taste for Byronism. In other climes, also there have been firmilians, and men need not be born in California to have the will in excess of the understanding and the understanding ill informed. There are people of all nationalities whom a pinch more brains and a trifle more of diffidence would not hurt."[22]

These observations are important because they show the power inherent in the western archetype, its capacity to provoke superlatives of assent and dissent, to create adoration or disgust, ecstasy or revulsion. "The will in excess of the understanding and the understanding ill informed." There, in a nutshell, is the East's immemorial indictment of the West. Many other descendants of Joaquin Miller, artists of greater intrinsic stature, would suffer both the applause and the denigration, even as they drew to themselves the glare of attraction that accrues from the extremity of their position.

More specifically it was all to happen again fifty years later, though in New York rather than London. There would be the same disappointment of two unsuccessful early works, the same private printing of a few copies sent out for review, the same sensational breakthrough in a deeply knowledgeable and sophisticated publishing establishment. The concurrence, the continuity, witnesses to the archetype in play. As for Joaquin Miller we can say that if he testifies principally to a literary abortion, something else was nonetheless at work in support: the spirit of place. As Untermeyer concedes, his poetry did not fail to capture "the grandeur of his surroundings, the spread of the Sierras, the lavish energy of the Western World."[23]

Actually, it isn't too surprising that its first real manifestation in the West should occur at the level of the persona rather than that of realized achievement. By the 1820s James Fenimore Cooper had immortalized the figure of the frontiersman in the Leatherstocking Tales, and when the image went West, it was almost certain to achieve a kind of pre-figurement in a literary personality. This is because the ethos itself valorizes participation over discrimination which means that the emerging archetype demands authenticity of life style as the basis for expression. We can say that the archetype is clarifying its image even though it has not yet found its voice.

Critics speak of the two moments of flowering in nineteenth-century Californian literary history, the Bret Harte–Mark Twain period of the Gold Rush with Joaquin Miller for its poet; and at the end of the century the Frank Norris–Jack London revival with Edwin Markham for *its* poet. I want to introduce Markham by pointing first to the fictional poet based on him who Norris introduced in *The Octopus*. His name is Presley, and though often spoken of as ineffectual, his essential passivity and accessibility enable him to survive the violence and permit Norris to use him as the key observer, and in some ways the judge, of virtually all the action in the novel. Early in the book we are given the substance of Presley's literary ambition. It is obvious that here we stand in the presence of the archetype itself:

> It was his insatiable ambition to write verse. But up to this time, his work had been fugitive, ephemeral, a note here and there, heard, appreciated, and forgotten. He was in search of a subject; something magnificent, he did not know exactly what; some vast, tremendous theme, heroic, terrible, to be unrolled in all the thundering progression of hexameters.[24]

It is typical of Romanticism that the subject takes

precedence over the executive powers of the writer, as in Classicism. The Romantic poet looks to the subject to move him, sweep him off his feet and into dionysiac transcendence of his own limitations:

> But whatever he wrote, and whatever fashion, Presley was determined that his poem would be of the West, that world's frontier of Romance, where a new race, a new people—hardy, brave, and passionate—were building an empire; where the tumulous life ran like fire from dawn to dark, and from dark to dawn again, primitive, brutal, honest, and without fear. Something (to his idea not much) had been done to catch at that life in passing, but its poet had not yet arisen. The few sporadic attempts, thus he told himself, had only touched the keynote. He strove for the diapason, the great song that should embrace in itself a whole epoch, a complete era, the voice of an entire people, wherein all people would be included —they and their legends, their folklore, their fightings, their loves and their lusts, their blunt, grim humour, their stoicisms under stress, their adventures, their treasures found in a day and gambled in a night, their direct rude speech, their generosity and cruelty, their heroism and bestiality, their religion and profanity, their self-sacrifice and obscenity—a true and fearless setting forth of a passing phase of history, uncompromising, sincere; each group in its proper environment; the valley, the plain, and the mountain; the ranch, the range, and the mine—all this, all the traits and types of every community from the Dakotas to the Mexicos, from Winnipeg to Guadalupe, gathered together, swept together, welded and riven together in one single mighty song, the Song of the West. That was what he dreamed, while things without names—thoughts for which no man had yet invented words, terrible formless shapes, vague figures, colossal, monstrous, distorted—whirled at a gallop through his imagination.[25]

It is true that Norris wrote specifically to show how the insubstantiality of that vision is exploded before the iron actuality of economic life, one of the almost casual byproducts of the stranglehold the railroads held on the wheat ranches of the West. But the fact that this preview is almost a paraphrase of Edmund Wilson's intuitions about the grandiose aspirations of the western sensibility shows how true to the mark it actually was. This truth goes deep, and is only a western version of a perennial American myth, one which poets will be trying to realize as long as there is an America. William Carlos Williams' long poem *Paterson* was written to the score, and Pound's *Cantos* effect it for Western Civilization as a whole. Following Williams, Charles Olson made his own attempt in the *Maximus Poems* to register the entire life of a community and a region. The difference in these attempts and Presley's vision is only one of range, and is territorial. Norris understood perfectly that the scale of the imagination was hinged directly on the scale of the western earth itself.[26] From a height Presley surveys the vast ranches around him, only to find them made small as he gazes:

> Then, as the imagination itself expanded under the stimulus of that measureless range of vision, even those great ranches resolved themselves into mere foreground, mere accessories, irrelevant details. Beyond the fine line of the horizons, over the curve of the globe, the shoulder of the earth, were other ranches, equally vast, and beyond these, others, and beyond these, still others, the immensities multiplying, lengthening out vast and expanded, Titanic, before the eye of the mind, flagellated with heat, quivering and shimmering under the sun's red eye. At long intervals, a faint breath of wind out of the south passed slowly over the levels of the baked and empty earth, accentuating the silence, marking off the stillness. It seemed to exhale from the land itself, a prolonged sigh as of deep fatigue. It was the season after the harvest, and the great earth, the mother, after its period of reproduction, its pains of labour, delivered of the fruit of its loins, slept the sleep of exhaustion, infinite repose of the colos-

sus, benignant, eternal, strong, the nourisher of nations, the feeder of an entire world.[27]

Nothing touches the subliminal responses of a poet like maternal immensity, and nothing is more baffling in terms of specific application. Presley is both exalted and confused.

> Ha! Here was his epic, his inspiration, his West, his thundering progression of hexameters. A sudden uplift, a sense of exhilaration, of physical exaltation appeared abruptly to sweep Presley from his feet. As from a point high above the world, he seemed to dominate a universe, a whole order of things. He was dizzied, stunned, stupefied, his morbid super-sensitive mind reeling, drunk with the intoxication of mere immensity. Stupendous ideas for which there were no names drove headlong through his brain. Terrible, formless shapes, vague figures, gigantic, monstrous, distorted, whirled at a gallop through his imagination.[28]

It is important to notice that twice Norris closes the vision of Presley with the rise of negative images as counterparts to the glimmering ideality of the mind. It will be in terms of these, rather than of the former, that apotheosis, when it at last is given, will be offered.

A bit further on in the book Norris will have Presley repudiate his vision when, through experiencing direct social violence, he will have discovered "The People." But this repudiation does not ring true. In the passages above, what Norris is trying to communicate is too compelling with him to be denied. One gets the feeling from them that the poet in him is relatively unconscious and undeveloped, not thoroughly articulate. He surges toward the rhythms of exaltation but because of the factual orientation of his mind they are never really developed. Actually he was coming very close. Even such passages as those above, in the hands of a good editor could have been pruned into the litheness that characterizes his fictional episodes and his psychological grasp. But his secular convictions were more positively developed than his vague religious and pantheistic yearnings. He realized where the higher octave lay —his whole book demonstrates it—but he did not have the religious conviction to rise to it. And perhaps at the turn of the century the religious atmosphere was as yet too flaccid to be compellingly utilized in creative expression.

And yet if this be true how does one explain the Norris that we actually have? For if *The Octopus* is not as accomplished a work as *Moby Dick*, it is definitely in the same class. As a novelist Norris is certainly no less assured than Melville—a comparison of the opening pages of both works is convincing of this—it is as poet that he is outranked. For it seems evident that in *Moby Dick* the poet is in advance of the novelist, whereas in *The Octopus* the reverse is true. Thus the factuality of Norris's mind is quite adequate to the work of direct action and social delineation, whereas when he tries to serve the diamon in a manner consonant with its impulse, though he does not altogether fail, he badly falters.

The answer is partly explained in the fact that in Melville's time the ancient antagonist for the American was still the Wilderness—the elemental cunning, the fierce obdurate hostility to man latent in all unspoiled nature—whereas by Norris's time, after the continent was subdued, the antagonist had become not the Whale, but the System. And the encounter with the system was better engaged in prose than in verse. For this reason his attempt to render the celebration of the elemental in *The Octopus* has a strained inflated character which his decisiveness in coping with the Southern Pacific Railroad does not.

As one reads on, one muses that perhaps the difference is that in *The Octopus* the secondary symbol corresponding to the Whale is the Wheat, and there is little resistance in this symbol—nothing of the elemental cunning and brute malevolence and awe which Melville found in pitting against the Whale.

We feel we have encountered the underlying problem of pantheism as a literary context, a problem we sense also in Whitman. Lacking an inherent duality, pantheism is unable to utilize the full potential of polarity. Everything tends to bleed away in a vast indistinguishable awe of the All. Thus pantheists are generally constrained in their aesthetic strategy to turn to lesser opponents. It comes as no surprise, we conclude, to find the ancient metaphysical struggle shifted to the modern social one.

And then, suddenly, it happens. In the final chapter of the book the passivity of the wheat is dramatically converted from an inert organic abstraction to a cunning and triumphant antagonist. S. Berhman in his cupidity stumbles and is plunged into the hold of a ship being loaded with the loose, free-flowing grain, grain which he exploited from the apparently infinitely passive earth. In a trice that passivity is converted to living malevolence. Like our subjugated earth that endures tyranny until man's own apathy possesses him, and he succumbs in bemusement to his own success, then the underlying instinct finds its moment. And Norris rises to meet it. Listen to the pulse of implication as the writer in his immemorial role of definer and register of consequence meets his long-sought creative opportunity:

> Then began that terrible dance of death; the man dodging, doubling, squirming, hunted from one corner to another, the wheat slowly, inexorably flowing, rising, spreading to every angle, to every nook and cranny. It reached his middle. Furious and with bleeding hands and broken nails, he dug his way out to fall backward, all but exhausted, gasping for breath in the dust-thickened air. Roused again by the slow advance of the tide, he leaped up and stumbled away, blinded with the agony in his eyes, only to crash against the metal hull of the vessel. He turned about, the blood streaming from his face, and paused to collect his senses, and with a rush, another wave swirled about his ankles and knees. Exhaustion

grew upon him. To stand still meant to sink; to lie or sit meant to be buried the quicker; and all this in the dark, all this in an air that could scarcely be breathed, all this while he fought an enemy that could not be gripped, toiling in a sea that could not be stayed.[29]

It is one of the prime moments in American literature, but more than that it is the western archetype manifesting itself in a moment of unprecedented clarity. Once again we see it verified in the crucible of apotheosis.

When Frank Norris adopted a contemporary figure upon which to model his conception of the western poet, he did not use Joaquin Miller, who was still alive and famous, and who, as we have seen, was the archetype's inceptor. Writing on the eve of the twentieth century the times were already too late for that. In fact he considered Miller a fraud, dismissing him with a scarcely veiled sneer as a "certain bearded poet, recently back from the Klondike," and conspicuous among the swarm of effete literati buzzing about wealthy San Franciscans, who, "perspiring in furs and boots of reindeer skin, declaimed verses of his own composition about the wild life of the Alaskan mining camps."[30] Instead, he chose Edwin Markham, a man who had not rushed off to Alaska to record the ordeals of the argonauts, but had stayed resolutely at home to confront the troubles at hand, which, though economic rather than geographic, were nonetheless awesome. While Miller chanted in the Klondike, Markham remained to write the poem that would focus man's attention on the place where nineteenth-century industrialism had left him—his relation to the moral wilderness his economic techniques had created.

Markham is no longer highly regarded. He was, however, the first poet of the West to produce a poem that has entered world literature. Seventy years after his composition "The Man with the Hoe" is still read and believed around the world. And as long as men remember Lincoln they will remember Markham's tributary verse to him. Yet the fact remains that as literature it cannot compare with Whitman's tremendous eulogy to the same man. Markham was essentially a conformist in everything he publicly did, whereas Whitman made his unconformity his life, one of the chief clues to his dazzling originality.

Louis Filler, in his sensitive study of Markham,[31] points to the little known "The Ballad of the Gallows-Bird" as his finest achievement, and while it does draw upon the darker sources of Markham's vision for an increase of power, it does not show the requisite mastery of the ballad form in which it is couched to rival other modern attempts in the same form. It never burns pure, as the form is made to burn pure through personal obsession in, say, "The Ballad of Reading Gaol." Markham could have compensated by drawing more deeply on the regional archetype and releasing some of the flowing energy that Joaquin Miller wasted. Instead he went East. He was a better poet than Miller, but more pedestrian in his life and in his verse. There may be regions of the world for which a pedestrian gait suffices, but the West is not one of them.

Nor would Erskine Scott Wood, who, in *The Poet in the Desert,* was soon to make the first attempt to accommodate the techniques of Whitman to the fulfillment of the western archetype, achieve success. In all these cases there is partial realization. The archetype is clearly throwing up images, masks, seeking to find a projection that will realize its essence. The problem is that though each of these efforts aspires to the role, none achieves sufficient concentration to pull the immense forces unleashed by the scale of western perspectives into cohesion. Right up through the first world war the archetype is still searching for its voice. Norris possessed the insight into violence that was demanding expression, and knew how to make it count, but his religious instincts were essentially unshaped. London too was lured by the prospect of violence, but compelling as his delienation of it could be, there is a contemplative deficiency that binds it to earth in the end. Markham possessed the social passion that the leveling democratic ethos turns against class distinctions, but had no real grasp of the crucial role of violence in the conversion of passion into exaltation.

Not only so, but these men were all of them deeply involved in particular issues. Passionately concerned with the reform movement, the great overriding social issue of the day, they shaped their efforts to that correction. This preoccupation, it must be confessed, salutary in itself, narrows the vision as it focuses the energy, and though it can be transcended, as Dante transcended it, not many who attempt it actually succeed. Norris, for instance, was too incautious to be wary of its pitfalls. Having scaled out the archetypal vision of the western poet only to reject it, he finally allows Presley to compose his masterpiece. It is called "The Toilers" and we know he had Markham and "The Man with the Hoe" in mind when he did it:

> Now at last he had achieved. He saw why he had never grasped the inspiration for his vast vague *impersonal* Song of the West. At the time he had sought for it, his convictions had not been aroused; he had not then cared for the People. His sympathies had not been touched. Small wonder that he had missed it. Now he was of the People; he had been stirred to his lowest depths. His earnestness was almost a frenzy. *He believed.* And so to him all things were possible at once.[32]

This is one of the tenets of doctrinaire Naturalism and Norris has stumbled into it. I do not mean that such a tenet is lacking in truth, but only that as a tenet it is received by the artist rather than achieved by him. In the first chapter, rather too abruptly, Norris has given us Presley's revulsion from the people in his encounter with Hooven, an immigrant German landholder. "These uncouth brutes of farmhands and petty ranchers, grimed with the soil they worked upon, were odious to him beyond words. Never could he feel sympathy with them, nor with their lives, their ways, their marriages, deaths, bickerings, and all the monotonous round of their sordid existence."[33] It is hardly enough to give Presley's subsequent conversion the force that Norris attributes to it.

Has Norris, then, only set us up for a subsequent reversal, as we have seen reversed the great fantasy of the Song of the West? No, for Presley immediately seeks to confirm his awakening consciousness by recourse to the mystic Vanamee, whom Norris more than once compares to the desert prophets. Vanamee does not hesitate. Even before the poet speaks he has intuited the transformation:

> Something has happened to you, something has aroused you. I am right, am I not? Yes, I thought so. And this poem of yours, you have not been trying to make a sounding piece of literature. You wrote it under tremendous stress. Its very imperfections show that. It is better than a mere rhyme. It is an Utterance—a Message. It is Truth. You have come back to the primal heart of things, and you have seen clearly. Yes, it is a great poem.[34]

To the present day reader these capitalized social abstractions are as suspect as was Presley's vast poetic revery, for since Norris's time we have seen them debased by a cynical political proletarianism. This penchant effectively unmasks the more inflational element in Norris's vision, indicating that though the terms have changed, the underlying impulse is the same. For until it is authenticated by tragic violence the inflational tendency, with its liability to excess and exaggeration, cares little for the content—it inflates the social consciousness as readily as it inflates the metaphysical one. Notice too the simplistic anti-intellectual bias. The poem is not "literature." Emotional stress is superior to critical discernment. Imperfections are the guarantors of validity. It is not a "mere rhyme." This is one of the underlying facets of the western archetype, the American archetype, actually. These simplistic criteria present a temptation to any who aspire to diamond-in-the-rough authenticity. Confirmed by imperfection the poet is reassured of Truth:

> "Thank you," exclaimed Presley fervidly. "I had begun to mistrust myself."
> "Now," observed Vanamee, "I presume you will rush it into print. To have formulated a great thought, simply to have accomplished, is not enough."
> "I think I am sincere," objected Presley. "If it is good it will do good to others. You said yourself it was a Message. If it has any value, I do not think it would be right to keep back from even a very small and most indifferent public."
> "Don't publish in the magazines, at all events," Vanamee answered. "Your inspiration has come *from* the people. Then let it go straight *to* the People—not the literary readers of the monthly periodicals, the rich, who would be only indirectly interested. If you must publish it, let it be in the daily press. Don't interrupt. I know what you will say. It will be that the daily press is common, is vulgar, is undignified; and I tell you that such a poem as this of yours, called as it is "The Toilers," must be read *by* the Toilers. It *must* be common; it must be vulgarized. You must not stand upon your dignity with the People if you are to reach them.[35]

Norris adds that before Presley went to bed that night he addressed his poem to the Sunday editor of a daily newspaper in San Francisco.

History records that the publishing of "The Man with the Hoe" was quite different. Markham and his wife attended a literary cocktail party on New Year's Eve of 1898 in San Francisco, presumably among the people whom Vanamee thought the poem too vital for. Present at the gathering was Bailey Millard, editor of William Randolph Hearst's *San Francisco Examiner*. As Louis Filler recounts it:

> Millard did hear the poem in the emotional circumstances of New Year's Eve, helped on by the poet's distinguished figure and earnest face, and most of all by "his great vibrant voice as he slowly read the verses, the tremendous power of which moved me forcefully."

This was Markham's greatest moment, and as with every man he was not conscious of it. No matter how hard thereafter he strove, and his striving was not in vain, everything to follow was anti-climactic. Filler continues:

> The poem appeared in the *Examiner* for January 15, where it was given impressive type and Millard's own introduction. Markham wrote Millard with gratitude, and with no sense of an important event having occurred. He was delighted with the publication. It gave him faith "that there is something worthwhile in my stuff," for it had been treated so graciously. He thought Millard had caught his spirit perfectly: "I am indeed, I hope, jealous of justice!"[36]

Jealous of justice he might be, but his moment has occurred, and he must accept it—though he never recognizes it, still, he must accept it. It is the mystery of the destiny that governs the life of every public man. Be he artist or politician, it makes no difference—the mystery is the same. It is the moment of apotheosis, and it comes but once.

Yet it can be no surprise that Norris felt moved to improve on the actual creation of "The Man with the Hoe," for its impact was so emphatic as to virtually demand a more mythical origin to explain its powerful effect. As Filler goes on to say, the poem was not simply a nine days' wonder—it was the tocsin of a generation:

> "The Man with the Hoe" went round the world, binding the sorrowful people and the pitiful and

the revolutionary into one single perception of humanity's problem and its dangers. There had been no such staggering intellectual challenge in America to the social contract—affecting so many classes of people—since *Uncle Tom's Cabin.*[37]

Well, yes. But the very reference makes us realize we are not yet in the presence of a *Moby Dick* or a *Leaves of Grass.* But notice again the power of the western archetype to strike with breakthrough force from outside the structure of the literary establishment. Joaquin Miller had effected it in London. Now Markham effects it from San Francisco. But Markham's success is essentially different than Miller's, for the nominal appeal is to other sources of value.

What we are witnessing is the displacement of an archetype by one of its splinters, a sudden manifestation that in its emergence obscures the whole from which it flows. When "The Song of the West" with Presley's adolescent vision is put aside and "The Toilers" is elevated to center stage, we know that it is not merely a case of a Joaquin Miller being upstaged by an Edwin Markham in Norris's purely personal scheme of literary values. The impact of "The Man with the Hoe" upon its time proves that. Something crucial is being worked out in the ethos of the West. The throes of broad pantheistic affirmation are being displaced by the intrusion of the concrete actualities; social conviction is replacing rugged individualism, and a constricting Naturalism is displacing the broad native largesse as civilization closes in. But it is a mistake to think that these factors represent a basic shift in the underlying impulsion.

For it is evident that Naturalism itself is simply a child of pantheism. Given Norris's explicit adhesion to Zola the almost overwhelming celebration of pantheism in *The Octopus* is proof of that. The glorification of brute nature and the celebration of an inexorable Fate which are typical ingredients of Naturalism derive directly from the intuition that the cosmos has displaced a personal God as the clue

242

to divinity. The glorification of nature that pantheism encourages is but a step to the glorification of
the masses, who are the most elemental class and
hence closest to nature. Thus the social struggle becomes holy and the resultant inrush of violence
becomes significant to a mentality that has long
found religious violence meaningless—provides, in
fact, the true authentication to life. Consequently
Edmund Wilson finds this element the most convincing in what otherwise is for him the general
Californian illusion of value:

> . . . the labor cause has been dramatized with
> more impact by these writers on the Western
> coast than it has been on the whole in the East,
> where the formulas of Marxist theory are likely
> to take the place of experience . . . I mean the
> tradition of radical writing which Californians
> like Storm and Steinbeck are carrying on after
> Frank Norris, Jack London and Upton Sin-
> clair . . .
>
> This tradition dates from Henry George, who
> saw the swallowing of the whole state by capital
> accomplished in record time during the sixties
> and seventies of the last century. In our century
> the labor war has been fought out in California
> more nakedly and savagely than—except for the
> most primitive parts of the South—perhaps any-
> where else in the country. The McNamaras,
> Mooney and Billings, the Wobblies and Vigilantes,
> the battles of the longshoremen and the fruit
> pickers, the San Francisco general strike—these
> are the events which have wrung blood and tears
> in the easy California climate; and it is this con-
> flict that has given Mr. Storm his orientation to
> the Pacific vacuum among the direction of the
> larger world, and that has communicated to Mr.
> Steinbeck the impetus which has carried the Joad
> jalopy into the general consciousness of the na-
> tion.[38]

Wilson does not mention Markham in this context, but he might well have. "The Man with the
Hoe" was as famous in its day as *The Grapes of*

243

Wrath was to be, and a substantially superior work of art to boot. But it is too isolated in the author's achievement, and does not bulk broad enough in scale, nor dense enough in specific gravity, to take a place beside *The Grapes* or *The Octopus* in accommodating to the western archetype. The subjects of those works, with their naturalistic presuppositions, are such as could find adequate expression in prose, which by virtue of its ordination to the concrete, the explicit social condition, is the vehicle of the trend. But the pantheistic base, the ground from which Naturalism derives, is ultimately amenable only to expression in poetry, and Markham, as we have observed, was not destined to become its voice. For the great poet of the West could not emerge until the overriding pantheistic sublimity that had displaced a personal God in modern consciousness, and the underriding actuality of the awful violence inherent in the phenomenal world, had shattered the hypnotic materialistic complacency upon which Victorian social assumptions were based. The shattering was accomplished not by revolution or reform, but by the tension of its own contradictions, and it was massive. Even now, almost six decades later, its effect goes unmeasured. Historically it is called the first world war.

In saying that the first world war effected a social liberation from the past I do not mean that the artistic impulse, in following the line of its creative intuition, ever waits for a war. As early as 1912, the Revolution of the Word had instituted the cleansing of creative speech, ejecting from poetry its padded fixtures and restoring it to a fit medium for the expression of powerful truths. But before the artist could be listened to, it took the war to precipitate the sexual revolution and tear the fabric of Victorian decency, exposing men and women in the hostility of their mutual aggressions. While this eruption was raging around the world, out on the Pacific, the lip of the last migration, its implications were achieving form in the consciousness of a suffering ṛecluse who was to give them a passion, a violence, and a resolution consonant with their intrinsic substance. When the mother of Robinson Jeffers died in 1921, liberating, as the death of the mother so often does, the creative energy fixated in the soul of her son, the breakthrough poem which Jeffers poured out gave the western archetype its fiercest clench and its prospective apotheosis.

Yet even as one says it, one hastens to add, "But not in terms of its prefigurement." For the direction Jeffers took could not have been predicted either from the persona of Joaquin Miller or the naturalistic dream of Frank Norris or the social benignity of Edwin Markham. All the expansive energy of affirmation of these western visionaries seems negated in Jeffers, and yet actually his deceptive strategy has been to press negation to its conclusion in order to reach its other side and touch the core of affirmation which the archetype keeps specifying.

For Whitman's priority had already appropriated and given expression to the affirmative aspects of these root obsessions of the American psyche—not necessarily exhausting them, but rendering them extremely difficult to extend. That is one reason why Miller and Norris and Markham could do so little with them. But because the peculiarly western ingredient of violence lay undeveloped by Whitman, Jeffers could make it operative through a reversal of strategy in achieving the same end—the bounds-breaking liberation which is specified at the heart of the Transcendentalist impulse, and which all the vaunted American obsessions were instituted to achieve. Thoreau had taken these same negative predispositions—disdain for the masses, contempt for enthusiasm, disinterest in causes, aloofness to material wealth—and made them operative through contemplation. But Jeffers carried contemplation a step further—he appropriated the uses of violence to the rupturing of forms, and the consequent liberation of the numen inhering in the natural object, the point-focus of the underlying pantheistic intuition.

Actually Jeffers' historic moment could not have

245

been better. The new astronomy was even then revealing that what were called nebula in outer space and thought to be clouds of cosmic gas were actually galaxies dwarfing our own and chilling the mind with the prospect, leaving the hapless human race in a more insignificant position even than the one to which nineteenth-century science had reduced it. The War had gone far to breaking down the inherited cultural matrix, securing thereby the painful atomization of consciousness that is the private citizen's personal hell and the creative artist's supreme opportunity. Depth psychology had begun this atomization sufficiently long for its tenets to have acquired serviceability in the artist's hands without yet becoming stale, as they were soon to become stale in fiction. The sense of whole new outer and inner worlds, opened for the poet to explore, chart, and memorialize in verse, was irresistible. The cynicism and cultured doubt endemic in the twenties were in full cry, awaiting the castigating hand of a prophet. Lawlessness, induced by Prohibition, gave sin a spur and righteousness a cause. The new sexual freedom sprung by the atomization of consciousness, coupled with the techniques of dream interpretation, opened the cellar of the collective imagination like a Pandora's box. In this potent and explosive situation Jeffers stood up in his vantage point of isolation of the western coast and pulled the outer and inner prospects into massive compression.

And in retrospect it seems that the predispositions in the soul of the prophet themselves could hardly have been bettered. The long life of his mother forced him to bank his interior fires, endure her omnipresence till death could grant him release from the unconscious maternal authority over his soul. Thus two inferior books enabled him to jettison the purely cultural overlay of received poetic forms and be free for a new technique when this breakthrough moment arrived. The son of a Presbyterian theologian, he had grained in his nature the long Calvinist distrust of human aspiration. Furthermore his scientific education and curiosity gave him an acceptance of, and an adhesion to, the world view of science when most humanists were fighting tooth and nail in an effort to salvage some vestige of value from its materialistic sweep. Jeffers used Scientism in the way Norris used Naturalism: to eliminate the complacency of inherited illusion and expose the underlying core of force and counterforce in a material universe. And yet he had the pantheistic insight of a divine cosmos operating with Calvinistic obsessiveness: religious passion of a kind and intensity that Whitman, a benign Quaker, could never match.

Thus he assails all the American assumptions with the massive right of his invective consciousness —American optimism, American service, American wealth, American power. But when they are gone it is seen that these native obsessions have been somehow attested to, evoked in the sense that their root-obsessions in the American psyche have been given expression in the interior violence of the poet. How does he do this? By recourse to an obverse interiority —a symbolic *progression* under-structuring the violational *regression*.

The opening pages of "Tamar" take us instantly into the domain of the unconscious—that is to say, the unreal world. Whereas the attempt of his predecessors had been to authenticate a strange but real world, in Jeffers the weird atmospherics of his narratives are creations of sheer mood and are highly unreal. This enables him to register the excoriate violence with a nightmare intensity which, being dream-like, does not contradict reality. No writer was farther from the tenets of Naturalism than Jeffers. This is strange because his adoption of the presuppositions of science is unique. But these precepts do not obtrude on his dreamlike credulity.

If it is asked how the quality of unreality, when cited as an honorific, can be applied to the regional archetype, which is of necessity rooted in space and time in the phenomenal world, it can be shown that the dream itself, with its unreal meshing of the most familiar objects in an atmosphere of unreality, points to the answer. This is an attempt which Natu-

247

ralism never undertakes. For instance, in the shoot-out at the irrigation ditch, the apotheosis-point of *The Octopus*, the action is in no sense unreal; it is rendered with the superb factuality of Stephen Crane. And even in the more poetic passages—for instance Vanamee's apprehension of the mystic approach of his lost love, Norris almost laboriously strives for factuality. With Jeffers one is never led to dwell on the actual at all, despite his precise specifications of place on the Carmel Coast. In fact the closer he approaches to factual reporting, as in the saloon fight in the minor narrative "Myra," the more untypical he becomes. No, Jeffers gaze is true enough, but it is the gaze of a seer, not the gaze of a reporter. And in "Tamar" the seer's gaze is terrible and intense.

And who is the protagonist of this fearful drama? Not an epic figure from the winning of the West, no Fremont or Kit Carson or Jedediah Smith. Jeffers will have his heroes, indeed, but now, fresh from the material impress in the death of the mother, the poet seizes back on the *anima*, the feminine principle in the deeps of the masculine unconscious, and thrusting her forward puts her through violation after violation until all the dross of her conditioning is purged away and she burns pure fire. The dross is incest—always, in Jeffers, symptomatic of the pride of man, the race's obsession with itself rather than with God—and it is scoured in the anguish of consciousness, the acid not of morality but of metaphysical truth.

This intuition to place the crucial role in the figure of woman is not untrue to the archetype, for woman, symbolizing Instinct over against the masculine Intellect, fulfills beautifully the western penchant for "the will in excess of understanding, and the understanding misinformed," the moot liability which, in the impasse of cerebration, enables the questing spirit of man to transcend the rational context and achieve apotheosis. If we have the perspicacity to accept the unreality of Jeffers as something creative, in the way we have learned to do with, say, Yeats, then we will not fall into Wilson's mistake of dismissing it all as an instance of the "Californian vacuum."

"Tamar" is the story of a young girl who grows up on the gnarled coast of Point Lobos, a promontory of such natural grandeur as to have earned the appellation "the greatest meeting of land and water in the world."[39] The story begins with her seduction of her brother and ends with the bringing down of the whole house of her family in a holocaust of fire. Coming when it did it served as a kind of benchmark for much of the incipient violence in American writing that was to follow. As such its excessiveness is frequently cited and condemned, together with the infected imagination of its author.

However, there is a similar Californian narrative, one fairly widespread among the coastal Indians, which may be read in Theodora Kroeber's *The Inland Whale*.[40] It is called "The Loon Woman" and narrates how a young squaw seduces her brother and ends, in the version of the Yurok tribe at least, with her frenzied dancing around the blazing house of her family, much as Tamar drew the same fire to herself in expiation. In instancing sources Jeffers nevers pointed to this tale. Actually, the power expressed in both narratives is really too impersonal to be accounted for by derivation, or by the mere coincidentally perfervid imagination of two artists, one of whom happened to be an aboriginal. The similarities are, rather, archetypal. Jeffers himself suggests the regional root:

> Was it the wild rock coast
> Of her breeding, and the reckless wind
> In the beaten trees and the gaunt booming
> crashes
> Of breakers under the rocks, or rather the
> amplitude
> And wing-subduing immense earth-ending
> water
> That moves all the west taught her this
> freedom?[41]

Thus the sheer panoramic scale of western perspectives is directly adduced to account for the bounds-breaking psychology of the protagonist. And indeed the same power infused into the form produces that straining of measure and syntax in a line like "the amplitude/And wing-subduing immense earth-ending water," which feels through to the root instinct in language and mirrors the uncoiling impulsion. Compounded in the regional archetype the poet articulates his own prophetic witness:

> O beauty of the fountains of the sun
> I pray you enter a little chamber,
> I have given you bodies, I have made you
>   puppets,
> I have made idols for God to enter
> And tiny cells to hold your honey.
> I have given you a dotard and an idiot,
> An old woman puffed with vanity, youth
>   but botched with incest,
> O blower of music through the crooked
>   bugles,
> You that make signs of sins and choose
>   the lame for angels,
> Enter and possess. Being light you have
>   chosen the dark lamps,
> A hawk the sluggish bodies: therefore God
>   you chose
> Me; and therefore I have made you idols
>   like these idols
> To enter and possess . . .[42]

But a more technical consideration is the essential difference in point of view between "Tamar" and "The Loon Woman." In the latter the motivation is the narrator's horror before the crime, the fact of incest—what might be called the archetype operating at the primary collective level. But in "Tamar" the point of view has changed from horror to celebration. This sense of celebration in the very themes of disaster interlacing the narrative fabric of "Tamar" is done at the symbolic level, and has remained largely unnoticed. I myself, though overwhelmed by the affirmation in Jeffers' diction as he pursued his violational ends, was quite unaware of the deep symbolic progression of the action until I read the work of Robert Brophy, whose doctoral thesis at the University of North Carolina is soon to be published. In this work Brophy unfolds the symbolic continuity beneath the massive texture of the narratives. Now a critical article, actually a kind of footnote to his "Tamar" chapter, has just appeared in *American Literature*. Brophy notes that Jeffers, in the Introduction to his *Selected Poetry*, pointed to Shelley's "The Cenci" as one of the sources of his inspiration, and follows up this lead:

> "The Cenci," as a whole, questions, as does "Tamar," the most cherished values of civilization: authority, law, and divine providence. Shelley's play rejects the "great chain of being" (in its hierarchial presuppositions), paternalism, sacred customs, and codified truth; Jeffers's drama presents a cyclic, inhuman world which is overwhelmingly Dionysian. Beatrice, as also Tamar, finds worth only in self-judgment, a stance apart, subjective morality, individual insight, indifference to institutions, divinity of experience, apocalyptic salvation.

Here we see the transcendentalist impulse reducing the protective limitary boundaries of human convention in order to touch a transmoral expansiveness that is illimitable. The instrument is violence, specifically that ultimate of moral violence which is most horrendous to the Judeo-Christian conscience: incest, the sin of sins.

> Incest, then, serves as metaphor in both dramas, partly for what civilization has wrought in terms of self-regarding, inverted values and institutions, partly for the mold-breaking, transcendent repercussions precipitated by the act. The act of incest is not defended; at best it is considered indifferent, a necessary part of a process

that brings about transfiguration. It does, however, effect by its degrading impact a personal
emptying (both women becoming nothing of what
they had been before). From this zero-point both
victims progress to transhuman heights—Tamar
viewing her plight as though from the Evening
Star, Beatrice aloofly from beyond the inquisi-
torial tribunal. This is incest's function within
both works.[43]

If we think of "The Loon Woman" as an example
of aboriginal collective taboo and the consequences
of violation, and "The Cenci" as Romantic revolt, a
principled attack on crystallized conventional values, we can see in "Tamar," with its extension of
scale, its pantheistic background, and its awesome
infusion of violence, the western archetype at the
threshold of apotheosis.* Spread-eagled, Tamar in
her nightmare sees herself after her miscarriage,
impaled on a kind of cosmic phallic crucifixion:

> The afternoon
> Was feverish for so temperate a sea-coast
> And terribly full of light, the sea like a
> hard mirror
> Reverberated the straight and shining
> serpents
> That fell from heaven, and Tamar
> dreamed in a doze
> She was hung naked by that tight cloth
> bandage
> Halfway between sea and sky, beaten on
> by both,
> Burning with light.[44]

It is doubtless this infusion of violence and monumental scale into such episodes that leads Edmund
Wilson to speak of "Cloud dramas that fade out to

* I speak of the threshold of apotheosis rather than its
actuality because that would not be effected until *The
Women at Point Sur;* but for the purposes of this essay
"Tamar" is the breakthrough point, and must stand for the
fact of apotheosis's imminent arrival.

sea, leaving only on our faces a slight moisture and in our ears the echo of hissing." In reality such episodes are not without their inevitability. For symbolic inevitability, when authentically derived, extends, as Brophy shows, with the scale, subsumes the expansion within which it is cast, and dwarfs its context. It is the peculiar office of the western artist to press this expansion, strictly by virtue of the consequence of its inevitability, to the maximum.

Jeffers' career was meteoric in an almost classic sense. He emerged like a rocket with four rapidly ascending works, "Tamar," "The Tower Beyond Tragedy," "Roan Stallion," and "The Woman at Point Sur," a narrative he claimed for his personal masterpiece. After this he leveled off with four others, "Cawdor," "Dear Judas," "Thurso's Landing," and "Give Your Heart to the Hawks." His prestige at this time was so high that the Gregorys could compare it to the position of Victor Hugo in Europe a century before.[45] Then the tide turned. The Depression brought a new social consciousness and the Spainsh Civil War a new internationalism and Jeffers, an unreconstructed isolationist, rapidly fell from favor.

Soon such strictures as Wilson's against him were common. After the war the New Critics made his name a touchstone for uncouth sensationalism, verbosity, and bad taste. In 1948 his own publishers took the humiliating step of repudiating his book even as they issued it. At mid-century, when John Crowe Ransom, dean of the New Critics, summed up the fifty years of American poetic achievement, Jeffers was not mentioned. More astonishingly, in 1955, when Howard Hoffman issued his authoritative work *The Twenties*, which noted the most minute literary movements of that decade, Jeffers is not even in the index, despite the fact that Horace Gregory, who was there, says his narratives "swept through the furnished rooms and studios of Greenwich village with the force of an unpredicated hurricane."[46] This kind of exclusion simply could not happen to an eastern writer of comparable reputation. However, the fifties saw the passing of the New Critical hegemony and the sixties ushered in other perspectives. After Jeffers' death in 1962 his posthumous poems were cordially received. The process of reaffirmation has begun.

But critical recognition is not here pertinent, since its doubtfulness regarding the entire western movement is the premise upon which this paper is founded. The important thing is that the archetype we are tracing has achieved apotheosis. What attests to it is the scale of the imagination, the eruptive intensity of the energy, the monumental output, the aloof, transcendent passion, the overwhelming pantheistic vision—all these are unmistakable evidence that the force so long abuilding has at last found its voice. As we noted earlier the British reviewer who, reading Joaquin Miller with his heart in his throat and extolling "the supreme independence, the spontaneity, the all-pervading passion, the unresting energy, and the prodigal wealth of the imagery that stamp the poetry before us"[47] was possessed of the archetype and responding to it. It was, unfortunately, premature. His words would take another fifty years to be validated in Jeffers.

Actually, recognition is a secondary and essentially attestory phenomenon—it inhibits more than it stimulates creativity. Still, it is necessary, because it represents a kind of apotheosis in its own right, an apotheosis at the collective level that must follow and validate the apotheosis first achieved in the soul of the poet. Both are required for literature to be culturally operative, but ofen the estimative or critical instincts of a nation are fixated by the impress of extraneous factors, and are not truly responsive, so that recognition is delayed. This period of deferral is important because it allows recognition to congeal into true acceptance. Shakespeare achieved apotheosis in English literature; but the critical faculties of his time were preoccupied with French culture and it took 150 years before recognition truly crystallized and became universal. Whitman achieved apotheosis in American poetry with "Song of Myself" in 1855, and claimed it. But the claim was rejected as ridiculous, then vehemently disputed right up to his book's first centennial, when accreditation can be said to have at last occurred. With Jeffers it will not take so long, but neither will it come easily.

How, then, are Whitman and Jeffers related? I say that by virtue of the law of apotheosis they define between them the positive and negative polarities of the American poetic achievement, as Shakespeare and Milton define the positive and negative polarities of English poetic achievement. Whitman and Jeffers, like Shakespeare and Milton, are not really comparable, for Jeffers' place must stand upon his narratives, a form Whitman never attempted. True, Jeffers is best in his shorter poems, as Milton in his shorter poems is best, but it was not in terms of them that either achieved apotheosis in their respective national traditions. Therefore Jeffers must suffer the travail of unrecognition in terms of his narratives and, given their nature, it will be sternly contested. But recognition or no, the important thing is that apotheosis has occurred, and having occurred constitutes a true crystallization, forms a permanent prism.

For, drawing the light to it, apotheosis transmits those rays through the menstruum of its surging synthesis, and all who work further in the field must work in its shadow as well as its light, whether they recognize it or not. As Americans, and insofar as they remained Americans, Pound and Eliot were both heirs of Whitman, though they defined themselves against him. So too were Cummings, Williams, Stevens, and Aiken. And Frost? Frost assimilates to Thoreau and is a precursor of Jeffers—the negative facet of the American psyche which he articulates did not achieve apotheosis until Jeffers carried it to the ultimate, and opened up the pantheistic affirmation inherent in its scepticism. Only then could the divinity caged in the nuclear material entity show its true face, and the Godhead blaze through. Whitman is the sunrise in the East, but Jeffers is the sunset in the West. It is bloody and violent, but it is the last light given us. We deny it at our peril.

Early in this essay I declared that after the concept of the archetype the concept of apotheosis is the most decisive idea employed. To that concept I must now add a third, deriving from it and fulfilling it—the concept of reduction. A powerful artistic movement is like a river. It has its source in a single spring, augments into a stream, swells to a torrent, then diffuses in its own delta eventually to lose its individual drops in the oceanic anonymity of the race. It is all in the nature of things. The final phase is as vital to the whole course of the movement as the flood crest itself, but it is not nearly so dramatic to experience.

In the foregoing pages so much space has been devoted to the phenomenon of emergence because, as I have said, more can be told of an archetype from its inception than from its proliferation, regardless how manifold are the latter effects. For after the summit of expression in any given movement those who follow can only reduce the vision of the great inceptors, the giant figures of the trend. Their function is to individualize the elements that were so lavishly and inchoately bestowed on the initiating protagonists. The Romantic movement in English poetry found its source in Blake and achieved its apotheosis in Wordsworth and Coleridge. After them Byron, Shelley, and Keats begin the narrowing and refining function. This is, I submit, a process of reduction, and it implies an enforced limitation. Though we value a Keats quite as much as a Wordsworth we often fail to understand that his historic situation is infinitely more constricting. To leave it out of account when estimating his achievement is fatal.

This is not confined to the problems of technique or style: formalistic derivation. The artist emerging in the reductive phase finds the prestige of the giants from whom he derived extremely difficult to contest. The glare of réclame blazing about their figures fixates the gaze of the public and threatens that inner certitude every artist needs to evoke the maximum creative energy. For the artist never works in a vacuum; he responds to the unconscious needs and stimuli of his time. In the reductive situation none who follow ever seem in the eyes of their contemporaries to be of quite the same stature as the great masters who stunned the world with their originality. So it is today. The proliferation of sheer genius that manifested in the energies of the great Modernists is past. Many consummate artists have arisen to follow them, but they appear in the public mind more like ornaments than rival contestants. The prestige of the giants is undisputed.

Of those to whom it has fallen to reduce the western archetype, the first name to be mentioned is that of Jack London. A close contemporary of Norris, but lacking his education and philosophical training, nevertheless London implemented his thought with the current pantheistic adumbration of his time—Darwin's recent "survival of the fittest" doctrine and the materialistic monism of Ernst Haeckel, among others—so that in the words of Franklin Walker he "became one of the outstanding examples in American literature of the successful illustration of social and biological theories exemplified in a life-situation."[48] More crucial for our purpose is his explosive liberation of the violence that is the natural consequence of these values.

Only minimally confined by his hastily acquired and shaky intellectural structures, London pursued the work of reduction with fantastic energy, an onslaught of raw vitality. In him the primitivistic element in the western archetype drives down to its archaic root. His voracious appetite impelled him to assail every sensation in rapid succession, forcing each to yield its kernel of stimulus as the effluent of apotheosis. The opening chapter titles of his breakthrough book, *The Call of the Wild,* seem to chart this progression: "Into the Primitive," "The Law of Club and Fang," "The Dominant Primordial Beast." Thus was begun the school of naked experience, a reduction that was to extend through many popularizers down to such figures as Saroyan and Kerouac. It is a method singularly effective in registering the shock of encounter, but it is essentially episodic, and runs to diffuseness, easily deteriorating into out-and-out shapelessness.

Enormously popular, London witnesses to the process by which the reducer of an archetype sometimes enjoys more immediate success than the more visionary artists who precipitated it. In many ways he deserves that success, for he was a powerful story teller, and his reductionist onslaught on nuclear experience is in its very simplicity a more effective literary method than any save the most superior aesthetic formality. Thus his first success, *The Call of the Wild*, burns with an intensity his more ambitious attempts like *The Sea Wolf* cannot equal, and is only incidentally blemished by Naturalism's tedious penchant for abstraction then in vogue. In any case, he is a better writer than conventional highbrow criticism allows. Not long ago I picked up *The Sea Wolf* in a depot, idly wondering what had moved me when I read it as a youth. Instantly I was on the deck of the ferry *Martinez* with the red-faced man, gripped in the moment of impending collision with the steamboat:

> "Grab hold of something and hang on," the red-faced man said to me. All his bluster had gone, and he seemed to have caught the contagion of preternatural calm. "And listen to the women scream."[49]

My heart jumped. I knew I was in the presence of a remarkably vivid literary intelligence.

London's values were those typical of his period, but of the men who have sustained reduction into our own time none is more widely known than John Steinbeck, an incomparably more sophisticated writer, but one profoundly disturbed by his fated role. Edmund Wilson, as we saw, pointed to the influence of Norris on him, but his first significant novel, *To a God Unknown*, is clearly derived from Jeffers. In this book the essential ingredients, chiefly the overwhelming pantheistic violence, are emphatically in play, and if they are not in quintessential expression they do advance the archetypal flow from turn-of-the-century preoccupations to the changed attitudes of the twenties; for though the book was not published until 1932, it is in essence a late response to the mood of the preceding decade.

London burned with a kind of primal purity, but with Steinbeck it is rather as if the archetype has scorched him but never truly annealed him. There is an unconscious obsessive singleness in Norris and London and Jeffers that gives their excesses and failures a glaring consistency, but some inner division in Steinbeck neutralizes his toughness. Like a sensitive scion who has by the accident of birth inherited a brutal responsibility, he retains an inner softness that none of his themes, for all their violence, can ever purge. Thus he is more aesthetically cogent in a palpably tender and evocative narrative of childhood like *The Red Pony* than when gritting out an epic attempt like *The Grapes of Wrath*.

There are those, however, who will insist that I have got the western syndrome all wrong, that as far as fiction is concerned the inception point lies with Norris's *McTeague*, by common consent a superior novel to *The Octopus*, and that the point of apotheosis, if it has indeed occurred, must be seen in *The Grapes of Wrath*. Certainly it was an apotheosis point of some kind. In *Fiction of the Forties* Chester E. Eisinger writes:

> The thirties may be said to have crested with the publication of *The Grapes of Wrath* in 1939, certainly the finest statement of the social indignation and faith in the common man that marked the sociological fiction which dominated that decade. This kind of fiction went into a chilling descent immediately thereafter.[50]

Moreover, the book's staggering impact on the nation at large, and particularly on the inner sanctum of publishing, New York City, attests, as nothing previously from the West had done, the power of the archetype when it begins to swell, reverberating across the country and crashing on the East Coast with the force of a tidal wave. *The Grapes* is not the first instance of this phenomenon, nor yet the last, but none has had a mightier impact.

Speaking for myself, however, I cannot see the apotheosis of western writing in this book. It is too effortful. It rings true to the times but not to the vibration I am tracing, though it is indebted to that vibration for its resounding success. There is an ideological forcing that denotes the top of the mind rather than an instinctive upwelling. In true apotheosis a sense of discovery as well as consummation suffuses the texture of utterance, transmuting the formative thesis into electric consequentiality. This, I believe, does happen in *The Octopus*, despite its programmatic Naturalism, transcending the obvious faults with heightened participation. In *The Grapes of Wrath* it is the program that triumphs, and it is massive, but to me it is confirmed more by history than by aesthetic realization.

Nevertheless, I do hold Steinbeck, for all the negative implications, to be a primary western writer, and his case is more interesting, as regards the archetype, for his failure to sustain achievement and its attributed effect on the rest of Californian practice, than the customary uneventful consistency of a writer's declining years. Warren French writes in his critical study *John Steinbeck:*

> Two important facts about the phase of Steinbeck's life are that he was a Californian and that he wanted to be a serious writer. His birthplace could have inspired him. There is something special about the Golden State beyond the legends fostered by its Chamber of Commerce. A big, beautiful land, it was; and as Steinbeck and other writers have emphasized, the last frontier. Epics

might be written about the tumultuous episodes in its history—the dispossession of the sedentary Spanish settlers, the Gold Rush, the struggles of the railroad empire-builders, the San Francisco disaster, the trouble with migrant laborers and imported minority groups. Many of its writers— Frank Norris, Gertrude Atherton, Stewart Edward White, Upton Sinclair, Robinson Jeffers—have called for and sought to produce an American epic.[51]

Jeffers certainly never called for, nor consciously sought to produce, an American epic; but the author's instinct to place his name in the list is not untrue to his realization. Steinbeck's name, however, belongs there by every right:

> Steinbeck, when he has written of the problems that confront man in his epic struggle with unreliable nature and his own uncontrollable passions, has not been unique in his own country, but a contributor to a vigorous tradition. His break with this regional tradition has had a disturbing effect upon his career; it has also, in the absence of a successor of comparable stature, had a disturbing effect upon the state's cultural pretensions.[52]

I do not deny that when a major writer abdicates, something is shaken in the interior processes of genesis so that the flow of continuity is threatened. But my view of the reductive phase following apotheosis leads me to see the problem in a different light than does French. My essay will attempt to show that the continuum is not broken by Steinbeck's defection, but has proceeded in consonance with the laws of dispersion and diffusion that naturally follow the crest. I see, therefore, the full meaning of Steinbeck's deterioration after leaving the West as a striking certification of initial archetypal presence. And I see his break not attributable simply to the lure of success, though I think he payed for it with all the liabilities of success, but rather to inner cleavage which found a false solution in the enormous success it actually gained, and of which the softness I have mentioned acted as forerunner.

However, it cannot be denied that this softness was early accommodated into genuine creativity. The first device, as Whipple noted, is the time-honored one of aesthetic distance. Writing of the work preceding *The Grapes of Wrath* he instanced the essentially uninvolved character of Steinbeck's violence, and speculated upon the aesthetic strategy by which it is achieved: "Proper distance, I think, is the secret of this effect—to place people not too close and not too far away." It is an ostensibly Classical virtue, and points up the difficulty in appraising Steinbeck's relation to the western archetype, which of itself is incorrigibly Romantic:

> Surely no one writes lovelier stories, yielding a purer pleasure. Here are tragedy and suffering and violence, to be sure, but with all that is sharp and harsh distilled to a golden honey, ripe and mellow. Even cruelty and murder grow somehow pastoral, idyllic, seen through this amber light, as one might watch the struggles of fishes and watersnakes in the depths of a mountain pool.

Wilson, we recall, impugned this same detachment, declaring that "The *paisanos* of Tortilla Flat also eat, love and die in a golden and boundless sunlight that never becomes charged with their energies." But Whipple sees it in a more favorable light:

> Beyond question, Steinbeck has a magic alchemy, to take the sting out of reality and yet leave it all there except the sting. Perhaps it is partly the carefulness of his art, with endless pains devising and arranging every detail until it fits perfectly and is smooth and suave as polished ivory. But probably it is more the enchantment of his style, of that liquid melody that flows on and on until even such experiences as a man dying of thirst in the morning sunlight among remote and lonely hills can seem not altogether ugly, because it had become a legendary thing that happened once upon a time.[53]

262

My own feeling is that the golden ambience is concealing an essential contradiction in the nature of the artist. Violence compels because the western archetype decrees it, but its psychological consequences are denied through the imposition of aesthetic distance and the cultivation of a marmoreal style.

It is apparent, then, that the case of John Steinbeck differs in kind from that of any western writer who preceded him. As such it witnesses to a factor essential to an understanding of the archetype, actually of any archetype, when considered in terms of its broadest artistic registration, and in order to make it clear I propose to expand our terms of reference by introducing a broader equation, even as I utilize the opportunity to bring into focus the salience of the individual factor. This further equation is most aptly called the Charismatic and the Institutional.

We have stressed the fatality of archetypal power, its omnivorous and overwhelming character, dwarfing the limitations of the mind that seeks to engage it. As an emphasis it is not untrue, for clearly the archetype is the inclusive or unifying factor, capable of subsuming the point of view of the individual intelligence. Yet the individual mind cannot ever be wholly denied. It brings to bear against the awesome numenousness of the archetype its own critical awareness, and it does so in terms of another influence altogether (actually another archetype) superimposed by the cultural collective from without. The one power is the evocative Dionysian creative force that we are tracing, the regional western archetype, but it emerges as only one element in the broad generality of the Charismatic. The other power lies in the stabilization of structure, the traditional Apollonian format into which the molten power must be poured in order to achieve configuration, hence the Institutional. Both, as we have said, are simply more inclusive archetypes in their own right, and both, therefore, contest for dominance in the soul of the writer; but they can only be resolved there in terms of the synthesizing factor, the creative intelligence of the self-realizing person.

Steinbeck's career is instructive in that it demonstrates how the dilemma raised by the convergence of two such impulsions can enervate the force of either. More than any western writer before him he stands consciously at the crossroads. The earlier writers were moved more or less unconsciously to the working out of their creative solutions. Conforming as they did to the colonial period in nationalism they possessed no real formalistic alternatives. They simply expressed themselves in terms of the literary conventions they brought West, as they clothed themselves in the sartorial conventions that came round the Horn.

The masters of apotheosis, on the other hand, in a sense found the problem solved for them—sheer eruptive creativity specifying original forms of expression, insights achieving manifestation by virtue of the blaze of conception. The witness of all such men, when they attest to it, is that the resultant form was not really their own, was in fact something "given." In apotheosis, form is born of idea, not by means of craftsmanship, though craftsmanship is there, but by unalloyed creative force, spontaneous inspiration.

By the time of Steinbeck, however, consigned by destiny to the reductive phase, the possibility of selective choice has truly emerged, and it must be faced—has, indeed, become undeferrable. This fact can be singularly opportune, for diversity is the real benefit of the long reductive period; but on the immediate downhill side from apotheosis opportunity presents itself as dilemma no less than as solution. In Steinbeck the dilemma compromises both opportunity *and* solution. But his example renders the complex decipherable in a way no western writer before him allows.

In approaching it let us repeat that in the study of regionalism the archetype we have been tracking, the Charismatic, is unquestionably the primary one. The opposed force, the Institutional, must be accounted secondary. Even when in the ascendency, as we see it triumphant in T. S. Eliot's famous pronouncement that he had become a Classicist in literature, an Anglican in religion, and a Royalist in politics, its function is to provide the matrix within which the primary archetype is received and transmuted. What is needed for resolution is the third factor already indicated: the creative intelligence of the individual man, the shaping mind. And this creativity we have characterized as that which brings to bear the ultimate synthesizing factor: the critical spirit.

For it is this critical spirit that presides over the convergence of the two archetypal impulsions, welding their energies. In the artist's creative ordeal these two forces are synthesized according to his purely personal sense of values, his estimate of aesthetic balance and of social relevance, emphases dictated not only by the structure of his conditioning but by the power of his intrinsic critical spirit. If he leans toward subjectivity and enthusiasm, we call him a Romantic or Dionysian, typifying the broader Charismatic movement. And we group these elements together not as if they possessed no distinction among themselves, but as affinities under stress. For since every concept is rooted in a sense impression, it follows that both the infra-rational and the supra-rational share the dynamics of the unconscious, and are therefore compelled, for all their intrinsic duality, to emerge more or less simultaneously. This charged explosive mixture, so potent and yet so problematical, is what the Charismatic is. Its very indeterminacy constitutes the reason the Institutional evolved to structure it out, shape it into serviceability.

Conversely, if the man leans toward objectivity and dispassionate judgment, we call him a Classicist or Apollonian, representing the Institutional, compressing in the same way the infra-rational and the supra-rational elements derived from the collective tradition, but ordaining them to the first task of canalizing the eruptive Charismatic thrust.

But if the man is truly great, regardless of the side from which he originates, his powers of critical synthesis transcend those distinctions to achieve unitary form, a crystallization that contains both but ultimately triumphs over either. This triumph, at its point of maximum fruition, I have called Apotheosis, and I capitalize it now to show that when it occurs the Charismatic and the Institutional have been subsumed in a mode of utter transcendence. Steinbeck, emerging just after the crystallization-point in western literary tradition, sought to approximate its teriffic implications, and he brought great talent to the task. But his attempt was enervated by his indeterminate position in the period, a position which produced the divided allegiance within him, and which delivered him over not to apotheosis, which was even then beyond him, but to equivocation.

Why? Because the problem for the artist who follows apotheosis no less than for him who precedes it is the prestige of received solutions, the decisiveness of aesthetic forms confirmed by the authority of the Institutional, the secondary archetype. This holds true whether these forms were originally Apollonian or Dionysian. For the Institutional, in its processive structuring, constantly absorbs the force flung into it, as Max Weber noted in his perceptive phrase "the routinization of the charismatic." Most writers of the West, whether immigrants or natives, have coped with that dilemma by forthrightly opting for the Apollonian solution, content to exercise their executive powers in the perfecting of received forms. The roster of their names is long, running from Ambrose Bierce to Ken Kesey. They achieved brilliance in many modes, but they stand outside the scope of this paper, for our purpose here is to trace the primary archetype in its protogenic emergence and its subsequent evolution.

Steinbeck's case is unique in that by virtue of his closeness to the archetype's moment of poetic apotheosis in Jeffers he understands and addresses himself to its challenge, but because of his excruciating situation after the fact he toys with received solutions, formulas, models. The hesitation between the two archetypal impulsions prevents the necessary creative faith that prime genius requires. He belongs to the West by birthright and affinity, but he fights shy of its ruthless directive by an equally inexorable need to conform. This underlying conformism first surfaced in stilted models like "The White Quail," and then in studied solutions of aesthetic distance and the marmoreal style. After *The Grapes of Wrath* he finally and irrevocably "went East," and it was only a matter of time until he verified the move with "The Making of a New Yorker."

More important, for our purposes, was the fact that almost immediately after his removal his work deteriorated. He soon lost his most devoted early admirers, not just through disinterest but through disillusionment. As Lawrence Clark Powell, noted librarian and bookman, and the most genial and sensitive of West Coast literary chroniclers, was to say:

> I once had the best John Steinbeck collection in the country, up through his *Grapes of Wrath*, at which time he fell into a slump of success and produced a series of books that could have been written by any popular novelist. My collection went to Harvard.[54]

In these words we detect the disappointment of many an *aficionado* who was distressed not simply with the course of one who had gone astray seeking popular success (for Steinbeck more than most had girded himself against it), but the course of one who, when success came, succumbed to it with a kind of relief, who almost deliberately "lost his soul."

For popular success stands opposite the individual critical spirit as alternate or rival, just as the Dionysian and Apollonian archetypes stand opposed. There is no more seductive solution to the anguish of blocked archetypal tension. It is an anguish which

267

genius must sustain to achieve full stretch, and which creative form, like an angel of deliverance, arrives to resolve. But lacking such an angel the recourse to mere virtuosity, which talent implements and success, like a devil of ensnarement, arises to confer, is insidiousness itself. This seductivity had nothing to do with the composition of *The Grapes of Wrath,* for it was truly a committed work. But when such an effort has been conceived and executed, when acclaim resounds but the realization dawns that the jewel of apotheosis is somehow denied; when no clear goal toward which to carry the quest is forthcoming; when inactivity is intolerable and silence terrible, the stakes, in that awful impasse, take on an entirely different complexion. It is then, and not before, that the devil smiles, and the door swings open.

To speculate on what Steinbeck might have achieved had destiny taken him East as a boy, as it took Robert Frost from San Francisco to New England at the age of twelve, is fruitless. What is certain is that when the move did come, it came too late to help anything but his fortunes. In that regard, however, it proved consolatory indeed. He lost the critics but he retained the crowd, and by the devil's privilege, which fosters the peculiarly unrealistic European notion of what the American archetype actually is, he held both the critics and the crowd abroad. "Although he suffered a long period of adverse criticism, particularly in the United States," says *The Oxford Companion to American Literature,* "he remained popular and esteemed in Europe, and in the year when he published his account of a tour of 40 states, accompanied by his poodle, as *Travels with Charley in Search of America* (1962), he became the seventh American author to win a Nobel Prize."[55] The conjunction of that book and the world's highest award naturally shocked the critical sensibilities of his native land. But purely in terms of what William James called the Bitch Goddess Success, it can hardly be beat.

Steinbeck's problem is illustrated by that of Theodore Roethke, not a westerner by birth, but a poet who emerged on the Coast from another segment of the cultural hemisphere. Had Roethke remained in Michigan and responded to the regional spirit, he could have done for the Midwest in poetry what Dreiser achieved for it in the novel, a synthesis which neither Carl Sandburg, nor Edgar Lee Masters, nor Vachel Lindsay possessed the critical spirit to effect, and which, therefore, remains unrealized. But ambition and the glare of prestige drew Roethke East where he adopted the neo-metaphysical aesthetic then in vogue, an aesthetic markedly at variance with his regional ethic. Later in life he moved to Seattle, and there attempted to accommodate to the western archetype, shown in the lengthening of his poetic line, and the relaxation of his sharply focused aesthetic attitude. It was too late. Although he consistently celebrated the primacy of intuition over intellect, he could never really let go. His forms, East or West, were the paradigms certified by a conscious prestige. Toward the end he saw this, recognizing instinctively that he had chosen a wrong path. The last piece in his *Collected Poems* is called "Supper with Lindsay," a kind of dream in which he has Vachel Lindsay say, "We need a breed that mixes Blake and me."[56] In the interpretation of dreams this constitutes a clear indictment of the midwestern expatriate by the midwestern dead. Roethke knew Blake, knew him chapter and verse— but what did he know of the extravagant posture of Vachel Lindsay? Only the mute recognition of a kindred soul, covertly acknowledged. That guilt split him. Having memorialized the spontaneity of childhood in a monument of Establishment prestige, the syndrome tore him apart. The man won every award available to an American poet, and his artistic triumph was, for all intents and purposes, complete, lacking only Steinbeck's supreme culmination of the Nobel Prize. Steinbeck's defection brought him the adherence of the lending library millions, and Roethke's brought him the adherence of the cultural elite, but the result, if not actually the same, was close enough to be instructive. Though they approached the altar from opposite directions their genuflections were identical. The Bitch Goddess got them both.

The defection of Steinbeck was not so crucial for the West as that of Roethke was for the Midwest. As a region the latter has never achieved apotheosis in poetry, and hungers, therefore, in the hollowness he failed to fill. Nevertheless, as French suggests, with Steinbeck's going something in California was shaken, and the Nobel Prize could only intensify that shock. Such an award, if appropriate, tends to strengthen or increase achievement, and not just individual achievement but collective achievement as well. Thus the entire South gained stability from Faulkner's Nobel Prize, was culturally firmed up, as it were, by the authentification given its sectional potential. Universally regarded as deserved, it confirmed not only the region but the authentic power of the Institutional to fulfill its legitimate office.

But the indeterminacy of Steinbeck's position in his own land shrouds his award with a disquieting embarrassment, aggravating the sense of fundamental equivocation. It troubles his career rather than crowns it. And yet unquestionably it is a testimonial to the fact that in his own way he did serve his region. His softness, the signature of his equivocation, rendered the diffusion of the western archetype far wider than the fierce austerity of Norris and Jeffers could ever have effected. If that softness was protecting a core of compromise, it did so through the cultivation of a genuine humanization, and it was efficacious.

Only partially so, however. And this because it was only partially certified within himself. When humanization fails, humanity relapses into caricature. But in a minor attempt like *The Red Pony* where no forcing was involved, Steinbeck did make the process of humanization complete. Finding a subject that permitted him to relax the aesthetic distance which his terror imposed between him and the archetypal force, he withdrew to childhood, the period of maximum awareness preceding the objectivization of consciousness, and for a moment the interior contradiction was transcended. Roethke, too, found in childhood the material for his most haunting poetry; and thus each momentarily became the archetype's chosen voice, if not in its magnitude and scale, then in its accent of essential purity. As Whipple says of the four stories of which *The Red Pony* was composed when first published in *The Long Valley*:

> These stories concern a little boy and his ponies, his parents, his grandfather, and the hired man. They are so well told it is hard to see how they could be better. Delicate and sure, they attain perfection in their kind. And here is no detachment, no distance. The writing is reserved and economical, but it leads straight into the characters and the relation between them.[57]

Thus in a retrospective reverie Steinbeck was able to focus essential truthfulness. The decrees of his critical spirit achieved harmonization with the brutal thrust of the archetype itself, resolved with a minimum of contradiction from the acquired culture. Each, in a manner of speaking, absolved the other. It is the kind of unforced attestation that denotes an esthetic triumph. On the basis of it, if on nothing more (and of course there is much more), Steinbeck's place as a true proponent of the western archetype is confirmed. He accomplished for it what no one had before, bringing its latent tenderness, its palpable sensitiveness, into universal comprehension.

But following the aesthetic pinnacle of *The Red Pony*, he was not able to maintain the cool synthesis his critical spirit achieved there. Rather, having foregone the factor of aesthetic distance to pursue living participation, it was as if the archetype convulsively embraced him. Dazing his critical spirit, it shotgunned him into a monstrous marriage, which, after the mauling consummation of *The Grapes of Wrath*, he escaped by flight. What he had courageously renounced was the protective zone, the device of aesthetic distance that enabled him to hold violence at arms length; but what was wrung from him despite himself was the celebrated marmorial style. In *The Red Pony* that style enables the monologue of a simple cowboy instructing a child to become a kind of music:

> "Carl says he wants you to start right at the beginning. That's the only way to learn. Nobody can tell you anything. Like my old man did with me about the saddle blanket. He was a government packer when I was your size, and I helped him some. One day I left a wrinkle in my saddle blanket and made a saddlesore. My old man didn't give me hell at all. But the next morning he saddled me up with a forty-pound stock saddle. I had to lead my horse and carry that saddle over a whole damn mountain in the sun. It darn near killed me, but I never left no wrinkles in a blanket again. I couldn't. I never in my life since then put on a blanket but I felt that saddle on my back. [58]

But in *The Grapes of Wrath* the same type of man is proletarianized into a colloquial puppet capable of a kind of grunting:

> What do ya think a guy in business is? Like he says, he ain't in it for his health. That's what business is. What'd you think it was? Fella's got— See that sign 'longside the road there? Service Club. Luncheon Tuesday, Colmado Hotel? Welcome, brother. That's a Service Club. Fella had a story. Went to one of them meetings an' told the story to all them business men. Says, when I was a kid my ol' man give me a haltered heifer an's says take her down an' git her serviced. An' the fella says, I done it, an' ever'time since then when I hear a business man talkin' about service, I wonder who's gettin' screwed. Fella in business got to lie an' cheat, but he calls it somepin else. That's what's important. You go steal that tire an' you're a thief, but he tried to steal your four dollars for a busted tire. They call that sound business.[59]

Ludicrous? On the contrary it proved stunningly effective. *Time* magazine wrote of *The Grapes* (as quoted on the Bantam jacket blurb): "Great . . . impassioned and exciting. It is Steinbeck's best novel, his toughest and tenderest, his roughest written and his most mellifluous, his most melodramatic, his angriest and most idyllic." We perceive that again, as by a kind of magic, ruggedness of stress validates sincerity, and imperfections emerge unabashedly as the guarantors of authenticity. So, indeed, they are. But it is amusing to see the Establishment, for all its insouciance, proving tractile when it finds something it can promote. We conclude that once more the archetype has scored.

It is true that the recourse to a particular issue, the plight of the Oklahomans in California, enabled Steinbeck to pull together the cleavage within him, and produce thereby a rugged massiveness, the consequence of participation, more convincing than the aesthetic distance which previously gave violence its ambience in his work. But as we saw with Norris and London and Markham, the accent of the particular issue can narrow even as it authenticates, so that the sensitivity of *The Red Pony* becomes brutalized under a doctrinaire ideology. For the doctrinaire, whatever its subject, always inflates, and under the expansion of inflation more gets expressed than was intended. In Steinbeck's case he is delivered over to a reckless archetypal bludgeoning when he sought only to deliver himself to the issue. As a result he creates stereotypes rather than characters, character being submerged within the simplifications of the theme.

Of course, the same tendency may be faulted in Jeffers, but actually it does not hold true for him at the religious level. In his peak narratives Jeffers' pantheist passion goads his figures to a kind of somber incandescence, in a sense rendering character incidental. This could have happened for Steinbeck had his social passion been of a truly revolutionary temper, but he did not have the revolutionary's absolutist thirst. His oft-reiterated "non-teleological" premise permitted him to forego the imperation of transcendence, which every revolutionary needs to press through to finality. One feels the notion was adopted more to salve his divisive conscience than to serve as fundamental artistic conviction. In *The Grapes of Wrath* the urgency of the social crisis enabled him to draw enough impetus from the spirit of the time to mount and sustain his assault, but not to burn through. In the book's climax the old mother can only grit out its painful message: "We ain' gonna die out. People is goin' on —changing a little, maybe, but goin' right on." With no more visionary force than this to impel him, it is no surprise that Steinbeck, when the economic crisis passed with the war boom, could not prevent the revolutionary zeal from passing with it.

War itself bewildered him. It is generally held responsible for his impending failure of nerve. Certainly, he did nothing with it, and went on searching for the subject that would enable the impasse to jell into perceptive truth. In the opening pages of *East of Eden* he seems to have found it. We feel the old vibration, and we thrill to it, only to see it abruptly jettisoned. The intervening potboilers had exacted their toll, and the creative faith necessary to make action burn, instead of simply unwind, was gone. Looking back on *The Grapes of Wrath* from this perspective, we understand why none of its characters has been elevated into incandescence, has only, in a sense, been wrenched into caricature. For that is one of the chief liabilities of the archetypal approach.

And indeed when one thinks of the caricature of living beings in such works, one is awed before the terrible dehumanization of archetypal power. It becomes a debasing thing. Like a hypnotist at a country fair inducing yokels to do ludicrous things, it exceeds compassion—the puppetizing of the individual in an obsession with its own applicative power. We see the southern archetype abused the same way in Erskine Caldwell, *Tobacco Road* and *God's Little Acre* exhibiting the same inflexible contempt; we see Faulkner descending to it in *Sanctuary*. For truly the regional archetype does have the power to brutalize, render inhuman or subhuman, when the artist's attempt at humanization doubles back upon himself. Unclear within, motivated more by cynicism or proselytizing zeal or ambition than by aesthetic demand, he debases what he seeks to exalt. Jeffers, too, succumbs to it when he is angered politically, as in the horrid narrative "The Love and the Hate," savagely brutalizing human personality in a bitter self-righteous mania.

That Steinbeck himself recognized this simplistic descent, and from the beginning was defensive about it, is indicated by the following anecdote:

> He came out of the back room of Gelber, Lilienthal's bookstore on Sutter Street in San Francisco, thirty three years old to my twenty-seven. He spoke with a kind of growl that was nevertheless soft and courteous: "I've just finished a tract, not really a novel at all. It's called *The Grapes of Wrath*."[60]

An artist's heart is revealed more by his apologies than by his program.

The speaker is William Saroyan. As a participant in the reductive phase he too was called on to humanize the archetypal passion, and he earned thereby his own vast international public. But Saroyan was never troubled by Steinbeck's inner cleavage. It was as if his Armenian heritage, a heritage scarred by alienation in the xenophobic San Joaquin Valley, endowed him with the charismatic intensity to arrive instinctively at his true position despite the distraction of emergent possibilities his period offered. In his first book *The Daring Young Man on the Flying Trapeze*, we see the archetype in its stress of essential violence, a young man walking the streets and dying of hunger; but as it was with Steinbeck this was not to be Saroyan's forte. Rather, he is an authentic precursor of the Beat Generation, advocating the "Go, go, go!" philosophy twenty years before its apotheosis in that movement, placing accent on spontaneity of response and expression, rupturing traditional forms, particularly in drama, by assailing them electrically with passionate energy, inculcating the western expansiveness by infusing it into the most trivial human situations and forcing them to expand until they yield their nuggets of universality. As Alfred Kazin sums up the impact of Saroyan when he arrived in New York in the thirties following the sensational breakthrough of *The Daring Young Man:*

> That story had caught on because of Saroyan's extraordinary dependence on his own feelings. There is no past, he said, and the future is dark; there is no other writer, there are no teachers for us, no examples; there is only me, now, this moment, this crazy alternation of dread and ecstasy. I am alone, and making my writing out of *being* alone. I occupy the streets of the city as I occupy my room and occupy my body; there is only me, going up and down between the dread of becoming nothing and the ecstasy of realizing my kinship with this body, this earth, this place, this moment.[61]

It seems almost a paraphrase of the ethos of the Beat Generation. As such it is more Whitmanesque than Jeffersian, but no one would ever take Saroyan for an easterner. And the extreme extroversion evidenced in Kazin's account seems a Depression version of Joaquin Miller walking up and down among the London literati. Saroyan, however, rides the wave of the future whereas Miller exemplified a dying romantic past. But once again the manifest persona is validated in the guts of its creative expression.

Other writers at work in the thirties and forties to humanize the archetype include the Oregon novelist and poet H. H. Davis, whose *Honey in the Horn* was the Pulitzer prize novel in 1935. As the cross-section of a period and a people, it is like a page from Presley's great Song of the West, and Davis's volume of open-form verse, *Proud Riders,* carries the haunting evocation of the western spaces.

William Van Tilburg Clark, the Nevada writer, who did his doctoral thesis on Jeffers, uses a more somber lens and gains in depth. His first novel, *The Oxbow Incident,* is sometimes said to have displaced Owen Wister's *The Virginian* as the classic example of the western. However, both works lie outside the scope of this article, for as traced here the central factor is not subject matter but attitude, not accuracy of depiction but a sweeping dionysiac energy, and these two models are incontestably objective. But Clark truly enters the archetype in *The Track of the Cat,* the real reduction of Jeffers narrative verse to prose fiction. Here he takes up the old theme of a malevolent presence in nature as pursued in *Moby Dick,* though the possibility of apotheosis is denied him by Melville's priority in this. The animal presence here is a giant puma haunting a Sierra Nevada cattle ranch. The situation is Jeffersian—a closed family context immured in an aloof impersonal natural grandeur, enforcing a sharp balance and containment of tension, until the contrarities surface explosively when the presence of the cougar intrudes upon them. It is interesting that Clark's move from objectivity to participation betrays him into certain distinct Jeffersian mannerisms which he never used in *The Oxbow Incident*— the swift brushstrokes of terse conversational violence to limn the opposed characters, for instance. His chief figure, Curt Bridges, is taken from a standard Jeffers type like Reave Thurso or Cawdor. But also the humanization of primeval characters is palpable, the mother being more sensitive than her prototype in the old vulturine mothers who haunt Jeffers' houses. Other elements also find synthesis— the step-by-step plotting of the demise of Curt is reminiscent of Norris' following of McTeague through the final phase of that book. But despite these derivations the work of reduction is true and evocative. The result is synthesis rather than apotheosis, which is just what Clark's historical position calls for. It is hard to see how the process of reduction could be more sensitively accomplished.

Of the western poets who closely follow the moment of apotheosis and devolve from its implications, the chief is Kenneth Rexroth. Although not a native he found his voice in San Francisco, for the ingredients of an illimitable pantheism and an incipient violence provide the determinants of what he writes. Although he repudiates Jeffers, the stance, the point of view of the isolated consciousness subsumed in the western landscape is Jeffers' own.[62] But his reduction, or refinement, of the Jeffersian moment of cosmic awareness is efficacious, because in savagely defining himself over against Jeffers he is freed from stylistic imitation even as he refines the point of view.

In Rexroth the tenets of Modernism and Experimentalism are much more crucially employed than in Steinbeck or Saroyan. An awesome erudition, a powerful nostalgic sense of history which infuses much of his mood with a tragic classicism, it is nevertheless always the Californian earth and sky and sea that form the vital imagery infusing his verse with its power. In him the western expansion casts over history as well as space. Not only so, but the sexual violence which Jeffers introduced into American poetry is subjectivized, refined in the erotic movement deriving from D. H. Lawrence, but infused by Rexroth with the western pantheism:

> At the wood's edge in the moonlight
> We dropped our clothes and stood naked,
> Swaying, shadow mottled, enclosed
> In each other and together
> Closed in the night. We did not hear
> The whip-poor-will, nor the aspen's
> Whisper; the owl flew silently
> Or cried out loud, we did not know.
> We could not hear beyond the heart.
> We could not see the moving dark
> And light, the stars that stood or moved,
> The stars that fell. Did they all fall

We had not known. We were falling
Like meteors, dark through black cold
Toward each other, and then compact,
Blazing through air into the earth.[63]

Rexroth's masterpiece is his long poem *The Phoenix and the Tortoise*. Written in wartime, cast on a deserted California beach on the night of Holy Thursday, 1942, all the facets of his extremely complex mind and sensibility, the undersurge of his sexual passion and the overreach of his spiritual thirst, are orchestrated in a sequential meditation that seizes up the haunting moment of time in history as the key to impasse, the mind's bafflement before the fact of material flux. Denis Donoghue has spoken of how "in one of the recurrent 'moments' of American literature the imagination confronts reality in the guise of a poet gazing at the sea." Jeffers made that "moment" his abiding stance, but Rexroth attributes to it the wealth of intellectual preoccupations deriving from our European heritage, distinctions that lie outside the concretistic thud of Jeffers' thought.

Actually, *The Phoenix and the Tortoise* is a kind of American synthesis of the particular Modernist tendency it represents, the tendency of which *The Waste Land* is the thesis and *Four Quartets* the antithesis. In no other American poem are the manifold complexities of the modern intellectual dilemma so resonantly subsumed. At the root of those difficulties is the penchant for substituting the process of verbalization for the process of logic. It is a displacement which, in effect, places upon the sensibility the role of monitor to the reason rather than vice versa, for sensibility, not logic, governs the sensory roots of language. The result of this displacement we see in *The Waste Land*, its repudiation in *Four Quartets*. But in *The Phoenix and the Tortoise* the archetype rises to redeem the deracinated intelligence from the cross of Eliot's contradiction, for it puts the monitoring sensibility in tune with the pulse of cosmic flow and delivers the spirit from the impasse of consciousness where Eliot's fear of physical passion had left it. Fundamentally Lawrentian in its solutions, if the poem does not have the full diapasan of affirmative celebration Rexroth would later sustain, it is because the darkest year of the world's worst war would not permit that kind of exultation. But coming when it did its intellectual courage was heroic and for the lacerated intelligence of our time its healing effects are incalculable.

After World War II Rexroth began the first attempt to focus the archetype, now definitely constellated, into an explicitly formulated literary movement. Not that he deliberately conceived it as such, for his prospect was ultimately international, but his emphasis in art on the autochthonous, to use his word, his appropriation of the anthropologist's concept of Pacific Basin Culture as pertinent to the West Coast literary situation, and his instince to ground his movement within the mystique of place, San Francisco, made it the inevitable expression of the emergence we have been tracing.

The principle poets of this first group were Rexroth, Robert Duncan, Phillip Lamantia, Thomas Parkinson, Richard Moore, and myself. James Broughton was active but did not participate, and the newly arrived Jack Spicer stood aloof. Although this movement was short-lived, blowing apart within a year or two not so much from ideological differences as from the exacerbations of explosive temperaments, the regionalist incentive was discernible in its indictment of the East Coast Literary Establishment, and the accentuation of lifestyle, validated as personalism, over against the New Critical impersonalism in poetry then in vogue. The poet's role as *vates* was affirmed, his prophetic stance as refresher and invigorator of stultified literary and social forms was asserted. Anarchism and pacifism were adopted as political programs against the military-industrial complex, and a relaxed bohemianism was favored over against the "correct" posture of the Academy.

I participated in this group from 1946 onward. My own origins stemmed directly from Jeffers in the mid-thirties, when I implemented the reduction of his violence by subjectivizing it, controverting its cruciality through interior travail. Later, recognizing the apotheosis of pantheism in the incarnational instance, I espoused Catholicism, and, from the bastion of the Dominican Order, pursued an erotic mysticism as the most viable emphasis in a West-oriented religious quest. But it was my conviction, at the time of the new movement, that it truly embodied the archetype I had consistently espoused, that led me to identify with it. No matter how vehemently some of the others might reject Jeffers in the crystallization of their own literary identity, it did not dampen my belief that each of them constituted a genuine continuation of the impulse of which he was but the master voice. Failing in the attempt to establish a counter movement to the reactionary literary current which the New Criticism was just then promoting with great success, nevertheless enough energy was generated to incite a counter attack in *Harper's* called "The New Cult of Sex and Anarchy,"[64] beginning a baptism of fire that would culminate in the trial against "Howl" a decade later.

Although a literary magazine, *The Ark*, was begun, the primary emphasis was personal, tending more toward poetry reading than to magazine publication as a means of dissemination. This accent on the spoken rather than the printed word, this devolution from the fixed standard of the page and its emphasis on dispassionate analysis which the eye implements, meant of course a rise in the *participation mystique* which this archetype favors, and which would later become one of the principle features of the Beat Generation. There were poetry readings earlier, of course, but attendance was usually confined to persons who knew beforehand the poet's representative works. Now the poetry reading was transformed from recital into *encounter*. This elimination of lecture hall distance between speaker and audience, this dependence on the primacy of voice, was crucial to the development of things in San Francisco. As we noted earlier it was Markham's direct reading that moved the editor of the San Francisco *Examiner* to instigate the breakthrough publication of "The Man with the Hoe." So it would be with *Howl,* which was "published" when it was first read in the old Six Gallery in the San Francisco Marina in the fall of 1955, and which gained a powerful reputation on platform well before it was issued in print. But in the earlier postwar period all of us were more earnestly and self-consciously literary than the later stance of the Beat poets would reflect.

Of this group Robert Duncan emerges as the most important figure, and is, after Rexroth, the chief poet of the San Francisco movement. He published sporadically through his early years, almost consciously protecting himself from a premature exposure, so that his emergence was slow. Yet today he stands among the foremost poets of the nation. His recent collection of early poems declares his approximation to the western archetype in many instances, the pantheism and violence manifesting in remarkably vivid impressions and images. More than any of the others he experimented directly in all poetic forms certified by Modernist precepts, calling it a special mark of the poet to body forth the dominant influences that have shaped his thought. But although these influences rise and blend and subside across the long course of his poetic practice, he remains ineluctably true to his origins, and retains the stamp of his heritage in all he does. Here, in a passage taken from the close of his powerfully celebrative "Heavenly City, Earthly City," the mode is adapted from Wallace Stevens, but the archetypal western source is unmistakable:

Turbulent Pacific! the sea-lions bark
in ghostly conversations and sun them-
    selves
upon the sea-conditioned rocks.
Insistent questioner of our shores!
Somnambulist! old comforter!
You wright in passion's storm and pas-
    sionate calm
your reasonless change and seek to restore
the aspiring man to your green remote.

The individual ape in the human sea
is worn, is worn by a non-committal tide,
and shows in his unnecessary watching
    face
the necessary convolutions of that sea,
the memories of forsaken lands.

The praise of the sun is a nostalgic poem.
Sometimes the sea seems mild and light
as a luminous harp upon which the sun
    plays
threaded with indolent wires of gold
across the ruddy music of its waves
and its voices merge in a pulsing counter-
    point
to sing the wonders of the sun,
the beasts of the sun and the watry beasts.

Sea leopards cough in the halls of our
    sleep,
swim in the wastes of salt and wrack of
    ships,
and sun themselves upon the resounding
    rocks,
or lie in the thoughtless shallows of the
    sun.
These are the tides of the poetic sea.
I drift. I drift. The praise of the sun
is purposeless. I dream of those forsaken
    shores
wrapt in the mind's redeeming haze.

283

Sea leopards cough in the halls of our
    sleep;
disturb the course of the nostalgic sea,
casual hints where harmlessly they swim
of some brooding fear in the fiery deep.[65]

After Duncan, Phillip Lamantia shows the deepest
accommodation to Modernist aesthetic principle.
Like myself he gained his literary identity before the
formation of the Rexroth group. An avowed surrealist, nevertheless he espoused the group's principles
and wrote the article in the British magazine *Horizon* which introduced the movement to international
attention.[66] His western origin shows in a certain
somber opulence of tonality, rich verbal texturings
of regional ingredients, almost gluttonous urgencies
coiling from sentient recesses in a wilderness-sat-
urated imagistic resource. Yet what Parker Tyler
wrote of him shows how the archetype in its process
of reduction and dispersion, transmutes from traditional regionalism to revolutionary internationalism:

Phillip Lamantia, discovered by Charles Henri
Ford and myself when he was fifteen and instantly welcomed by Andre Breton into the ranks
of the surrealists, has always written with the
voice of revelation. This is dangerous at any time,
even the most enlightened and tolerant of times,
and such a vocalist is due to suffer from the
world's ceaseless timidity. But the danger of daring is the active root of Lamantia's poetry. It is
violence as victory—a victory over what is terribly true. Only this apocalyptic sort of poetry can
sear and soothe, break and mend, destroy and
create at once. Lamantia's language automatically
divorces itself from periods and localities, vogues
and conventions; it is so vital exactly because it
has little relation to the evolutions of taste and
the rise of reputations—all of which belong to
time and place. With every line, with every image,
it creates the world where poets are always born
and which, if wise, they never leave: Elsewhere.[67]

This "Elsewhere" which Lamantia creates, is the terminus of the expansionist vision which the rupturing of form is directed to liberate into consciousness. Wherever Lamantia wanders it is the San Francisco origin that makes inevitable in him the precise degree of apocalyptic eroticism and pantheistic celebration, and through him fuses the other elements emerging in the breakthrough period of the fifties. As Allen Ginsberg wrote of him in *Poetry:* "Since I'm cited as stylistic authority I authoritatively declare Lamantia as American original, soothsayer even as Poe, genius in the language of Whitman, native companion and teacher to myself."[68]

This is true. And the relevance lies in the fact that although the movement was, as I have said, short-lived, it proved to be the point of group-inception, the nuclear impulse that generated the celebrated San Francisco Renaissance of ten years later, simultaneously launching the Beat Generation as the culmination of everything begun in the immediate post-war period. At that time the world had been too preoccupied with the massive problems of reconstruction to give serious attention to the message Rexroth's group was enunciating. It would take the disillusionment of the Korean War, the disgust of the McCarthy period, and the blandness of the second Eisenhower administration to produce that—an age of affluence so pervasive that *Life* magazine's cover article on the Beat Generation, when it came in 1959, would hail it as "The Only Rebellion Around."[69] Rexroth had called *Howl* "the declaration of faith of a new generation," a statement that provoked much scoffing at the time. But after a decade of riots and confrontations *Life* magazine is not asking for any more rebellions; and if anyone remembers Rexroth's prediction, he is no longer scoffing.

The opening document was the San Francisco issue of *The Evergreen Review*[70] in 1957, wherein the work of the post-war group was joined by that of impassioned newcomers like Ginsberg, Kerouac, Ferlinghetti, McClure, and Snyder. With the obscenity trial of *Howl* that same year, the movement achieved apotheosis, and the popular image of the Beatnik was born. Ginsberg and Kerouac did not stay long on the Coast, though certain of Kerouac's writings exhibit the western archetype in its pure manifestation. It seems certain that had he chosen to remain he would have brought the strain to perfection, but he was chosen for another, more transcontinental, witness. This illustrates how a native like Steinbeck may have only an accommodated relevance to the regional archetype with which he is universally identified, living on in its aura, whereas another writer, who held it in his capacity to become the true voice of that same archetype, may not, in retrospect, be associated with it at all.

For Kerouac the West was crucial, not only in the sense that it received him first, as Seymour Krim has written, noting that "Transcontinental though Kerouac was, the West Coast, and the Frisco area in particular, were to prove culturally more ready for him than the East." No, more basically than this, in works like *The Subterraneans*, he became for a magic interval the archetype's, chosen voice, and registered its vibration as few before him succeeded in doing. Thomas Parkinson is quite mistaken when he defensively protests that "When Kerouac writes of the West Coast he does so with a tourist's eye; it is all copy, raw material to be exploited, not substantial."[71] Actually the western atmosphere and the youthfully burgeoning author took to each other with a beautiful affinity. If the West may not be claimed as Kerouac's inception point into creative life, it was certainly for him the place where he fulfilled himself. Krim well observes:

> California looks toward the Orient; its young intellectuals and truth-seekers are far more open to untraditional and experimental concepts than their counterparts in the New York and New England cultural fortresses, and it was to be no accident that the Beat chariot fueled up in S.F. and then rolled from West to East in the late 50s

rather than the other way around. But more specifically for our knowledge of Kerouac, it was on the Coast, especially from Frisco north to the high Washington State mountains, that climate and geography allowed his *Dharma Bums* (1958) to combine a natural outdoorsy way of life with the Buddhist precepts and speculations that plays a very consistent part in all of Kerouac's writings and especially in *Desolation Angels*. In this propitious environment Kerouac found a number of kindred neo-Buddhist, antimaterialist, gently anarchistic young Americans whom we would never have come upon in New York, Boston or Philadelphia; they discussed and brooded upon philosophy and religion with him (informally, but seriously) and brought—all of them together, with Kerouac the popularizer—a new literary-religious possibility into the *content* of the American novel that anticipated more technical studies of Zen and presaged a shift in the intellectual world from a closed science-oriented outlook to a more existential approach.[72]

That this phenomenon of West-to-East reversal is truly the archetype in play and not merely an ephemeral Beat fad is shown by the same accent manifested in even such East Coast preserves as higher learning: "Whatever happens in American higher education," writes *Newsweek* magazine, "usually happens first in California, and then eventually engulfs the nation." It is chauvinistic to insist that the symptom is not incompatible with quality?[73] Sheer originality is indeed too evanescent to be compatible with permanence. But under the stress of apotheosis, originality fuses significance into realized achievement.

With Allen Ginsberg the western encounter was to be an even more decisive crystallizing factor than with Kerouac. The latter had achieved his breakthrough statement, *On the Road,* before he arrived, and can be said to have come with his aesthetic focus well in hand, but with Ginsberg San Francisco meant ignition. It changed him from potentiality to act, brought him to creative realization. This attribution of western impact, it is true, is again disputed. Thomas F. Merrill, in his scholarly work on Ginsberg, declares that: "Despite the fact that it has been fashionable to say that *Howl* exploded on the American literary scene like a bombshell, that San Francisco finally 'turned Ginsberg on' and that this poem heralded in the Beat Generation, it is difficult to find in this admittedly extraordinary poem much that had not been anticipated in inchoate and sometimes even mature form in *Empty Mirrors*"[74]—a reference to Ginsberg's early, but then unpublished, poems.

Thus the scholar with his documents before him. But he is reckoning without the archetype, and it was the archetype alone that seized the fragmentary and tentative materials of *Empty Mirrors* and fused them into the long cumulative cry of anguish and jubilation that is *Howl*. But Merrill is right when he stipulates that *Howl* is not a genesis; it is an amplification. "Part of the reason for considering *Howl* an amplification has nothing to do with literature at all. The furor surrounding its publication was like a shot heard round the world."[75] We've encountered that phrase before in this study, spoken in connection with another San Francisco poem, "The Man with the Hoe," published fifty-seven years earlier. And by its presence we understand that in both cases the archetype has touched its nerve in the social body, that something larger than literature has been sprung into existence. With "The Man with the Hoe" the values were conscious ones, but the Revolution of the Word that had occurred between the composition of the two poems had shifted the point of preoccupation, and the values set clanging in *Howl* were right out of the lacerated unconscious of modern man.

Ginsberg himself has testified to the importance of his San Francisco interval in the unfolding of his creative destiny. His meeting with Orlovsky, that crucial love affair of his life; his finding of the psychoanalyst Sidney Hicks, who impelled him into the freedom he needed; his friendship with the poet

Gary Snyder; his recognition by Rexroth, so different a mind and man from his Columbia University mentors—all these factors he has spoken of as constituting the loosening elements that opened his mind, prepared the laying bare of his soul. But what the poem itself attests to is something else—an invasion, the terrific effusion of psychic force that transmutes the crazed imagery into incandescent fire.

For the dark, violational element introduced into the archetype by Jeffers was in *Howl* thrust down to a deeper, more explosive dimension. It was Ginsberg's insight into the operative power of the obscene that gave him the leverage to effect a revolution in American poetry, precipitate a new concept of the poem. This element was welded into the sense of surrealist explosion that was so much the operative force of his New York intellectual background—not so much surrealism regarded as a sophisticated literary idiom, but surrealism as an attitude, a method of holding together the shattering consciousness of the modern sensibility. Henry Miller was even then living at Big Sur, and in his explosive novels he had introduced the same element of comic obscenity that is both outrageous and yet in deadly earnest for all its slapstick. But no one had done that for poetry; no one had welded it into abiding verse form. Yet paradoxically the form of *Howl* is unquestionably traditional, and it was born of the situation in which Ginsberg found himself in San Francisco, drawing on his New York past, but finding in the West the freedom to make it count. In his travail of unrest and creative ordeal he reached back into the roots of his Hebraic past and came up with the true prophetic idiom. It was the moment of self-finding, a prophet utilizing through his own emergent voice the impact of his identity.

Interestingly enough, the best words ever spoken of *Howl* were said at its obscenity trial in the moment of its emergence. During the second Eisenhower administration things were culturally very tight, and artists and critics, recovering from the

McCarthy era, rushed to the defense of a poem attacked by the Establishment. Rarely has an unknown poem by an obscure poet known such high praise before it has been assessed by the scholarly community. But as soon as the trial was over and the battle won, a reverse set in. The poem began its work of effecting a critical reevaluation of the course of poetry, and the defensive reaction was intense. For a few years you could hardly find anyone who would say a good word for it, but gradually its liberating role was effected, and already we are finding it discussed seriously in the critical forum.

And so, like the dignified and lofty "Man with the Hoe," the obscene and outrageous poem *Howl* has taken its place in world literature, each, so far, more on the basis of its crystallizing effect upon the crisis of consciousness of its own time, than on any consensus as to its aesthetic supremacy. "The Man with the Hoe" looked back upon the literary values of the immediate past, and the consciousness that it caught at crisis-point was Victorian in essence and formality; whereas *Howl*, while not really instituting any technical innovations, rides the wave of the future. Its tragi-comic roar of anguish and celebration reverberates beneath the search for wholeness and honesty that typifies so much of the defiance and shame of our life, a defiance and a shame in which the role of San Francisco and the West continues unabated.

Of the direct descendants of Ginsberg on the Coast the chief is Charles Bukowski of Los Angeles. A German by birth, he retains a blunt, almost gutteral accent, the adhesion of his blood ("I am hammered home not upon wisdom / but upon defamation"). His verses seem closer, in fact, to the genius of Henry Miller in their stark, almost pornographic directness, a marked distinction from Ginsberg's joyously lyric Hebraic sources. Reading him we feel a hunched fumbling for utterance. Suddenly finding it, the poet coughs out an epithet of astonishing violence and repudiation ("I am sad because my manliness chokes me down / to the nakedness of revulsion"). But his bluntness is the shield of a terrible sensitivity, a primal wound. Unlike any other writer on the Coast he seizes us with a brute-like patience, an almost animal anguish. His gouts of throttled speech conceal the endurance of a gored ox:

> in the slow Mexican air I watched the bull
>   die
> and they cut off his ear, and his great
>   head held
> no more terror than a rock.
>
> driving back the next day we stopped at the
>   Mission
> and watched the golden red and blue
>   flowers pulling
> like tigers in the wind.
>
> set this to metric: the bull, and the fort of
>   Christ:
> the matador on his knees, the dead bull
>   his baby;
> and the priest staring from the window
> like a caged bear.
>
> you may argue in the market place and
>   pull at your
> doubts with silken strings: I will only tell
>   you
> this: I have lived in both their temples,
> believing all and nothing—perhaps, now,
>   they will
> die in mine.[76]

Kerouac and Ginsberg did not long remain in California. The ground swell of the Beat Generation ran, as Krim has noted, from West to East, and it is only natural that its two instigators should follow that groundswell back to the place of their origins. For if creativity may with some justification be said to constitute the power of the West, it is undeniable that *judgment* constitutes the power of the East; and

no American idea, no matter how intensely prophetic, can be said to have fulfilled its destiny until it
has been certified in that estimation. This is the
power that draws so many creative artists, once they
have discovered themselves in the ethos of a region,
to seek immolation in a new encounter, pursue a
verdict at the seat of judgment. It is the prophet's
destiny. Christ left Galilee to suffer crucifixion in
Jerusalem. The western artist in New York can expect nothing less.

But as for the Beat awakening, though Kerouac
and Ginsberg turned East, other arriving poets did
remain. Lawrence Ferlinghetti and Michael McClure
have each made San Francisco their base where,
joined by later comers like David Meltzer, they continue to extend the consciousness they tapped here
and helped define. Ferlinghetti is more cosmopolitan in his sources than the western archetype usually tolerates, but as he assimilated into the San
Francisco attitude he adopted the Californian spread
in his large, declarative poems, humanizing the
comic and ironic element that we saw introduced
in *Howl*. McClure registers the dark sexual libido
in its omnivorous pre-verbal urges, approximating
its crudity by recourse to a correspondingly blunt
typography, which nevertheless he arranges with
deceptive sophistication.

The cluster of serious, deeply committed poets
drawn to San Francisco and productive here in this
later phase of the western reawakening is too multi-
various in composition to mention individual names,
but of the purely native voices the chief are Gary
Snyder, Phillip Whalen, and Lew Welch. These men
were all associated at Reed College in Portland,
though Snyder was born in San Francisco. All share
the open form and prophetic stance which the
archetype exacts, but Snyder reveals more crisply
than any other figure certain directions taken since
its constellation in the postwar group. Although
Rexroth and Duncan are superior as poets, it is necessary to treat Snyder in more detail because he

represents the terminal literary situation of the archetype at present, witnessing both to his skill as a reducer of perspectives established before him, and as its creative embodiment in his own right.

For he typifies that aspect of the westward thrust that actually leaps the Pacific to retouch the origins of civilization in the Orient. Jeffers had looked westward to the vast expanse of water, and Kerouac and Ginsberg both responded to the sweep beyond, but more than any other American poet Snyder has followed that gaze to its conclusion. This oriental insemination makes him, among the young, one of the most influential poets writing today, though he has not been as widely publicized as, say Ferlinghetti, or even Duncan. In *The Southern Review* Thomas Parkinson published the major article on him so far to appear. He writes:

> Gary Snyder has not had so much public exposure, having spent most of the past decade in Japan, where he writes and studies. He has become a legend for several reasons: first, he is not merely interested in Buddhism but has studied Japanese and Chinese so thoroughly that he is fluent in conversation Japanese and translates easily from both languages. . . . The western world with its dualism and antimonies he has made alien to himself. His knowledge of Zen Buddhism is not that of a dilettante but, insofar as this is possible for an occidental, of an adept. He is at present completing a study of the history of Zen rituals for the Bollengen Foundation, based on records that have not been available to an occidental nor systematically studied by anyone.[77]

But this impressive overlay of acquired culture, be it noted, is unable to enervate the root-force we have been delineating, and Parkinson begins, unconsciously enough, to encapsulate the traditional image of the frontiersman as history has given him to us, sure sign that the archetype, far from exhausted with the arrival of civilization, remains singularly in play:

Second, he is skilled in the use of his hands. If he were put down in the most remote wilderness with only a pocket knife, he would emerge from it cheerfully within two weeks, full of fresh experience, and with no loss of weight. There is a physical, intellectual and moral sturdiness to him that is part of each movement he makes and each sentence he phrases. He is gracious, soft-spoken, incisive, and deeply intelligent. Third, he is an extraordinarily skillful poet, and his work develops steadily toward more thorough and profound insight. If there has been a San Francisco renaissance, Snyder is its Renaissance Man: scholar, woodsman, guru, artist, creatively maladjusted, accessible, open, and full of fun.[78]

While the honor surely belongs more properly to Rexroth himself, since he was all these things before Snyder emerged to give them quintessential expression, nevertheless the fact that the attribution can be made attests to the ongoing character of the archetype as it constantly refreshes itself in new variations of its primal impulse. It is no disparagement to Snyder to note that Parkinson's summary is all Joaquin Miller strove to be. But something else has been acquired in the processive realization:

> For when one thinks of Snyder, the personal and biographical obtrude in a way they do with Duncan or with Levertov—their work remains intelligible within the traditions of European poetry; Snyder presents a different set of references and beings. It is necessary to call on different habits of thought, and to think of the poetry as creating a different set of human possibilities. Nor is it a simple matter—insofar as such matters are simple—of translating Eastern into Western nomenclature; Snyder is Western in many direct and palpable ways. He has effectively done something that for an individual is extremely difficult: he has created a new culture.[79]

If anything can be challenged in Parkinson's essay, this statement is surely doubtful. But since Parkinson wrote there is appearing on every side the attestation that a new culture is indeed being born. Of these attestations Charles A. Reich's *The Greening of America* is best argued and best known. Gary Snyder does not figure in Reich's account; it is an East Coast formulary and proceeds speculatively on the basis of evidence that has come into the author's ken. But from the West Coast point of view Snyder has for two dozen years been hewing out the guidelines along which the greening of America must proceed, and his work has not been in vain. Seen in this light, Parkinson is not far wrong when he credits Snyder with a kind of single-handed creation of a new culture. Before him there were ideas, yes, and images, too; but more than anyone else of his generation he has, with his life, put those ideas and those images to the test:

> The culture was there in potentia for anyone who cared to seize upon it; to paraphrase Trotsky, Pacific Basin Culture was lying in the streets and no one knew how to pick it up. The paintings of Mark Tobey (prewhite paintings) and of Morris Graves and the sculpture of Richard O'Hanlon prefigured what Snyder would do, and Kenneth Rexroth had an intuitive grasp. But the peculiar blending of Zen Buddhism with IWW political attitudes, Amerindian lore, and the mystique of the wilderness was Snyder's special articulation. He had associates—Phil Whalen, Lew Welch, Jack Kerouac, Allen Ginsberg—and he has followers, especially James Koller. Along with Creeley and Lowell, he is a primary influence on the writing of young people now, though as a spiritual rather than technical force.[80]

Once again, be it noted, we see how the archetype enforces a subjective, or spiritual, rather than an objective, or technical, effect. But the effect is at last taking:

> His voice is so clear and firm that it is fatally easy to imitate, so that the Gary Snyder poem that his

apprentices discover and write has a certain mechanical quality—a reference to Coyote or Bear,
a natural (preferable wilderness) setting, erotic
overtones, plain colloquial language, firm insist-
ence on an objective imagery, an anecdotal frame,
short lines modeled on the Chinese Cantos of Ezra
Pound with much internal rhyme and alliteration,
very little dead weight (the prepositional phrase
held in abomination).[81]

We see here how the influence of Zen cleans up the
maundering rhetoric of the archetype in its native
emergence, enforcing a chastening effect that all
the scolding from the literary establishment failed
to achieve. Yet strangely enough when the sources
of this style are mentioned no reference is made to
William Carlos Williams, who, from the East Coast
perspective, is usually considered about the only
credible father figure the Beat movement had.

The sources of the style are Pound and Rexroth,
Pound technically, Rexroth for general political
orientation and stress on beach and high country
—the segment of *A Range of Poems* called "The
Back Country" is dedicated to Rexroth. The proxim-
ity to Pound and Rexroth come partly from
genuine indebtedness to them but more largely
from immersion in the same origins: he started
from the older poets but returned to their sources
to see and shape them in a special form.[82]

Toward the end of his essay Parkinson defends
Snyder against the charge most frequently leveled at
him, one for that matter leveled against all the
primal writers of the West, namely, that his preoccupations are irrelevant to the needs and uses of
an established urban hegemony, and are therefore
out of harmony with humanity as it is. Parkinson,
rather, takes the view that Snyder is deeply in tune
with the most sensitive portion of humanity today,
the undefinable group of people "including historians, novelists, poets, artists, various scholars, and
many others" who are seriously seeking some proper

answer, or, as he says, at least a set of questions appropriate to the world in its current stage of history, but who insist on seeing that world not simply in the oversimplified urbanized form of today, but against the background of all human possibilities. In support he quotes directly from Snyder himself:

> As a poet I hold the most archaic values on earth. They go back to the late Paleolithic: the fertility of the soil, the magic of animals, the power-vision in solitude, the terrifying initiation and re-birth, the love and ecstasy of the dance, the common work of the tribe. I try to hold both history and wilderness in mind, that my poems may approach the true measure of things and stand against the unbalance and ignorance of our times.

And Parkinson's own conclusion is just:

> He is calling upon the total resources of man's moral and religious being. There is no point in decrying this as primitivism; it is merely good sense, for the ability to hold history and wilderness in the mind at once may be the only way to make valid measures of human conduct. A larger and more humble vision of man and cosmos is our only hope, and the major work of any serious person. In that work, Snyder's verse and prose compose a set of new cultural possibilities that only ignorance and unbalance can ignore.[83]

If one of the suggestions of this essay is true, namely, that the western writer stands as term of the American impulse, and that as term he constitutes its mainstream rather than a merely peripheral and incidental relevance, then this suggestion seems confirmed in both the Beat and the Hippie movements that flowed from the San Francisco Renaissance in the late 1950s. For the fact that these movements originated in San Francisco means only that their point of inception occurred here. They represent the diffusion of the archetype from isolate artistic expression down into intrinsic social manifestations. Of course this diffusion is first received by the young.

For the mass media could not have made the Beatnik and the Hippie household words were it not for their subsistent relevance to the American ethos. The historic line from East to West proceeds by a movement that is largely unconscious (an underground or behind-the-scenes phenomenon) and this is what has deceived writers like Edmund Wilson. But once crystallized in a work of major stature, what I have called its apotheosis, then it begins to openly redound back into the East, and keep redounding, as the new generations become imbued with its charism. Since this is the history of America vis-a-vis Europe, it should come as no surprise that it is the history of the West Coast vis-a-vis the East Coast. The Beat and Hippie movements have reverberated across the world, changing the image of youth from the conventional son-of-his-father to a provocative synthesis of archaic and primitive effects: beards, beads, and buckskins, with long hair for the signature, and independence as an attitudinal stance. Encounter is the clue to apotheosis. The western archetype, surely, must be acknowledged in these effects.

The Beat Generation, taken as a whole, and abstracting from the achievement of individual members, may be characterized as a reduction from the pure apotheosis of the archetype back toward the accent on persona. This, as we saw in Joaquin Miller, was one point of origin. Though the Beats were still an achievement-oriented movement, and furthermore an essentially literary movement, the place given in their ethos to life-style, which may be taken as a persona manifestation, was pronounced. After its brief flare the Generation dispersed as a creative phenomenon, but its image did not die, and following its demise at the beginning of the sixties the cluster of poets remained to consolidate its effects and sustain the sense of momentum it had instituted.

But the eruption of the Hippies at mid-decade, while certainly a true extension of that impulse, represents a sweep that makes direct literary continuity difficult. For the movement represents a manifest triumph of the persona over achievement per se, and in this respect the archetype has come full term. In fact achievement is repudiated as a threat to life-style, in the sense that achievement becomes programmed and militates against independence. Moreover it is in no sense a literary movement.

For though the hero of the Beat Generation was indeed the poet, the charismatic figure who took his place in the Hippie movement is the Rock musician. With the advent of oriental tonalities into the conventional Rock and Roll of the fifties, the young generation of the sixties found its own voice and gesture. Moreover its disdain for achievement and for leaders is belied by the consummate performance of its best musicians, and by the adulation poured upon them. Nevertheless in its hands literature suffers cruelly, for its lyrics indulge an uncritical casualness in order to counterbalance the catalyptic intensity of its sound, sanctioning the verbal cliché while eschewing the musical one. Some poet-musician must before long emerge from its ranks who can articulate the primal vehemence of the Word as Old Torino declared it, and redeem from the intensity of its musicianship the literary degeneracy it tolerates. That this task will be difficult in the extreme is indicated by the fact that in the Occident even the best music, from Gregorian chant to High Opera, has habitually swamped conceptual articulation in the omnivorous totality of its sound.

But even as the point of inception shifted from poetry to music in the wake of the Beat Generation, it was manifested in the same mystery of place that had dominated the former phenomenon: the San Francisco scene. In a survey of the brief history of this music called "Rock 1970" by Jon Landau in *Rolling Stone* the writer declares:

In the mid-Sixties San Francisco was the only city to develop a consciousness about the importance of rock. That cultural awareness was the cushion for all other developments. Rock was not only viewed as a form of entertainment; part of that collective outlook held that music was the essential component of the "New Culture." The almost religious fervor that surrounded Rock in 1966 and 1967 was occasionally frightening. Like the infatuation with drugs, there was a sense of discovery going on that made it seem like nothing could ever be better and that nothing would ever change. Things were so good, who could ever get tired with them.[84]

While yet another critic writing in the same paper speaks of the phenomenon of the Rock Festival that "began with the Magic Mountain Festival on Mt. Tamalpais near San Francisco in June 1967, the first of the modern American music festivals that are widely believed to have begun with Monterey" and which culminated in "the sense of generation? class? culture? at Woodstock."[85] It is impossible to avoid the conclusion that this is the same archetype we have been tracing in literature, the same eruption of dynamic creativity and spontaneous discovery finding its inception in a new medium.

In this brief summary of the ethos of the West as a literary region I have tried to identify its essential character as manifested to the nation as a whole. In the lateness of its development, sensing the closing of possibility behind it as the rest of the country matured, and longing for finality, the West cried "Eureka!" thereby placing its emphasis on the primacy of discovery, convinced that in discovery lay apotheosis. In the judgment of the East it achieved not apotheosis but extravagance, an excess of sentiment articulated in a superfluity of utterance. But this cannot be denied: even as an extravagance it is one that is built upon the aspirations of the nation as a whole, extended to the outmost margins, and projected against the possible as a profound hope of the motives that impel us all. Herein lies the real force behind its gigantic visions and its resounding words.

Josephine Miles, in her *Eras and Modes in English Poetry*, concludes with a chapter called "The Poetry of Praise," in which she expresses how, of the three universal styles of poetry—the low or colloquial, the middle or observational and meditational, and the high or ceremonial—it is the high style that has been most unfashionable in modern times:

> The high style has been ignored, or at best, since Pope's *Peri Bathous*, has had an unfavorable press. Yet if we think of the high style also as *deep*, not only as empyrean but as subterranean and submarine, we may recognize its serious function for the present day. To clear and polished surfaces, it adds depths, however murky; to the objectivities of thought, action, and the thing in itself, it adds the subjectivity of inward feeling tumultuously expressed. Like the word *altus* in Latin, which means both high and deep, it relates the gods of the solar system to the gods of the solar plexus.

What idiom could more truly express the native pantheism than one which "relates the gods of the solar system to the gods of the solar plexus"? Nothing less could serve the thirst for apothesis that is the determining western impulse. Miss Miles concludes:

> This American poetry of praise has a long free cadenced line, full of silences, symbols, and implications. It has a cumulative structure, building up to a height of force and feeling, whether in imprecation or rhapsody. It has phraseology of resounding sound and of warm responsive sense, suggestive of heights and depths beyond the reach of form or reason. At its worst it can be dangerously loose, semiconscious, and irresponsible; at its best it can be powerfully aware of moving forces and meanings. Strong as it was in England

. . . it has been more widespread and central to tradition in America, with added impetus from poets of the Orient as well as of Europe.[86]

In the brief list of American poets who, for her, exemplify the high style, Miss Miles, herself a Californian, instances not a single westerner. Perhaps this is because at the time she was writing the Beat Generation had become so identified in the public mind with San Francisco and the West that she felt to do so would jeopardize her thesis in the eyes of the people she was trying to reach. No matter. So widely has this high style been practiced in the West that its prevalence here has become almost synonymous with the locale as a literary region. Without doubt one reason for this is the terminal situation which confrontation with the Pacific exacts of the westward-hungering consciousness. In conclusion, these lines of Jeffers not only illustrate this style, but they touch the impulsion behind it, and they express what virtually every writer identified with this region might select as the quintessence of what the western situation has to say to the rest of mankind:

> The platform is like a rough plank
> theatre-stage
> Built on the prow of the promontory; as if
> our blood has labored all round the
> earth from Asia
> To play its mystery before strict judges at
> last, the final ocean and sky, to prove
> our nature
> More shining than that of the other
> animals. It is rather ignoble in its quiet
> times, mean in its pleasure,
> Slavish in the mass; but at stricken
> moments it can shine terribly against
> the dark magnificence of things.[87]

Notes

[1] Edmund Wilson, *The Boys in the Back Room* (San Francisco, 1943). Revised and included in the author's collected essays *Classics and Commercials* (New York, 1950).

[2] *Ibid.*, p. 49.

[3] *Ibid.*, p. 51.

[4] Perry Miller, *Errand into the Wilderness* (Cambridge, 1956), p. 216.

[5] Josiah Royce, *California* (New York, 1948), p. 394.

[6] T. K. Whipple, *Study Out the Land*, with an introduction by Edmund Wilson (Berkeley, 1943), p. 59.

[7] Letter to Porter Garnett dated 15 August 1911, in the Bancroft Library, the University of California at Berkeley.

[8] T. K. Whipple, *Study Out the Land*, p. 52.

[9] Alexis de Tocqueville, *Democracy in America*, vol. 2 (New York, 1958), p. 32.

[10] Christopher Davis, *North American Indian* (London, 1969), p. 69.

[11] Mari Sandoz, *Crazy Horse* (New York, 1942), p. 11.

[12] Margot Astrov, *The Winged Serpent* (New York, 1946), p. 3.

[13] Perry Miller, *Errand into the Wilderness*, p. 185.

[14] Josiah Royce, *California*, p. 6.

[15] D. H. Lawrence, *Studies in Classic American Literature* (New York, 1923), p. 124.

[16] Lionel Trilling, *The Liberal Imagination* (New York, 1950), p. 36.

[17] Mari Sandoz, *Cheyenne Autumn* (New York, 1953), p. vi.

[18] Louis Untermeyer, *Modern American Poetry* (New York, 1930), p. 11.

[19] *Ibid.*, p. 12.

[20] *Ibid.*, p. 76.

[21] Stuart P. Sherman, *The Poetical Works of Joaquin Miller* (New York, 1923), p. 25.

[22] *Ibid.*, p. 27.

[23] Louis Untermeyer, *Modern American Poetry*, p. 12.

[24] Frank Norris, *The Octopus* (1901; Bantam Books ed., New York, 1958), p. 5.

[25] *Ibid.*

[26] But this is itself an essentially American perspective. As Charles Olson was to write: "I take SPACE to be the central fact to man born in America, from Folsom cave to now. I spell it large because it comes large here. Large, and without mercy." *Call Me Ishmael*, 1947.

[27] Frank Norris, *The Octopus*, p. 29.

[28] *Ibid.*, p. 30.

[29] *Ibid.*, p. 433.

[30] *Ibid.*, p. 208.

[31] Louis Filler, *The Unknown Edwin Markham* (Yellow Springs, 1966), p. 183.

[32] Frank Norris, *The Octopus*, p. 247.

[33] *Ibid.*, p. 2.

[34] *Ibid.*, p. 250.

[35] *Ibid.*

[36] Louis Filler, *The Unknown Edwin Markham*, p. 101.

[37] *Ibid.*, p. 102.

[38] Edmund Wilson, *Classics and Commercials*, p. 50.

[39] From a brochure handed the visitor at the entrance to Point Lobos State Park.

[40] Theodora Kroeber, *The Inland Whale* (Berkeley, 1959).

[41] Robinson Jeffers, *The Selected Poetry* (New York, 1938), p. 9.

[42] *Ibid.*, p. 15.

[43] Robert J. Brophy, "Tamar," "The Cenci," and "Incest," *American Literature* 42:241 (May 1970).

[44] Robinson Jeffers, *The Selected Poetry*, p. 39.

[45] Horace Gregory and Marya Zaturenska, *American Poetry 1900–1940* (New York, 1946), p. 407.

[46] Horace Gregory, *The Dying Gladiator* (New York, 1961), p. 3.

[47] Stuart P. Sherman, *The Poetical Works of Joaquin Miller*, p. 27.

[48] Franklin Walker, Afterword to *The Sea Wolf* (New York, 1964), p. 345.

[49] Jack London, *The Sea Wolf* (New York, 1904), p. 11.

[50] Chester E. Eisinger, *Fiction of the Forties* (Chicago, 1963), p. 4.

[51] Warren French, *John Steinbeck* (New York, 1961), p. 19.

[52] *Ibid.*, p. 20.

[53] T. K. Whipple, *Study Out the Land*, p. 105.

[54] Lawrence Clark Powell, *Bookman's Progress* (Los Angeles, 1968), p. 126.

[55] James D. Hart, *The Oxford Companion to American Literature* (New York, 1965), p. 802.

[56] Theodore Roethke, *The Collected Poems* (New York, 1966), p. 274.

[57] T. K. Whipple, *Study Out the Land*, p. 110.

[58] John Steinback, *The Red Pony*, Bantam ed. (New York, 1948), p. 66.

[59] John Steinbeck, *The Grapes of Wrath*, (2d New Bantam ed., New York, 1969), p. 131.

[60] William Saroyan, *Days of Life and Death and Escape to the Moon* (New York, 1970), p. 124.

[61] Alfred Kazin, *Starting Out in the Thirties* (New York, 1962), p. 54.

[62] Thus Jeffers:

On the small marble-paved platform
On the turret on the head of the tower,
Watching the night deepen,
I feel the rock-edge of the continent
Reel eastward with me below the broad stars.
I lean on the broad worn stones of the parapet
    top
And the stones and my hands that touch them
    reel eastward . . .
In the East under the Hyades and rising Orion
Are many cities and multitudes of people,
But westward a long way they are few enough.

"Margrave"

Thus Rexroth:

The great geometrical winter constellations
Lift up over the Sierra Nevada,
I walk under the stars, my feet on the known
    round earth.
My eyes following the lights of an airplane,
Red and green, growling deep into the Hyades.
The note of the engine rises, shrill, faint.
Finally inaudible, and the lights go out
In the southeast haze beneath the feet of Orion.

"Requiem for the Spanish Dead"

[63] "Inversely, As the Square of Their Distances Apart," *The Shorter Poems of Kenneth Rexroth* (New York, 1966), p. 149.

[64] Mildred Edie Brady, "The New Cult of Sex and Anarchy," *Harper's* April 1947, p. 312.

[65] Robert Duncan, *Heavenly City, Earthly City* (Berkeley, 1947), p. 31.

[66] "Letter from San Francisco," *Horizon* (London, October 1947), p. 120.

[67] Parker Tyler, Introduction to *Touch of the Marvelous*, by Phillip Lamantia (Berkeley, 1966).

[68] Quoted on jacket of *The Blood of the Air*, by Phillip Lamantia (San Francisco, 1970).

[69] Paul O'Neil, "The Only Rebellion Around," *Life* 30 Nov. 1959, p. 123.

[70] *The Evergreen Review*, vol. 1, no. 2, n.d.

[71] Thomas Parkinson, "Phenomenon or Generation," in *A Casebook on the Beat* (New York, 1961), p. 286.

[72] Seymour Krim, "The Kerouac Legacy," in *Shake It for the World, Smartass* (New York, 1970), p. 193.

[73] *Newsweek* 23 Nov. 1970, p. 83. "The University of California is, in fact, probably the most successful public institution the world has ever known. 'It has shown,' says President Robben Fleming of the University of Michigan, 'what public education at its finest can be . . . .' "

[74] Thomas F. Merrill, *Allen Ginsberg* (New York, 1969), p. 86.

[75] *Ibid.*

[76] Charles Bukowski, "The Priest and the Matador," in *Penquin Modern Poets: Charles Bukowski, Philip Lamantia, and Harold Norse* (Baltimore: Penquin, 1969), p. 21.

[77] Thomas Parkinson, "The Poetry of Gary Snyder," *The Southern Review* July 1968, p. 616.

[78] *Ibid.*, p. 617.

[79] *Ibid.*

[80] *Ibid.*

[81] *Ibid.*, p. 618.

[82] *Ibid.*

[83] *Ibid.*, p. 632.

[84] *Rolling Stone*, San Francisco, 10 Dec. 1970, p. 41.

[85] *Ibid.*, p. 44.

[86] Josephine Miles, *Eras and Modes in English Poetry* (Berkeley, 1964), p. 224.

[87] Robinson Jeffers, "Thurso's Landing," in *Selected Poetry* (New York, 1938), p. 357.

regionalism in american literature: a bibliography

The most comprehensive bibliography for the study of regionalism in American literature is Clarence Gohdes' *Literature and Theater of the States and Regions of the U.S.A.; an Historical Bibliography* published in 1967 (see below). The following listing represents items appearing after 1965, approximately the last year included in Gohdes' bibliography, and items not included originally in Gohdes.

Adams, Richard P. "Southern Literature in the 1890's." *Mississippi Quarterly* 21:277–81 (1968).

Blake, Forrester. "Bibliography for Westerners." *Rendezvous* 2:33–42 (1967).

A general bibliography of western literature.

Boynton, Percy H. *America in Contemporary Fiction*. New York: Russell, 1963.

See "Two New England Regionalists," pages 21–34.

Bridgman, Richard. *The Colloquial Style in America*. New York: Oxford Univ. Pr., 1966.

Colquitt, Betsy Feagan, ed. *A Part of Space: Ten Texas Writers*. Fort Worth: Texas Christian Univ. Pr., 1969.

A sample of contemporary writing in Texas.

This bibliography has been prepared by Martha Kehde, a member of the staff of the University of Kansas Library, Lawrence.

Core, George, ed. *Southern Fiction Today: Renascence and Beyond.* Athens: Univ. of Georgia Pr., 1969.

A collection of essays by Walter Sullivan, C. Hugh Holman, Louis D. Rubin, Jr., and George Core.

Cowie, Alexander. "Local-Color, Frontier and Regional Fiction," in his *The Rise of the American Novel,* p. 536–98. New York: American Book, 1951.

A study of Edward Eggleston, George Washington Cable, Constance Fenimore Woolson, Thomas Bailey Aldrich, and "Charles Egbert Craddock" (Mary N. Murfree).

Derleth, August William. *New Poetry Out of Wisconsin.* Sauk City, Wis.: Stanton and Lee, 1969.

Dickinson, A. T., Jr. *American Historical Fiction.* New York: Scarecrow, 1963.

Durham, Frank. "The Southern Literary Tradition: Shadow or Substance?" *South Atlantic Quarterly* 67:455–68 (1968).

Eliot, T. S. "American Literature and the American Language," *Sewanee Review* 74:1–20 (1966).

Frederick, John T. "American Literary Nationalism: the Process of Definition 1825–1850," *Review of Politics* 21:224–38 (1959).

An historical analysis that, among other things, points out the necessity of regionalism for a national literature.

Friend, Llerena. "Posses All Over the Place: Publications of the Westerners," *Library Chronicle of the University of Texas,* 8:58–65 (1968).

Gohdes, Clarence. *Literature and Theater of the States and Regions of the U.S.A.; an Historical Bibliography.* Durham, N.C.: Duke Univ. Pr., 1967.

Heiney, Donald W. "Between the Wars: Regionalism and Rural Naturalism," in his *Recent American Literature,* p. 179–261. Woodbury, N.Y.: Barron, 1958.

Holman, C. H. "Literature and Culture: the Fugitive-Agrarians," *Social Forces* 37:15–19 (1958).

Describes how southern "regionalist writers" writing for the *Fugitive* magazine used the South as a subject to express universal themes.

Holmes, Edward M. "What Should Maine Writers Write?" in Richard S. Sprague, ed., *A Handful of Spice: Essays in Maine History and Literature.* (University of Maine Studies, no. 88) Orono: Univ. of Maine Pr., 1968.

James, Stuart B. "Western American Space and the Human Imagination," *Western Humanities Review* 24:147–55 (1970).
Authors' use of the prairie as a geographical characteristic to develop characters.

Jones, Howard Mumford. *Theory of American Literature.* Ithaca, N.Y.: Cornell Univ. Pr., 1966.
An old-fashioned definition of regionalism with sketches of ten regionalists.

———, and Ludwig, Richard M. *Guide to American Literature and Its Backgrounds since 1890.* 3d ed. Cambridge, Mass.: Harvard Univ. Pr., 1964.
See: "Special Aspects, Regionalism," p. 32–34; "American Literature, 1890–1919; Literature Written within the Genteel Tradition, the Regional and the Local," p. 125–26; "Some Continuing Elements, the Twentieth Century Regional Novel," p. 209–10.

Lavender, David. "The Petrified West and the Writer," *American Scholar* 37:293–306 (1968).

Leach, MacEdward. "Folklore in American Regional Literature," *Journal of the Folklore Institute* 3:376–97 (1966).
Describes the evolution of regional American literature from folk culture. A good bibliography.

Lee, Robert Edson. *From West to East: Studies in the Literature of the American West.* Urbana: Univ. of Illinois Pr., 1966.

Lucia, Ellis. *This Land around Us, a Treasury of Pacific Northwest Writing.* Garden City, N.Y.: Doubleday, 1969.

Martin, Jay. *Harvest of Change, American Literature 1865–1914*. Englewood Cliffs, N.J.: Prentice-Hall, 1967.

    See especially "Paradises Lost," p. 81–164.

Milton, John R. *Three West, Conversations with Vardes Fisher, Max Evans, Michael Straight*. Vermillion: Univ. of South Dakota Pr., 1970.

    Transcribed interview which took place at the University of South Dakota with three authors important to American regional literature.

Nolan, Paul T., ed. *Provincial Drama in America, 1870–1916: A Casebook of Primary Materials*. New York: Scarecrow, 1967.

Paluka, Frank. *Iowa Authors: A Bio-Bibliography of Sixty Native Writers*. Iowa City: Friends of the Univ. of Iowa Libraries, 1967.

Pattee, Fred Lewis. *A History of American Literature since 1870*. New York: Cooper Sq., 1968.

    A historical analysis which includes the concept of regionalism.

Peden, William Harwood, and Garrett, George, eds. *New Writing in South Carolina*. Columbia: Univ. of South Carolina Pr., 1971.

Rock, Virginia J. "Agrarianism: Agrarian Themes and Ideas in Southern Writing," *Mississippi Quarterly* 21:145–56 (1968).

    A bibliography dealing with "regionalism and and a consciousness of the 'Southernness' of Southern experience."

"Status and Future of Regionalism, a Symposium," *Journal of Southern History* 26:22–56 (1960).

    Briefly describes the historical, literary, and sociological concept of regionalism.

Veysey, L. R. "Myth and Reality in Approaching American Regionalism," *American Quarterly* 12:31–43 (1960).

Woodress, James. *Dissertations in American Literature: 1891–1962*. Durham, N.C.: Duke Univ. Pr., 1962.

    Subject divisions for both regionalism in literature and in drama.